THE HISTORY OF CIVILIZATION

LIFE AND WORK IN PREHISTORIC TIMES

THE HISTORY OF CIVILIZATION

General Editor C. K. Ogden

The *History of Civilization* is a landmark in early twentieth Century publishing. The aim of the general editor, C. K. Ogden, was to "summarise in one comprehensive synthesis the most recent findings and theories of historians, anthropologists, archaeologists, sociologists and all conscientious students of civilization." The *History,* which includes titles in the French series *L'Evolution de l'Humanité*, was published at a formative time in the development of the social sciences, and during a period of significant historical discoveries.

A list of the titles in the series can be found at the end of this book.

LIFE AND WORK IN PREHISTORIC TIMES

G Renard

Translated by
R. T Clark

Routledge
Taylor & Francis Group

LONDON AND NEW YORK

First published in 1929 by Routledge, Trench, Trubner
Reprinted in 1996, 1998, 1999 by Routledge

2 Park Square, Milton Park,
Abingdon, Oxfordshire OX14 4RN
&
711 Third Avenue,
New York, NY 10017

Transferred to Digital Printing 2008

Routledge is an imprint of the Taylor & Francis Group, an informa business

First issued in paperback 2013

British Cataloguing in Publication Data

ISBN 978-0-415-15571-7 (hbk)
ISBN 978-0-415-86968-3 (pbk)
ISBN Pre-history (12 volume set): 978-0-415-15611-0
ISBN History of Civilization (50 volume set): 978-0-415-14380-6

Publisher's Note
The publisher has gone to great lengths to ensure the quality of
this reprint but points out that some imperfections in the
original may be apparent

CONTENTS

LIST OF ILLUSTRATIONS

LIFE AND WORK
IN PREHISTORIC TIMES

INTRODUCTION

I. The Methods of Prehistory

IT is not so long ago that the origins of humanity were shrouded in as deep mystery as once were the sources of the Nile. Gradually, however, light has penetrated the darkness, and to-day it is possible, if not to know in detail this very distant past, at least to have such knowledge as though incomplete is yet sufficient to enable us to trace the broad outline of human development. Prehistory, which is history before history, embraces all the countries and all the centuries in which men lived before knowing how to set down in written documents what they remembered of their deeds and thoughts. Thus there exist two prehistories, one of which follows logically from the other.

The first is universal : it embraces all the world and all the races ; it goes back to the first beginnings of humanity ; it unfolds itself through hundreds and perhaps thousands of centuries ; it ends at the hour when the most civilized races learned to write, that is, some twenty-five to thirty centuries before our era if one reckons by the hieroglyphs, thirteen centuries at least, if one reckons by our alphabet. This may be called ancient prehistory. The second which may be called modern prehistory is sectional, local, and ends at different dates for different races and peoples, and extends in some remote corners of the globe to our own day. Its duration compared with that of the first is very short, not more than fifty centuries.

It is the first with which we are concerned. The second affords only an indirect means of explaining the first when we lack direct means of explanation, of clearing up the obscurity in which our beginnings are enshrouded, of explaining the older by the more recent past.

When we begin our study of ancient prehistory, however, we do not need to go back to the remotest ages. How did life begin on the earth ? How did the creature which was to become man make his appearance after fish, reptiles, and birds, a member of the vertebrates and a kinsman of the great anthropoid apes ? How and at what date did this distant ancestor, the original of all humanity, make his entry into the animal world ? Was he born of a single couple whose descendants acquired different characteristics and shapes because of the influence of the different environments in which they developed ? Or, as seems more probable, were conditions that favoured the birth and development of the human species found in more than one region, so that man, as a species, had several birthplaces ? These are very interesting questions, but we may neglect them. Here we seek to study only the efforts of this vertical animal, which, standing up on two legs, saw wider horizons opening before it, became capable of housing a fuller and heavier brain, and obtained such use of his two hands as enabled him to throw missiles and strike at long range. But it is a formidable task simply to chronicle the first results of his efforts to survive and to secure a better existence. The whole of human civilization is the result of this fierce effort by early man. The whole of it is the work of the arm or the brain, the building of towns and the harvest of the fields, the works of the artist, and the poet and the system of the philosopher. This multiple activity turned by man to the satisfaction first of material needs and then of higher needs is the subject of our study which we pursue by tracing its evolution in the life and organization of primitive societies.

It is a delicate and difficult subject to treat, and it needs to have brought to it scrupulous care and implacable and scientific frankness. We must get rid of all preconceived notions, take a firm stand to be content only with the truth and nothing but the truth, even if we have to abandon a belief that we absorbed with our mother's milk. No doubt the romance which Greeks and Romans, Persians and Hebrews wove around humanity's beginnings is a charming idyll, that of the age of gold which has only one flaw that it exists only in the imagination, an earthly paradise to which man unfortunately has lost the key. When the world arose out of chaos in all its youth and brilliance, the earth, says the legend, was lightened by the heavenly bodies, washed by the waters of the sea, clad in a garment of flower and grass and verdure, and nourished by light and transparent air. It was the centre of the universe, and awaited only a king. Man was born. For him everything existed. All was established for his sake. For him the sun rose, for him moon and stars spread a dim light in the night, for him the ocean kept itself within its bounds. He was a *roi fainéant* : he had nothing to do but to live and enjoy living. Nature or a complaisant deity saved him from having either to toil or to suffer. A need for him was merely the opportunity for a pleasure. He was hungry : the most savoury of fruits hung above his head within easy reach. He needed sleep : he had only to close his eyes as he lay on thick and perfumed turf while a warm breeze caressed his sleeping body. He woke at dawn to the sweet song of the birds. He wandered through his kingdom, which preserved always the beauty of eternal spring. He had his subjects, the animals, the docile instruments of his will. He had a mate who doubled his happiness by sharing it. He had his like, brothers who loved and respected him and were, like him, models of innocence and virtue. For many a century he lived this life of pleasure, and then full of years he died, just as he used to sleep. For him even death was tender and pleasant.

With certain variations this is the tale which the sacred books of the nations or the imagination of the poets present to us, and the majority of the stories add that man, after having enjoyed this unalloyed happiness, was deprived of it for sin.

The illusion of a miraculous Eden is so strong that it recurs from century to century. The companions of Columbus thought they had found an enchanted land, an El Dorado, where the fountain of youth would wipe out the ravages of old age. Rousseau, who proclaimed that all was good when it left the hands of the Creator, believed in a state of nature in which noble savages lived and died in peace and happiness. Diderot loved to celebrate the free voluptuousness of the happy island of Tahiti, where a century later Loti was to love Rara-Hu. Is all this the unconscious turning back of the man of the town towards the simple

and peaceful life of the man of the country ?   Or is it that
humanity, like the individuals who compose it, feels, as it
grows old an overwhelming nostalgia for its childhood
which seems to it to be so full of youth and freshness ?   Or
does humanity, tortured by its perpetual desire for happiness,
eternally place in the future the good old days not of yesterday, but of times before yesterday, which recede as one nears
that ideal of felicity which draws him on to a future goal
and sustains him in his high adventure ?

What is certain is that science has cleared all those legends
away.   For these idyllic and deceptive pictures of our past
it has substituted one which is harder, more manly, and
which fundamentally is more consoling, more fruitful in
useful results, than those vain mournings for the destruction
of a lost paradise.

What can we conclude from the slow rise of humanity
ascending by slow stages from a condition like that of the
beasts, not merely to power that will make it truly lord of
the earth, but to ideas of justice and of beauty which, like
pillars of fire, will lighten and guide its steps on its never-
ending journey towards a better state ?   Surely that toil is
the means by which it becomes more and more master of
itself, and of nature, that its past corresponds to its future,
that the progress already realized is the guarantee of the
progress that is to be, that despite lapses into barbarism
and survivals of the beast-nature there lies before it the
prospect of an improvement whose limits there is no means
of fixing.   This de-animalizing of the debased and savage
thing that is primitive man is a constant lesson of courage,
perseverance and hope ; it leads us, as it were, to make a
religion of human effort.

Imagine the life which at the beginning was led by this
wretched animal on two feet wandering in solitary wastes,
having to meet the menace of the lightning, the tempest,
the flood, the snares of the night, beasts and men, his brothers
and his worst enemies, sometimes the hunter and sometimes
the hunted, often forced to take refuge in a tree or a hole in
the rock, considering the day well spent if it came to an end
without wound or accident, and compare these painful
beginnings with what this animal has become, conqueror
of distance, victor over sea and land and air, and reaching

by the power of thought into infinities of time and space.
What a course he has run ! What an epic of energy and of
courage an epic that gives birth to hope ! The new knowledge
can stand proudly beside the old legends which it has vanquished. It tells a story not only truer but finer and nobler.

But what are the methods by which this new knowledge
has been obtained ? What are the sources in which it finds
its facts ? For ancient prehistory there are what we may
call *direct* documents. As has been well said, the earth lies
there to be read as one reads a book, but its leaves need to
be turned. First of all, there were discoveries made by
chance, when a quarry was being opened, a canal dug, or a
railway laid. Then later came methodical excavation, carefully carried out at a spot which seemed likely to yield
results. Thus there came to light the fossils, dusty and
clay-covered, whose date could be determined by the
thickness of the covering, and by the date of the stratum
from which they were unearthed. But a whole set of
precautionary measures were necessary. The excavation
had to be measured, the plan and section of the strata worked
out, the successive phases of the work photographed, the
other remains, animal and vegetable which are associated
with the traces of human existence and activity, described
with meticulous care, and then, without tampering with
them, the objects found had to be compared, classified, and
explained.

Now hundreds of sites have been explored. There are
peat bogs where tree trunks, skeletons, and utensils lie sunk :
lakes where the mud, like the lava of Vesuvius, protects
all that it has covered, the sands of rivers into which the
water has drawn and buried what used to be on the banks,
the rubbish-heaps in which the debris of man's food have
accumulated, the snail heaps of Algeria, the kitchen-middens
of Denmark, common on the coasts both of Europe and Asia,
and of America, the places where were slaughtered and eaten
wild horses and mammoths, the caverns where our ancestors
dwelled and which hold several strata of trampled earth,
not to speak of the walls which bear the first specimens of
painting and of sculpture, the burial places where men,

women, and children have been buried with the weapons and adornment which they wore when they lived.

From all these have come bones and all sorts of objects which to-day fill public and private collections, although some of them have to be regarded with suspicion for there is no lack of forged antiquities or of objects whose source has, to say the least of it, not been definitely established. Thus the student of ancient prehistory has to appeal for aid to kindred sciences : *geology*, which deals with the history of our planet ; *botany* and *zoology*, which describe terrene and marine flora and fauna ; *anthropology* and *palæontology*, which study the evolution of human and animal anatomy ; and of *technology*, which tells us of the tools and methods used in the various arts and industries.

To these relics of the past we can add a goodly number of *indirect* documents. These are the survivals of past practices that exist among civilized peoples. The *couvade*, the Basque practice whereby the husband retires to bed when his wife bears a child, a strange custom which is found also in Brazil, Guiana, and Greenland, recalls the belief in the intimate relation between father and child and the memory of a social organization where affiliation and relationship depended on the mother. The practices in this or that industry to-day help to explain how this or that tool was employed in older times. Thus the manufacture of flintlocks allows us to understand how flint was worked in earlier days. The stone scraper which is still used in Italy in the preparation of leather tells us how were used the similar instruments which were so plentiful among our distant ancestors. The religions especially are treasure-houses of old tradition and custom. A usage like that of stone knives in Egypt and Rome and Mexico takes us back into dim antiquity. Magic white or black, benevolent or malevolent, is perpetuated in the processions in which relics are carried to induce the rain to fall, in the practices of fortune tellers, in the exorcisms intended to drive the evil spirits from the bodies into which they had passed.

But soon written documents are available and with them we enter the sphere of modern prehistory. We have the guesses of philosophers and poets who, like Epicurus and Lucretius, divined what science has proved to-day. In

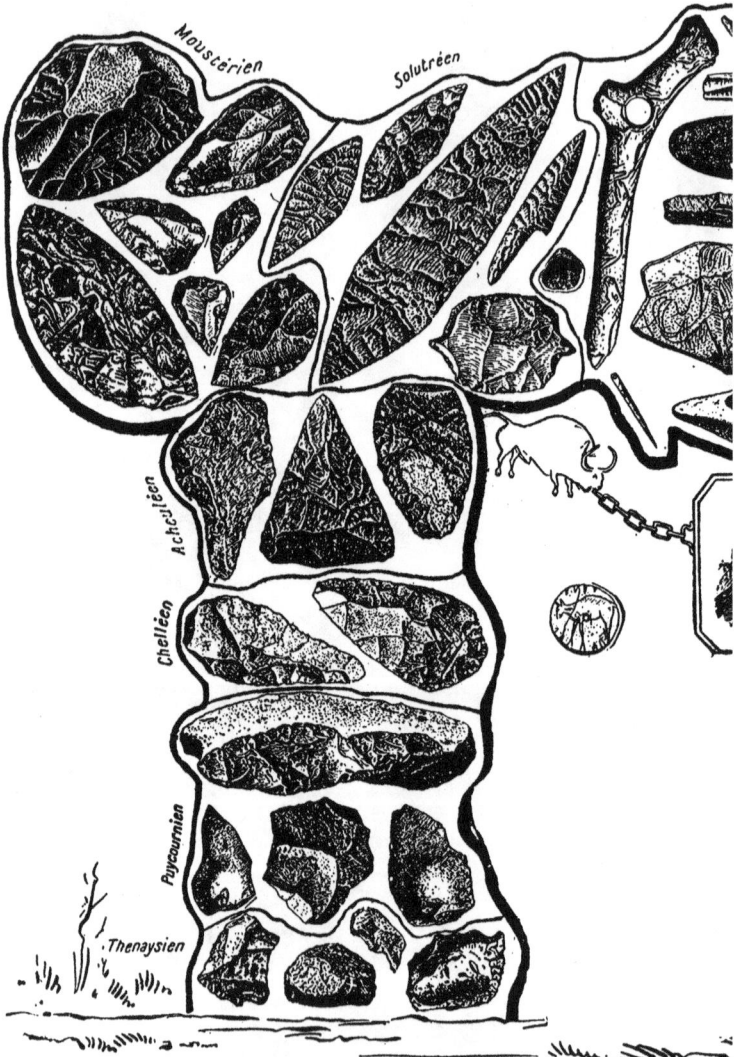

Fig. 1. Engraving made for a dinner offered to Gabriel de Mortile

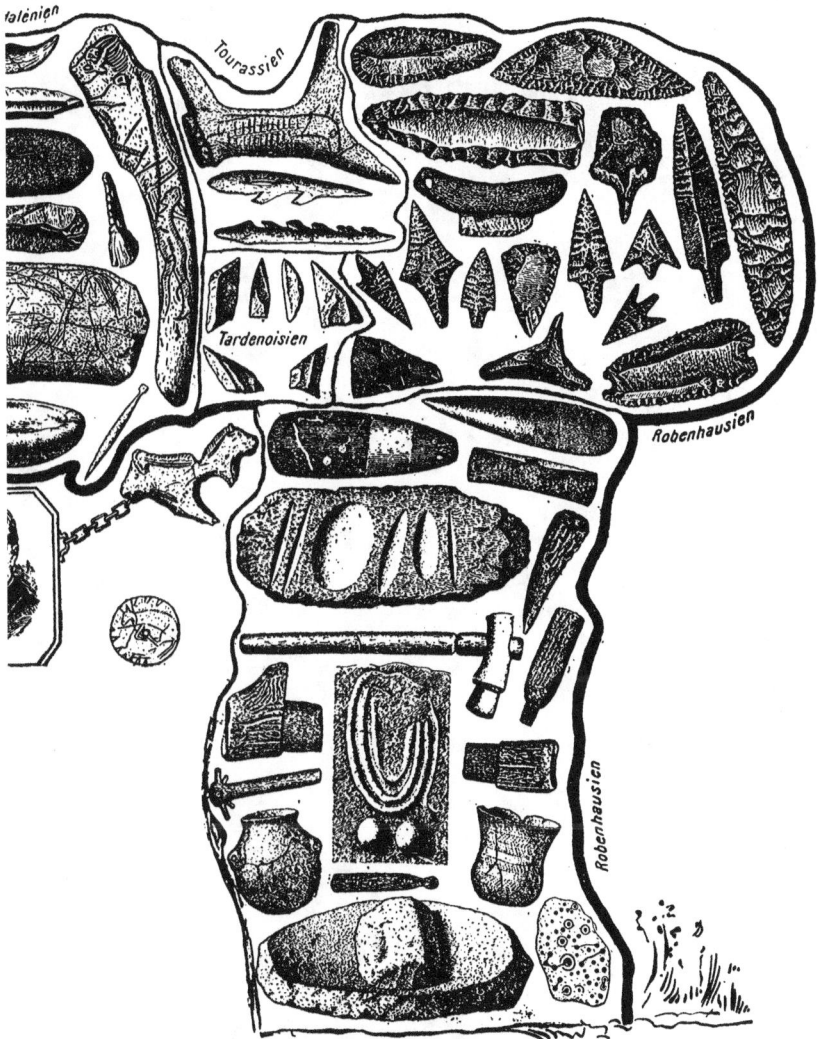

and giving an idea of the progress made by the science of prehistory in 1906.

Pliny the Elder, Strabo, Diodorus Siculus, curious guesses at truth can be found. The verses of Horace [1] are well known : " When living creatures crawled forth upon primeval earth, dumb shapeless beasts, they fought for their acorns and their lairs with nails and fists, then with clubs and, later, with the weapons which need had forged." The sacred books of the Persians, the Hebrews and the Hindus reveal to us psychologies which go back to the beginnings of humanity. A sacrifice such as Abraham's sacrifice of Isaac or Agamemnon's of Iphigeneia throw bright light on the bloodstained rites of early man. A hymn such as the Sanscrit one in honour of the god Agni, a legend like the Greek one of Prometheus tells us of the excitement aroused by the discovery of fire. When Herodotus describes the customs of the Scythians, when Tacitus takes us to the tribes that inhabited ancient Germany, they preserve the knowledge of usages which took their origin in the remote past.

In our investigation into the past we have also the help of a science which is equally of recent origin, that is, of ethnography. Its aim is to describe and compare the customs of the peoples and it affords us ample wealth of information. On the one hand there is what is called folklore, the mass of tales and popular traditions wherein are naively expressed beliefs and ideas which go very far back into the past, descriptions of games, costumes, and customs, and furniture, and tradition of all kinds which still exist among the peasantry in the very heart of the modern civilizations. Need one cite examples ? The ogre who delights in human flesh, who seeks to devour Tom Thumb and his brothers recalls the fact that cannibalism was once universal. The fires of St. John when the women quarrel over the coals, which I have seen in the Vélay accompanied by libations poured on the hearth are a memory of the cult of which the sun and fire, his representative on earth, were the objects. Equally certain tools still in use reproduce archaic types which date from the days when they were fashioned in bronze and stone.

On the other hand, the researches of folklorists must be completed by the accounts given by travellers who have been able to study the custom of peoples who are not at all, or only partially, civilized. These peoples have been called living

---

[1] *Sat.*, i, 3, 99 (Fairclough's translation).

primitives. We will say later how this description ought to be modified. But it is certain that they give us a great mass of information, a mass which increases with time. The Middle Ages knew the account given by Marco Polo of his wanderings in the Far East. The voyage of Vasco da Gama round Africa to India, the discovery of the New World, gave fresh stimulus to the burning curiosity which the appearance of unsuspected races stirred up in old Europe. From these times forward the accounts of travellers go on increasing. Soldier-adventurers who went out to conquer new lands, traders who sought gold and the produce of exotic climes, missionaries who went to win souls, readily tell us what they saw. To mention only French writers, Montaigne wrote on the Carribbean native, a few odd specimens of which he had seen in France, a chapter where in anticipation of Rousseau he pronounced a panegyric on the noble savages who could be cannibals and yet remain the noblest of the children of men. In the seventeenth century Regnard risked a journey to the Lapps and gave us the lively record of his experiences. Pallas in the eighteenth century carefully explored Siberia.

It is true that we cannot accept blindly all that the travellers tell us. The civilized observer often unwittingly distorts as he describes. The missionaries preoccupied with their religious work were the victims of many delusions and errors. As Rousseau says [1] : " To study men it is necessary to possess qualities with which saints are not invariably endowed." He regretted that there were not scientific explorers who would content themselves with stating what they could observe and no more of the customs of uncivilized peoples. It was a regret that his successors did not need to share. In the second half of the eighteenth century come the great French and English travellers who explore the ocean and seek to give a faithful account of what they saw—Cook, Wallis, Bougainville, La Pérouse. In the nineteenth century really scientific expeditions explored Africa, Australia, Tierra del Fuego, the lands of the Eskimos. The names of Caillé, Mungo Park, Livingstone, Stanley, Brazza, Étienne Richet, are famous names on a roll too long to reproduce. To-day we possess a vast accumulation of information on the laggards of civilization.

[1] *Discours sur les origines de l'inégalité.*

But here a grave question needs to be answered. How far do these alleged primitives give us an idea of what early man did and thought ? It has been held that they are degenerates, and the thesis has often been sustained by Catholic and Protestant theologians for whom the fall of man as the result of original sin is an article of faith. It is possible that certain peoples have known in former days a social state superior to that which they have to-day, although that is not easy to prove. But, as far as the enormous majority of those whom we proudly call savages are concerned, the supposition is perfectly arbitrary. They appear to us not as degenerates, but as backward peoples, who, having reached a certain level of development, have stopped, have marked time or have progressed only at a tortoise pace while the marching wing of humanity forged steadily ahead. Why this halt in development ? It appears to be due to a variety of causes. A race like the Pygmies, for instance, was badly fitted for the struggle by reason of their small stature. The inhabitants of the Congo and those of Tierra del Fuego were halted because the climate was in the one case too hot, in the other too cold. Ease of existence produces the same effect as extreme difficulty. Men who, as was the case in Tahiti, can dispense with effort because of an environment which supplies their needs without effort on their part lose all power of activity. Men isolated in the ocean or in the desert, left to their own devices, deprived of intercourse with other peoples, are driven back on themselves, and live in a state of ankylosis, in a mesh of unchangeable traditions and customs.

The result is that it is impossible to deduce from these the conditions prevailing among peoples better endowed and with more initiative ; for the latter had in them virtues of curiosity, daring, and invention thanks to which they were able to rise on the scale of humanity.

But, with these reservations, and they are very necessary, it is none the less true that everywhere one observes striking analogies between the rudimentary civilization of the backward peoples and those of fossil man as caverns and tombs reveal them to us. In many a case what exists in the present explains to us the past. It is equally true that the uncivilized races represent a degree of barbarism which their more

B

fortunate brothers reached and crossed and so there is authority for relating their customs to those which were practised and then abandoned by the progressive peoples. When we find among them arrows equipped with a stone point there is no longer any doubt of the use to which were put those lozenge-shaped flints which the excavations have yielded in hundreds, and which the incredulous at first denied to be the work of human hands. Their paintings on the Australian rocks, their dances, their fetishes, have enabled us to solve the puzzles presented by the mysterious designs and strange statuettes of earlier days.

Not only is their mode of life instructive. It is the same with their mode of thought, which permits us to understand the processes of those whom we cannot raise from the dead to question. They indicate to us what primitive man was, a creature of quick emotions, impulsive in character, ready to believe in apparitions and occult powers, and reveal to us the imperturbable logic with which these inexperienced minds drew the only possible conclusions, perfectly false ones, from false premises. Did not the natives of the Marquesas when they first met Europeans marvel at metal which they had never seen, and steal nails to plant in the ground in the belief that a tree would grow which would bear metal fruit?

Here becomes visible the great and difficult task which the prehistorian must undertake. It is not enough to ascertain facts, gather and class authentic objects. He must interpret them and to do so he needs two qualities which are contradictory, but which balance one another—an imagination ready to guess, able to divine what could be the processes of rude mentalities, and the events that could transpire under very varied conditions of existence; then to control these bold excursions into the unknown, he needs a spirit of criticism which will sift mercilessly all the hypotheses and, if it must be, end his work with a provisional mark of interrogation. Just as a naturalist who possesses a single bone can reconstruct the entire animal in virtue of Cuvier's principle, that in an organized being there is concordance of parts, so the prehistorian can, from the surviving fragments, reconstruct a whole civilization. Much ingenuity has been spent on this field and if sometimes there was excessive boldness, its results have been gradually corrected, so completely indeed that if the reader does not ask the miracle of impossible exactness of detail, he can have on prehistory a mass of certainties accompanied by a whole series of probabilities.

But we must take certain precautions in our study. It is useful to place oneself, so to say, at the level of these simple beings whose processes we seek to explain, whose method of feeling and reasoning we seek to understand. But as we have not always handy a noble savage to bombard with questions to which he either will not or cannot make answer, as it is in any case difficult to fathom the motives which determine his action, recourse may be had to the child. Just as the human embryo in its mother's womb passes through the lower and earlier stages of animal life, so the child in its games, its ideas of the world, its relations with its environment, unconsciously reproduces the infancy of humanity. Quite naturally it believes itself the centre of the universe ; it relates to itself all that passes around it ; it lends to inanimate objects will and purpose in relation to itself ; it strikes the door which has shut to on its fingers ; it loses its temper with the fire which will not burn ; it is as ready to cry as to laugh ; it is impatient, profoundly egoistical, easily cruel, cunning, untruthful ; it enters on life burdened with an inheritance of which it gradually gets rid. The man who understands children well is the better fitted to understand these grown children, primitive men. One can hardly fail to be struck by the resemblance between the figures that children draw on the walls and those of the grottos which depict the dances in which the contemporaries of the prehistoric artist delighted.

One can even descend lower in the scale of life. It is not in vain that we turn to animal psychology. The ancients did not disdain to do so. What does Montaigne write ? " Democritus believed and proved that the beasts taught us most of the arts, the spider to weave and to sew, the swallow to build, the swan and the nightingale to sing, and several animals to cure." In his turn Herder [1] says : " If man was able to make the animals subject to his law, he owes a good

[1] In his *Philosophy of History.*

deal of this triumph to the animals themselves, for from them he received his first instruction." These teachers, indeed, taught him much. The ant taught him to construct huts ; dogs, pigs, crows, vultures, and hyenas taught him to get rid of dead bodies and debris that engenders plague ; cats and elephants taught him to clean his body ;   the bear to steal honey ;   the hippopotamus and the stork to purge his stomach ;   sheep, asses, and horses to take advantage of mineral waters as happened, so it is said, at Barèges and at Challes. In the animal, and especially in a less known world, that of the insects, there are, says Maeterlinck,[1] " Architects, geometricians, mechanics, engineers, weavers, doctors, chemists, surgeons, who anticipated the majority of human inventions." Are not hives and ant-hills, if not models of social organization, at least striking examples of association to preserve life ?   In ages when the gulf that separates man from his inferior brothers was not so wide as it is to-day, he borrowed more than one thing from them which was well worth borrowing.

From all this, it may be seen that prehistory can be served by studies which do not appear related to it. But in this reconstruction of the past which it undertakes there are many errors to guard against and to avoid, and it may be well to take some precautions against making them. Firstly, when custom, a weapon, a tool, is met in countries often very far apart from each other, it would be rash to conclude that there has been imitation. The essential needs of man are everywhere the same, and it is natural that man, to satisfy them, should make use of analogous means. Nothing is easier to understand than that the materials of which they disposed, that the soil or climate which they enjoyed were, for certain peoples, the cause of precocious development. It is probable, even certain, that there were migrations, invasions, and infiltrations which brought new development in their train. In the historical period the Spaniards brought the horse to Mexico, which appeared a divine animal to the natives, so much so, indeed, that they sent a part of the first horse that was killed to the chief cities to prove to the people that it was not invulnerable. Later still the Europeans intro-duced into Australia the sheep and the rabbit. That occurred

[1] *L'hôte inconnu*, p. 226.

at a period relatively recent on which we have full information. Similarly bronze and iron came to our Western lands from more civilized lands in the East. But when we see the bow and arrow employed in Patagonia just as it was in the land which was to become France, the boomerang—that strange bit of curved wood which zigzags through the air and strikes to left and right, in front or behind—used at the present day in Australia just as it was in ancient Egypt, it is not necessary to suppose that this invention in ages when communication was peculiarly difficult, made the circumnavigation of the globe. It would appear, as far as one can judge, although documents are lacking for immense tracts and research in China,[1] Japan, and Central Asia has scarcely begun, that the scattered human groups everywhere followed analogous ways of development. Certainly it was an unequal way. According to climate, environment, race, some advanced more swiftly than others ; in its march the army of humanity has always had both advance guard and stragglers. Doubtless, too, the march was not continous. There were halts and retreats caused by a cosmic catastrophe, an epidemic, a famine, an invasion, which on many occasions interrupted the most regular and productive evolution.

From this two conclusions follow which seem contradictory. On the one hand, we must admit that the processes known in one country are, generally speaking, the same as we shall find elsewhere, that there is a logical succession of phases, through which evolution practically everywhere passes. On the other hand, we must recognize that certain peoples have had special destinies ; they have jumped stages and at a bound passed from one stage of civilization to one much higher, or have by some catastrophe been hurled back in a terrible regression.

To give concrete examples, it is very likely that men first of all used wood, shells, bones, stone, earth, and then, in the order mentioned, copper, bronze, and iron. But it is not right to speak of an age of stone, an age of bronze, an age of iron, unless particular care is taken to localize them, for it is quite certain that one people was still using stone

---

[1] The first excavations in China under the supervision of Fathers Licent and Teilhard yielded 18,000 kilos of fossil bones and articles (*Dépêche de Toulouse*, 14th Feb., 1926).

instruments, while another had already learned the art of forging tools and weapons of metal. That can be easily proved. When the invaders burned and wiped out the lacustran cities, their success was, it seems, made certain by the superiority which the possession of swords and shields of iron gave them. When towards the end of the eighteenth century Captain Cook landed at the Marquesas the natives were still in the stone age, while Europe had arrived at the machine age, and the age of steam and electricity.

If it is mere prudence, therefore, not to cut up the past into periods which will be false for one people just because they are correct for another, it is also prudent not to seek to attain an impossible accuracy of detail and especially of chronology. Once upon a time it was possible for historians like Bossuet to fix the year of creation as 4004 B.C. ; a theologian even gave the day of the month on which the rains that formed the Flood began to descend. This fantastic chronology is on a level with the information supplied by the Palestinian guide who will show you the tree on which Judas hanged himself and the place where Abraham tethered his ass when ordered by the Lord to sacrifice Isaac. To-day we reckon by hundreds and thousands of centuries [1] where our forefathers thought they were generous in allowing six thousand years. This invention, that custom, that implement, can be placed anywhere in a vast lapse of time. We must be content with vague approximations when we speak of time and place, of where and when the most important innovations took place. Who would dare say when or where man first learned how to make fire ?

But having thus pointed out the dangers against which we must be on our guard, we must go on to trace with care the limits of the subject which we propose to study, and the way in which we intend to study it. We intend to relate to the different human needs the different activities which were fated to satisfy them, to show how the need to drink, eat, sleep, and defend oneself against heat, cold, beasts, and other men, to clothe oneself, to have a place to live in, to preserve the species, and to express feelings and ideas gave birth to various industries and to different languages and groupings

[1] M. Verneau in *Les origines de l'humanité* considers that man appeared 100,000 years ago.

of mankind ; how, then, the domestication of animals, agriculture, hostile or friendly relations between one group and another, war, and commerce, have given birth to fortification, means of transport, common measures, and unwritten laws and customs ; how finally the division of labour not only assigned distinctive tasks to men and women and to specialists in the different trades, but gradually separated within each group chiefs and subjects, masters and slaves, manual workers and intellectual workers, of whom the latter were to become sorcerers, priests, doctors, and to regulate the social and religious life.

We will close our study at the moment, which varies according to country and people, when both peoples and countries enter into history. Even so the field of investigation is an enormous one. We shall enter on it boldly without claiming that we shall cover it all, and still less that we shall examine it in its entirety, but will be content if we can trace a living picture which is not without resemblance to what prehistory was. For of prehistory, and with more reason, one can say what was said of Montesquieu's *Esprit des Lois* : " The human race had lost its title-deeds, and it has found them again."

II. Beginnings and Principles of Prehistory

It is not enough to know the methods and the sources of information of prehistory. We must know how the science which studies it came into being and what divisions it has traced in the immense extent of time and space which it covers. Our science is a very young one, it is not yet a century old, and like every new science it has had to contend with many and serious difficulties. What the ancient Greeks and Romans had glimpsed of the origin of humanity had been forgotten or was despised, and in the darkness which veiled these origins if, by chance, a ray of light penetrated, it was like a lightning flash—swiftly lit and swiftly extinguished. Among the supermen of the Renascence, Leonardo da Vinci and Bernard Palissy seem on these matters to have known something by the intuition of genius. About the same time the Tuscan, Mercati, conjectured that the stones, sometimes called thunderbolts, or *cerauniae*, might well be primitive weapons, and, at the beginning of the eighteenth century,

the Jesuit Lafitau and the naturalist Jussieu compared them
to the weapons of savages.

In 1715 an English antiquary found near the Thames,
beside the remains of elephants, flints which seemed to have
been worked by man, but the memoir in which he reported
the fact passed unnoticed. What probability was there that
elephants and savages, their contemporaries, had ever lived
in Britain ? About the middle of the same century Eccard
and Goguet in France, remembering their Lucretius, opined
that stone, bronze, and iron had succeeded one another at
the beginning of human civilization. Buffon, who in his
Époques de la Nature had discreetly hinted at the antiquity
of the earth, advanced the view that the oldest inhabitants
of our continent " had begun by sharpening to the shape of
an axe those hard stones, those thunderbolts which are
popularly believed to have fallen from heaven and which
are in reality the first specimens of human art ". Rousseau
spoke of the stone axes with the cutting edge which were used
in the beginnings to cut wood, and asked if the orangutang
was man or beast.[1] In 1797 three flints, worked to the shape
of an almond, were discovered mingled with elephant bones
in Suffolk. John Frere described them in 1800, but in the
interest aroused by the wars in Europe his memoir was little
noticed.

When peace was restored, discoveries began to come thick
and fast from about 1820. In 1823 Ami Boué brought fossil
human remains from Austria to Paris, but the Academies
agreed to see in them only fragments gleaned from some old
graveyard. In 1828 and 1829 Fuornol and Christol dug up
from caverns in the south of France bones of men and of
rhinoceri, but the discovery attracted but little attention.
Then began the period of international discovery. In 1833
Schmerling made successful excavations in the caverns in
the neighbourhood of Liège. In Denmark Thomsen and his
pupil Worsae, in Mecklenburg-Schwerin Friedrich Lisch
from 1839 to 1849, laid down that the basis of European
archæology was the succession of what they called the three
ages, those of stone, bronze, and iron.

Then, little by little, were organized the data which were
available. But by virtue of the solidarity which exists between

[1] In the *Origine de l'inégalité parmi les hommes.*

all branches of human knowledge other sciences came to the aid of their latest brother and helped it to growth. Geology, whose masters played with estimates of millions of years, gave scientists the habit of plunging boldly into the mists of antiquity. Palæontology, whose master Cuvier had laid down the principle of the harmony of the organs of the living being, and from a simple fragment reconstructed the gigantic saurians of vanished centuries, spread the conception of whole species, which had once existed in these climates, but had been driven to distant regions or had perished altogether.

Science became bolder in its conjectures. It seemed as if it was on the point of discovering the origin of humanity, to win an easy triumph and to advance unhindered along the two roads of investigation open to it, the one pushing back the age of man into a remote antiquity, the other leading to the knowledge of his first labours.

It was not to be. Two forces ranged them against it in defence of tradition—theology and official science. What was to become of the Bible story in face of these revelations coming out of the strata which are the repositories of man's earliest archives ? Instead of a miserable six thousand years they spoke of an evolution which in time took thousands of centuries. Father Gratry and the Bishop of Oxford declared that to push time past the consecrated date was anti-Christian. Instead of a privileged creature who fell by sin from a golden existence, a hairy and savage creature was seen emerging with difficulty from the beasts. There was no solution save either to accuse of error books regarded as of divine origin, or by one of the miracles of compromise which separates one's mental processes into watertight compartments, to allow the truths of religion and the truths of science to live side by side, but kept carefully apart. It is easy to understand that priests and believers regarded with suspicion those investigators whom they held to be tainted with heresy. Some of them thought that there were men before Adam ; others blushed to think that they had ancestors so near in kin to the monkey. One need not be astonished. Without going back to the tragedy of Galileo, one need only remember how a year or two ago a Dayton teacher was tried and convicted for having taught the theory of evolution according to Darwin, which was attacked and condemned for not agreeing with the Bible narrative.

Equally the scientists enrolled in the great societies either out of deference to the Church or moved by that sense of discomfort which every new discovery brings to men comfortably established in their own conceit and on opinions which they have come to consider infallible, greeted with mocking laughter things which surprised and disturbed them. One must admit that they had some ground for scepticism. They could recall how in the eighteenth century a skeleton had been shown throughout France as that of a giant which actually was that of an enormous lizard, and that quite recently there had been found at Long Rocher in the forest of Fontainebleau stones which bore a rough resemblance to a horse and his rider, and that a simple freak of nature had been held to be a masterpiece of the art of remote antiquity.

Those who had to make headway against an implacable and well-armed opposition supported by the great name of Cuvier had need of hearts well armoured against sarcasm, contempt, and insult. Remember the experience of Boucher de Perthes, the real founder in France of the science of prehistory.   This   customs   official   was   a   passionate archæologist. He had been struck by the discovery of two flint axeheads fixed in staghorn which workmen had found when they were digging a canal outside Abbeville. Other digging, especially at Saint Acheul, in the same neighbourhood, yielded objects of a similar type and in 1838 he declared before the Mutual Improvement Society of Abbeville that these were human documents of the very first importance. Unhappy pioneer !   When he came to Paris to explain his discoveries, he was looked down upon as a member of a society in the provinces. He was accused of having been taken in by fabrications or, at the very least, of having incorrectly measured the strata in which the finds were made. He won over a few scientists, but Élie de Beaumont and the Academy of Sciences pronounced decisively an adverse verdict and soon the whole affair was forgotten.

During the revolution of 1848 Frenchmen were too busy to attend to things of the intellect, and nothing further happened till 1854. In 1853–4 the winter was a very dry one, and an unexpected discovery made the controversy flare up afresh. The waters of the Lake of Zurich had fallen so low that the people of Meilen thought it possible to reclaim some land permanently. In the mud in which they dug they were astonished to find quantities of objects in flint, horn, bone, and bronze, and stakes which appeared to have been piles which had suffered the effects of a great fire. A doctor, Ferdinand Keller, guessed that this had been the site of houses built on the water, the *lacustran dwellings* or *palafittes*,[1] whose remains had been buried in mud for centuries. He published an account of the discovery of this aquatic village, made himself, or inspired others to make, similar investigations in many lakes in Switzerland, France, Italy, South Germany, Holland, and elsewhere, to such purpose that a whole civilization was brought to light. About the same time, on the coasts of Denmark, artificial mounds [2] had been excavated in which was abundance of shells, fishbones, refuse, and cooking utensils—irrefutable witness of long connection with a people which had once lived in the neighbourhood. Later, quantities of these heaps were to be found on the Atlantic Coast from Portugal to Sweden, not to speak of Sardinia and Algeria, and the American coast.

Then the caverns like that of Aurignac near Saint Gaudens, were excavated, and greatly increased the prehistoric treasure heaps. It was no longer possible to silence such eloquent testimony. Boucher de Perthes with tireless obstinacy had converted some of his adversaries, and then in 1858 after two visits from English scientists who came to control his digging at Abbeville and Saint Acheul, his intelligence and his integrity were solemnly recognized, first in London and then in France, where finally only a few diehards were left to maintain their obstinate and prejudiced incredulity. In the same year, 1858, Broca founded the Society of Anthropology, whose *Bulletin* was to be the organ for spreading the new knowledge. In short one can fix 1860 as the date when the new science was established and took its place among its fellows. Henceforward it could advance. The School of Anthropology of Paris was founded in 1866.

From this time onward research has intensified and the

---

[1] An Italian word meaning constructions on piles.
[2] They are called *Kjökken-mödinger* in Denmark, *sambaquis* in Brazil, *paraderos* in Patagonia, and *escargotières* in Algeria.

books on it form a vast library. We cannot mention here the names of those who have brought stones to the edifice that the science is building. There are too many of them.[1] We ask those whom for the moment we pass by in silence to forgive us for we have to keep strictly to the essential and to indicate the general conclusions our science has reached, conclusions which risk being submerged by formidable masses of detail. Such a task is the more necessary as, in the early days of excavation, every station where something was found, aspired to give its name to a separate stage of civilization. Thus were created far too many local sub-divisions and, patriotism intervening, every country claimed the honour of having been at one time a centre of human development. Now it is absolutely impossible to determine the rôle which the various countries played in the early development of humanity. Our present knowledge is related especially to western and central Europe, to hither Asia, to the Mediterranean area, to America, and to Australia : India and north and central Asia, where several developments seem to have had their origin and the Far East, where investigations which seem likely to be productive, have only recently begun, may have more than one surprise in store for us. So we must indicate lacunæ in our knowledge and leave the door wide to the conjectures and certainties of the future when we seek to give a brief account of the phases through which has passed a prehistory which in certain lands still exists to-day.

In the first instance we must recall the four great epochs into which geology divides the history of the earth :—the *primary*, in which predominate the fish and the forests, which will later be buried and later still become coal ; the *secondary*, in which birds and reptiles appear, in which

---

[1] In a book written by a Frenchman and published originally in France it would, however, be base ingratitude not to mention some names ; of those who are no longer with us, Édouard Lartet, Piette, Cartailhac, Gabriel de Mortillet, Déchelette, Deniker, Letourneau, Élie Reclus, and, of the living, Marcellin Boule, Verneau, the Abbé Breuil, Capitan, Charles Frémont, Camille Julian, Louis Franchet, Jacques de Morgan, Salomon Reinach, Henri Bégouen. I could easily make the list longer, but as I proceed with my task I shall have the opportunity to name many others who do not deserve to be forgotten.

were formed limestone, flint, coal, and amber; the *tertiary* in which mammals and vertebrates appear on the earth, which is now firm; and the *quaternary*, which is still going on, in which men and animals in obedience to the climate, which suffers several drastic changes move sometimes northward sometimes southward, and live in turn under the sky or in caves.

The first question we have to answer, a question which arises in the study of human palæontology, is the date at which man made his appearance among the living beings which preceded him in the world. He may have had in the tertiary period a precursor, ancestor or collateral. Those who think that he had, base their belief either on skeletons or fragments of skeletons which have been discovered, or on certain flints and bones which seem to bear traces of the work of an intelligent being. Among these survivals which are called as witness to the existence of tertiary man, the best known is the fragmentary skull found at Trinil in Java, in 1891, which in 1894 was minutely studied by Dr. Dubois and Dr. Manouvrier. It has been considered part of the skeleton of a *pithecanthropos* or man-ape. In 1926 a second discovery was made at the same spot, this time of a complete skull, but it does not belong to a being of the same species.

Long ago the great naturalist Lamarck had indicated the possibility of the transformation of a four-handed animal into an animal with two feet and two hands. Darwin, in the *Origin of Species*, had adopted Lamarck's idea. Anthropologists since have shown how the gorilla, described as an imperfect biped and, still more, the chimpanzee, are anatomically related to man. One of the pioneers of palæontology, Edouard Lartet, published in 1860 his *Memoire sur l'ancienneté géologique de l'espèce humaine dans l'Europe occidentale*, and admitted the existence of tertiary man, a being possessing semi-simian characteristics. To those who felt humiliated by the bestial origin of humanity, Huxley addressed the ironic question: " Is it better to be a degenerate Adam or a perfected monkey ? "

Other fossil bones betrayed the resemblance between man and the ape. A skeleton dug up in Lombardy at Castenedolo, a jawbone found in 1907 near Heidelberg, other remains found at Piltdown in England (1912), at Taubach, near Weimar, at Brokenhill in South Africa, at Talgai in Australia, appear to belong to beings who are equidistant from men and from the ape.

As to the objects which seem to be the work of man certain flints have been found at Puy Curny, near Aurillac, at Ipswich in England, and at Otta in Portugal, in strata which go back to the end of the tertiary period. They have been called *eoliths*, a name signifying the beginning of the stone age. But are they really man's work? The controversy still rages. Certain striated bones found at Thenay (Loir-et-Cher) and at Saint-Prest (Eure-et-Loir) have been adduced as evidence. The Abbé Bourgeois believed that in their markings traces of intelligent work were visible. It was objected that the marks could have been made by wild beasts and that—which is more probable—they were due to the friction of earth and stones on friable material. A Belgian scientist, Rutot, believed that he had found a great many flakes of flint which were due to human work. But M. André Laville examined the heaps of stones, which were used at a cement factory at Guerville, near Mantes, and found among them fragments exactly like those which had been attributed to human work, and so their claim to be man's handiwork remains doubtful. The same holds true of the stones marked by fire which have been occasionally found in tertiary strata. It was remarked that a forest fire could explain the markings without having recourse to an intelligent being who knew how to make fire. The subject has been brought up again *à propos* the marks found on a whale skeleton found at Monte Aperto, in Italy. M. Lapellini thought that they could have been made by a flint. But it was remarked that they could just as well have been made by the teeth of a shark.

Thus the experts are divided. The question remains open, and it is prudent to regard either answer as doubtful until we can dispose of wider knowledge. But what is certain is the existence of human activity at the beginning of the quaternary epoch, that is to say, if one adopts the reckoning of Professor Verneau, about one hundred thousand years ago. Here one can classify human progress in seven stages [1] each dove-tailing into the other according to the

_____
[1] Wood, shell, stone, clay, copper, bronze, iron.

material which man used to make weapons, tools, and utensils.

His first material was *wood*. The club with which Heracles is armed in Greek legend, the stick which so long remained the badge of the commander in the shape of sceptre, cross, or marshal's baton, were the first instruments whereby man increased the power of his arms. Handles for tools, baskets, vessels and ladles of wood, plugs of bark and pointed stakes were very early invented and, if time which disintegrates vegetable matter, has destroyed many of the objects which the trees furnished to the first men, it is none the less certain that branches transformed into clubs were means of attack and defence whose efficacy none can deny.

Then there comes *shell* which furnishes not merely objects of adornment, but models for cutting tools.

Then, or at the same time, comes *stone* with bone and horn as subdivisions. It is not only a case of picking up stones and hurling them anyhow to bring down a fruit or to strike an enemy, but of making use of fragments at first those which of themselves afforded a point or a cutting edge and then of working and modifying them. As stone was for long in use and as it is durable enough to defy the action of time, we can mark the stone age off into divisions and subdivisions. According to the greater or less variety and fineness of workmanship of weapons and tools of stone, two great civilizations are distinguished : The first is that of splintered stone or *palæolithic* ; the second that of polished stone or *neolithic*. In its turn *palæolithic* in Europe is divided into three periods, *lower*, *middle*, and *upper* which we will briefly describe.

In the *lower palæolithic* when Europe had still a semi-tropical climate, man had reached a degree of civilization such as the Tasmanians had reached when the Europeans first made their acquaintance. He was a hunter and fisher, lived in the open air, had knowledge probably of fire and had learned to build rudimentary huts. In our regions he was contemporary with the bear, the hyæna, the hippopotamus, the rhinoceros with divided nostrils, the lion, and the mammoth. He used as tools rough-hewed flints which were mainly scrapers and punches with which he treated the skins of animals and also the *coups de poing*, as Gabriel de Mortillet called them, made of a cutting stone whose heel he covered with moss so as not to wound himself. For ornaments he had coloured seeds, the teeth of wild beasts and shells, perforated and threaded. As distinguishing names, the names of the first explored stations in what is now France have been chosen, *Chelles* and *Saint Acheul*. Under their names are classified objects which present the same characteristics as those found in these two stations, and which have been in use all over the world, in Belgium, Germany, Italy, Greece, Spain, Portugal, Britain, Africa, and America. Flints which seem to be older than those of Chelles are called *pre-Chellean* and M. Capitan dates then to 125,000 years before our era.

The *middle palæolithic* or *mesolithic* period saw man, under the influence of several returns of cold when glaciers came down to the plains of Europe, to Britain and as far as Lyons, bury himself in the caves, true nurturing ground of rheumatism, for whose possession he strove with the wild beasts, and access to which was often difficult and dangerous. It saw him eke out a painful existence, surrounded by reindeer which he had not yet domesticated, and probably reduced more than once for lack of game to eat his like. It saw him, however, accessible to larger and more complicated thought, for his skull, to judge by that of the skeleton found at La Chapelle aux Saints (Corrèze) which dates from this period, had a capacity of 1,626 c.c., while that of the pithecanthropos of Java had a capacity only of 855 c.c. and that of the anthropoid apes has one of only 622 c.c. Another skeleton found at Neanderthal in Rhenan Prussia makes him a relative of certain modern Australian tribes, so close a relative indeed, that a German scientist, Herr Schoetenschack, has ventured to make Australia the cradle of the human race.

To confine ourselves to Europe, however, the station of Moustier near Eyzies on the Vézère will suffice to give a name to a type of civilization which seems to betray a certain physical degeneration due to the rigour and variability of the climate. Nevertheless it is possible that the difficulties of existence due to the alternation of heat and cold have tempered the will and developed the inventive faculties of the men of this period. There are many stations akin to Moustier, stretching from Moravia to Spain, and everywhere the desire to preserve the dead from total destruction and from the hyænas, the scavengers of corpses and perhaps still more to preserve the living from the terror of ghosts, led men to place heavy stones on the tombs and furnish the dead with food, drink and arms in this underground life after death.

Then comes the *upper palæolithic* period. It is represented in our regions by the skeletons of Cro-Magnon (Dordogne), of Menton (Maritime Alps), and Paviland in Wales, by a race of invaders who seem to have come from the south and resembled Hottentots and Eskimos and by three station-types, Aurignac near Saint Gaudens, Solutré near Mâcon, and La Madeleine near Sarlat. In all the civilizations known under these three names there is technical regression in certain manufactured objects, for example, in the working of flint, but new tools appear, artistic ability such as had not been seen and great progress in the working of bone and ivory.

Man is revealed to us as still confined to the caves which are scattered throughout Europe, living on what he can gather and by hunting and fishing. His game includes the wild horse, the mammoth, the hare, the deer, and the buffalo. Inside his cave, however, or just outside, he indulges in painting, sculpture, and engraving, designing and colouring, no doubt for a magical purpose, stones, hands, and images of animals, and, though less commonly, human figures, modelling clay buffaloes and giving proof in these naive works of art of artistic sensibility and ability which raises him above his brothers. As we go on, utensils, tools, weapons, cups and lamps, engraving tools, harpoons, boomerangs, javelins with propellers become more perfected ; some of them have been dipped in poison, a step towards perfection in the art of killing.

One example will show how difficult and delicate is the exploration of the caverns. I take that of the Tuc d'Audoubert, in the Ariège department, which was explored in 1912. The entrance is barred by a watercourse, which is the re-emergence of a river, the Volp, hidden in the rocks. In winter it is impossible to get in, for the Volp is a raging torrent. In summer one must plunge in and proceed underground by the aid of a boathook for some seventy yards. Then galleries dripping with water open out before one where

c

it is just possible to walk dryshod. Then one comes to a cave of three storeys. The first is at the river level ; the second nearly three yards higher, and when one has climbed into the latter one finds oneself in great halls hung with stalactites and with walls covered with engravings representing horses. Then, by a narrow chimney, which rises almost straight, and then twists and turns, one climbs up using the ridges in the rock. A corridor is reached whose walls are covered with engraved bisons. The passage is· blocked by stalactites ; they must be broken or clambered over and one reaches the third storey, vast halls where are found the bones of bears and the marks of their paws, together with imprints of human feet and tools of flint, which are millennia old. That is not all. In a recess on a lower level which lies farthest away from the entrance, and which seems to be a sort of sanctuary, stand two clay buffaloes, a male and a female, accompanied by two smaller, half-finished sketches of the same animals. It was M. Henri Bégouen, a professor at the University of Toulouse, who with his sons accomplished this risky journey for which the scientist needs to be acrobat as well.[1]

In many of the caves the walls are covered with designs placed one on top of the other, so that it is not easy to determine which is the most recent in date. Besides outside on the cliffs there are drawings of a wolf and a lioness accompanied by marks whose significance we do not yet know.

To return to the inhabitants of the caves. The climate changes ; it grows warmer and becomes settled. The fauna and flora are very much like that which exists there to-day. Species disappear like the mammoths. Others, like the lion and hyæna, have emigrated southward ; others for whom

---

[1] *V.* also in the *Journal des Débats* for 9th October, 1926, an article by M. Bégouen on the cave of Montespan (Haute-Garonne) and in the *Dépêche de Toulouse* of the same date an article by M. Alexis Coutet on the same subject from the latter of which I quote what follows : " The excursion into the cave would hold attraction both for the Alpinist and the devotee of aquatic sports. The Ariadne's thread of this labyrinth is the stream, which, so to speak, is its foundation. It is also the only way in and one has to walk along it, all the time in icy cold water always ankle deep and sometimes rising almost to one's waist. After leaving the bed of the stream one has to clamber up steep rocks or scale slopes which wet clay makes terribly slippery. Then one crawls over outcrop as sharp as the teeth of a harrow ; one climbs steep cliffs ; one drags oneself up needle-like rocks or along sharp crests, crossing crevasses at the foot of which there is a black abyss, where one slip and one finally disappears with all one's bones broken by contact with the rocks."

cold has no terrors, like the reindeer and the white bear, have gone north. The men from our regions have, some of them, taken these roads also, which explains the resemblances between the cave-dwellers of old Europe and the Bushmen on the one hand and the Lapps and the Eskimos on the other. Was their place taken by another race less artistic and more practical, which arrived from the Baltic and probably from the East, bringing with it more advanced industries and more perfect tools ?   At any rate, by a slow transition humanity passes from the *palæolithic* to the *neolithic*.

The transition is represented by the stations of *Campigny*, near Rouen, where new tools show themselves, of *Mas d'Azil*, in the Ariège, of *La Fère-en-Tardenois*, remarkable from its tiny flints, and of *Gafsa* in Tunisia. There the world which was passing came in contact with the world that was to succeed it.

From this date we are in the epoch of polished stone. The lance-shaped arrow-heads reveal the regular use of the bow, introduced some time previously. The axes in diorite, jadeite, obsidian, materials which come from far countries, imply the existence of an extensive trade. There is painted pottery ; cordate and striped vessels, urns with human faces which may have been idols. Linen and flax are woven. The dog has been tamed, the first step to the domestication of animals. Sickles reveal the fact that regular agriculture exists. Have there not been obtained from the lacustran cities as remains of the civilization which is called Robenhausian,[1] not merely canoes made out of the hollowed trunks of trees, but evidence that their inhabitants knew apples, pears, and grapes, as well as millet, rye, oats, barley, and wheat, from which they made a sort of unleavened bread.

To this age belong the artificial caves cleverly constructed in tufa and chalk and used as individual or collective sepulchres. Then beside villages built on the water for greater security and which communicated with terra firma only by means of boats or a gangway, exists a sort of entrenched camps [2] which, pitched on isolated heights or forming a

---

[1] From Robenhausen on Lake Pfaeffikon in Switzerland.
[2] Examples : Chassey in the valley of the Saône, Catenoy in the Oise Department and the pueblos in North America.

promontory, served to protect the inhabitants against the beasts or that more dreaded foe, other men. Finally there are strange monuments which are burying places like the covered alleys and dolmens which are so numerous over an area stretching from Brittany to India, menhirs, upright stones sometimes painted, which are ranged sometimes in straight lines, as at Carnac, in the shape of a tortoise, as in America, or in a circle, as is the case with the cromlechs of Morbihan, Stonehenge, and the Deccan. We know neither by whom nor for what reason these monoliths, sometimes of gigantic size, were set up and arranged.

It is to this stage of civilization that apparently belong the peoples who have left on the coasts of the sea or on the edges of the Sahara those mounds which are the refuse of their kitchens (Kjökenmodings, shell-heaps, escargotières).

But already wood, shell, stone, horn, and clay are not the sole materials which man uses. Modelled clay has given birth to pottery and in the furnace have appeared hard and brilliant substances. Metal has made its appearance. As societies, no more than nature, do not proceed by sudden leaps, metal exists side by side with tools of stone.[1] It no longer, however, appears only under the form of brilliant particles of gold or copper, which rival as ornaments shells, the teeth of bear and wolf, and coloured stones. There is copper, soon to be rendered harder by its alloys with zinc, and, especially, with tin, which is the first metal to show itself in the shape of weapons and utensils of all kinds. Then there is bronze—copper and tin—which will be the dominant metal for several centuries and whose use implies the exploitation of mines, the blending of minerals, whose deposits are widely separated, the creation of the forge and the bellows. At first the stone tools are copied in metal. It is a rule that every new invention preserves traces of those which precede it. Thus the breadth of the railways was determined by that of the roads for vehicles and the memory of wax candles is perpetuated in the Jablochkoff electric candles.

But although bracelets, collars, vases, axes, and daggers of metal reproduce the shapes already in use, the sword, the

[1] The stations where this mingling is found have been called *œneolithic*. The word is a bad one, because it is formed of a Latin word and a Greek one, and in its resemblance to *neolithic* can easily give rise to annoying confusion. The word *chalcolithic* is much to be preferred.

helmet, the shield, the cuirass, the brooch, and the pin which serve to hold garments together gradually free themselves from imitation. The novelties pass from one people to another. Each, while retaining its own peculiar characteristics, borrows from its neighbour and that is why it is so obviously improper to speak of an age of bronze as it had been lived through by all the world, even by all Europe simultaneously. In Chaldæa, it began towards the end of the fifth millennium before our era, in Persia and in the Eastern Mediterranean in the third, and in Gaul only in the second. But bronze, which gave superiority to those who knew how to produce it, was in its turn dethroned. Iron, which if not rarer is at least more difficult to isolate, but is more resisting and more malleable, won supremacy. In Europe we see it winning the day in the tombs of Hallstatt in Bavaria and later in those of La Tène in Switzerland near Neuchâtel. No doubt the destroyers of the lacustran cities were armed with iron. Like all metallurgy it came from the East by the North and the Mediterranean. At first it was a precious metal. It made jewels adorned with geometric designs which rivalled in popularity those in ivory, coral, and mother of pearl. It was used for money as in the coins of Lacadæmon : several centuries later it was used to make the crown of Lombardy. At the same time it is put to common uses—spits on which to roast meat, hoes to till the ground, saws, knives, and chisels, the belting for wheels of chariots, shares for ploughs, bits for horses, swords, pikes, daggers, and the like. Who could have foretold what the new invention would mean ? It has been remarked that the invention of the screw [1] which about this time appears in Champagne was by itself the pivot on which turned all the progress of modern industry.

The peoples who knew iron knew also glass and the art of navigation. With them we come to the end of ancient prehistory, and indeed the date at which iron is introduced belongs in many lands to the historic period, that is to say, before they possessed iron, they had learned to preserve the memory of past events by engraving their annals on the monuments or the rocks and had even the rudiments of a script. The historian tells us how the Romans, before

[1] Van Gennep : *Le folklore*, p. 2.

acquiring their short swords of hard iron, fought with long swords of bronze which bent on impact and had to be straightened under the heel of the warrior. Iron entered India, it seems, with the army of Alexander. In America, where gold and silver abound, it was not known till after Columbus. In Oceania and in the north of Siberia it has not been in use for more than a century.

I have thus sketched to the end an evolution to whose details I shall return, and whose phases, as it is my duty to repeat, are determined only for Europe and, even in that restricted sense, one needs to use many an interrogation mark. What migrations of peoples took place, peoples who sometimes migrated in mass and journeyed over the world ? In what part of the earth was born this or that industry ? Some day, I hope, we shall know the answers to these questions.

Meantime I have intentionally neglected much work which deals with the description of the caves and of the tombs or with objects whose use is doubtful like the *bâtons de commandement*, with designs whose meaning we do not know. The neglect is in no way due to contempt for the work of the specialists who have studied these ; their work was necessary and is worthy of all praise. It brings many new facts and many conjectures which steadily reduce the area of the unknown, but it is only indirectly of use in the task I have undertaken.

We may study prehistory by a method which I will call analytic, which consists in examining one after the other a series of civilizations each of which extends over determined space and time. But one can also adopt the synthetic method which seeks to obtain a general view of the conquests which successively and locally man has won. Thus one can consider in turn the various activities by which man has sought to satisfy his needs and show how each was carried on until the time when it enters history not without projecting into our own times not a few curious survivals. It is the latter method that I have chosen and will try to work out in the course of this book. I do not flatter myself that I have brought to it any new facts, the fruit of my own discoveries. I intend to borrow lavishly from the works of those who worked this ground on which I in my turn am working in their train, and I pay homage to labours which did them honour. I confine my ambition to arranging and presenting in my own way what some of the research already made can offer. I ask only that no one shall expect from me more than I have tried to write, a provisional essay towards a prehistoric synthesis.

BIBLIOGRAPHY

BEUCHAT, *Manuel d'archéologie américaine.*

BOULE (Marcellin), *Les hommes fossiles.*

BURKITT, *Prehistory.*

CAPITAN, *Le préhistoire* : *L'Amérique précolombienne* (Collection de l'Histoire universelle du Travail : Alcan) : list drawn up by him of his memoirs and communications to learned societies.

CARTAILHAC, *La France préhistorique.*

DECHELETTE, *Manuel de d'archéologie préhistorique et celtique.*

DENIKER, *Races et peuples de la terre.*

DOIGNEAU, *Nos ancêtres primitifs.*

ESPINAS, *Les sociétés animales.*

LEVY-BRÜHL, *La mentalité primitive.*

LUBBOCK, *Prehistoric Man* : *The Origins of Civilization.*

MACALISTER, *A Textbook of European Archæology.*

MEYER, *Geschichte des Altertums.*

MORTILLET (Gabriel de), *Matériaux pour l'historie positive et philosophique de l'homme* : *Le préhistorique.*

NADAILHAC, *L'Amerique préhistorique.*

RECLUS (Élie), *Le primitif d'Australie.*

VAN GENNEP, *Le Folklore.*

VERNEAU, *Les origines de l'humanité.*

French Reviews : *Revue archéologique* ; *Revue anthropologique* ; *L'Anthropologie* ; *Revue d'Ethnographie* ; *L'annee sociologique.*

Foreign reviews issued by the various anthropological societies. The reports of the various international anthropological congresses. Museums : The Museum of National Antiquities of St. Germain-en-Laye ; the Museum of Ethnography at the Trocadéro ; the Palæontological section at the Museum at Paris ; the Gúimet Museum ; various museums in the provincial cities of France and abroad, and the collections of individuals, e.g. MM. Capitan, Doigneau, etc.

CHAPTER I

FOOD

THE most imperious need a living being feels is to go on living, and man is no exception to the rule. First and foremost, he must eat, drink, and preserve himself from being eaten. Hence a series of inventions, for hunger, thirst, and the instinct of conservation are the first and most potent stimulants to toil. Not without reason did Rabelais [1] call "Messer Gaster", that is, the belly, the first master of arts in the world, and see in him the inventor of all devices, trades and refinements. You cannot, he says, make him believe anything, remonstrate with him or persuade him, for he has no ears. He will have no delays when he calls ; when he issues an order, you must obey at once or die. The wild animals inhabiting the forest, the air or the water obey at the first sign. Everything turns upon him : "All for tripe " as Rabelais says in his own uncompromising manner.

First and foremost, then, man seeks his food. Fruits, grains, herbs, roots—these were his first nourishment. They are all *gathered* and in certain climates are enough. In the island of Ceram, a part of the Molacca archipelago, one sago palm will provide food for a man for a whole year. [2] In Tahiti the breadfruit tree grows wild, and the banana tree is there to supply dessert—a little paradise where there is no serpent. But such spots are rare. Elsewhere the task of finding food was one which occupied primitive man all the day, and left him no time for leisure. We can tell this by observing the primitive peoples still existing, the only kind of primitives that we can study.

To appease the demands of the belly everything was tried. " All goes into the belly," as the old proverb says—acorns, beechnuts, sloes, arbute-berries, walnuts, hazelnuts, chestnuts, geans, etc. Man competed for these with the birds and the pigs, and with the monkeys for dates and coconuts.

[1] Bk. iv, c. 58.
[2] Deniker, J., *Races et peuples de la terre*, 1st edition, p. 171.

But fruits are ripe only in their season, so, with the help of a pointed stick, primitive man dug up and experimented with roots—carrots, turnips, oyster-plants, radishes in our climate, manioc and potatoes in other countries. But it required experiment to ascertain definitely which were good. For lack of better food, herbs were eaten ; explorers in Australia have seen women returning to their huts carrying bundles of clover, although the tribe possessed no cattle, and in the same tribes it was the custom to wipe off the honey of flowers when it was impossible to steal the combs from the wild bees. No doubt there was much retching, indigestion, and deadly pain as a result of unfortunate experiment. How many people were poisoned by mushrooms or by the deceptive berries of the deadly nightshade ?

Certain writers have believed that in the beginning man was entirely frugivorous. Such was Rousseau's opinion, and it has been revived in our time. M. Frédéric Houssay [3] maintains that originally man lived in the trees, as Chinese tradition relates, that he fed himself with the fruit which he found, and he offers as proof of this view the number and shape of man's teeth. To this vegetarian diet he ascribes special virtues. It was the fact that this sort of provender is seasonal that taught man foresight in impressing upon him the necessity of storing up food for the winter as do squirrels, field-mice, hamsters, and certain birds in Texas, who store up acorns in the hollow trunks. He believes that the preservation of geans and sloes in a hole lined with clay was the origin of fermented liquors, and also that the study of plants gave man the idea of sowing the seed. According to this view man became carnivorous only under compulsion and because of a lack of vegetable food.

The hypothesis is interesting, perhaps for certain countries true, and can be partially accepted. But it is not a probable one in the case of humanity considered as a whole. Man is not constructed like the ruminant which passes its life in rechewing and digesting the vegetable food with which it gorges itself. The skulls of fossil men do not give one the idea of peaceful vegetarians. Their jaws are fitted with sharp teeth, which betray the flesh-eater. Man was omnivorous not from choice but from necessity. Where frost or drought

[1] *La Revue du mois*, March, 1906.

deprived him of the juice of plants, he devoured the eggs of
birds and reptiles, then he devoured little animals which were
easy to catch. Shellfish, salt and freshwater alike, oysters
and mussels, urchins and what the Italians call *frutti di mare*,
frogs and snails were hunted for just as they are to-day.
Mice, rats, spiders, earthworms, swallows' nests, locusts,
caterpillars, the larvæ of ants, the eggs of gnats, lizards,
and snakes varied the menu. Do not the French peasants
still call the common snake the hedge-eel, and do not the
Congo natives find the boa an exquisite dish ? [1]

These, however, formed but meagre resources. Famine
and long periods of starvation must have been common,
especially in winter or in very hot weather. The loin cloth
of hide which savages wear and which is seen on figures of
prehistoric men must often have been tightened across an
empty stomach. Sometimes the modern primitive men of
to-day have unexpected strokes of luck ; they happen on
the carcase of some big animal—ox, bear, or buffalo—and
the result is a terrifying scene of debauch. A whole tribe
has been seen living for over a week on the carcase of a whale
thrown up on the shore.[2] The Fuegans have been seen
carrying on their shoulders enormous lumps of flesh with
a hole through which their heads protruded. In Australian
feasts the prey was torn raw and, even when it was tainted,
was greedily devoured. There remained only the bones
which looked as if a multitude of ants had been at work
upon them.

It is not likely that primitive men were any more delicate
in their habits. Did they know how to hoard up food against
days of want ? We may doubt it. Their kin, those backward tribes of to-day, who help us to reveal the past of the
race, sometimes like a dog which buries a bone to return
to it later, hide the remains of their meal in the sand. This
act of intelligence is not outside the range of the most debased
of humanity but it is very probable that it was rats, ants,
and squirrels that taught them to provide for the winter.
In times of starvation it is possible that they allayed their
pangs with certain kinds of earth. In Spain in the
seventeenth century the women ate as a dainty bits of their

[1] Mandat-Grancey, *Au Congo.*
[2] Letourneau, *Evolution de la propriété,* pp. 33–48.

earthen water coolers, and in the overlong reign of Louis XIV the peasants of Franche-Comté eked out their rye by mixing clay in it before baking bread.

In a word the food supply of our ancestors seems to have been both poor and precarious. Did they suffer much as a result ? We cannot tell. Their improvidence saved them. Care for the morrow scarcely worried them. From orgies that were nearly fatal they passed to long periods when they had only roots to feed on or bark or insects. Nevertheless, hunger proceeded to reveal itself, as it always does, as the mother of invention. Carnivorous man proceeded to invent means of catching the animals on which he fed. *Fishing* and *hunting* were added to *gathering* as means of getting food.

Fishing was at first very simple, although that does not mean very easy. It began with the attempt to catch fish by the hand. The savages of to-day are splendid swimmers and divers. They seize the fish, kill it at a blow and eat it raw. Even yet in the Mediterranean fishers who catch a polyp deal with it just in this fashion. But it was soon seen that teeth and nails, man's natural arms, were insufficient for the task. Man bent his mind to prolonging them artificially. He invented auxiliary tools. The pointed and forked stick was used to kill or pierce the fish found under a stone or in a pool. Then with a creeper, a hair, or a strand of horsehair tied on to a flexible branch he invented the fishing line to which he added bait and a bent hook imitated from the thorns of the briar. After that he thought of a pointed stick for throwing and thus appears the harpoon, barbed and toothed, the point of which sticks in the flesh of the prey and the end of which is attached to a cord. Among the objects found on prehistoric sites there are quantities of stone and bone harpoons which, it seems, antedated the bow and the arrow.

Then came more complicated tools. Man invented the net [1] and the snare, making them of rushes, fibre, or osier. They were a sort of box net in plaited wood, a sort of cage which is easy to enter but impossible to leave. From what has been observed of the methods employed not merely by savages, but by fishers and poachers to-day, primitive man dammed a stream, drove the fish into the pool thus

[1] Fragments have been found among the debris of the lacustran cities.

formed and got in this way a miraculous draught, or
employing still more deadly methods, poisoned the water
of a pool to drive the fish dead or stupefied to the surface.
Finally, as one invention always produces another, the desire
to pursue the fish on its own element led to the invention
of the canoe.

Hunting developed in a similar fashion. It was not in
these days, as it is to-day, a pastime. It was a primary
necessity, the daily occupation of the men. At first man
found himself in a real state of inferiority as compared with
the big animals on which he hoped to feed. He had not
the strength of the bull or the buffalo, the swiftness of the
stag or the horse, the wings of the pigeon or the heron.
Beside the elephant, the rhinoceros and the mammoth
he was but a pygmy. But he possessed what will secure
for him the dominion of the world, intelligence, and he
gained the day over his adversaries however redoubtable
and however agile by sheer force of patience and ingenuity.

In the beginning he could count on nothing but his own
strength. Like the American Indian he took advantage
of the fineness of his senses. He could follow an animal by
scent ; the examination of a clod of turf told him that his
prey had passed that way. He used sight as much as the
sense of smell. Broken branches, the movement of the grass,
revealed things to him. His ear could catch almost
imperceptible sounds. He was also a fine runner, climber,
and jumper. He was able to run down the game he had
started. The Australian savages pursue the kangaroo for
days, and end by running it to ground and killing it.

He soon learned to add stratagem to the power which
agility of body gave him. Stratagem was necessary in the
case of winged game which, when he approached, could
soar into the air. What was he to do ? Lying flat on the
ground, motionless as a tree trunk, he caught the bird lured
within his reach by bait or he fascinated it by extraordinary
motions while his fellow coming from behind seized the
imprudent and half-hypnotized watcher of so unexpected
a spectacle. Or he would imitate the love call which brought
the female within reach, or the cry of the buzzard, or the
vulture which made the terrified prey blunder into the snares
he had carefully laid. He invented all sorts of limes, traps,

and snares especially for prey which he did not dare attack openly. A pit covered with grass delivered into his power the elephant or the tiger which fell into it and disembowelled itself on the sharp stakes. Traps of this kind are frequently painted on the walls of prehistoric caverns.

For the hunting of large animals bands were formed and battues were organized. The paths by which the prey came to the drinking places were riddled with treacherous holes. At Solutré at the foot of a precipitous cliff which overlooks the plain an enormous mass of bones was discovered. Those of horses were in great number in this charnel heap, and it is conjectured that the precipice being on the other side an easy slope and quite accessible the hunters had fixed up two hedges of stakes and by shouting and waving of torches had driven their prey in panic between them and driven them over the precipice. At Vistonice [1] near Brünn in Moravia there was found not long ago a vast heap of mammoth bones and it is thought that having only stone weapons the hunters had massacred in a similar way the enormous pachyderms. Two facts were gleaned from the examination of this station. First that the animals killed were for the most part young, either because young animals are easier to surprise or because they are more tender to eat and, secondly, that the animal when killed was cut up on the spot and that the hunters took away only the brain, the nerves, and the most edible parts, and also the tusks which provided a fine store of ivory, but abandoned the rest. This confirms what earlier discoveries had suggested that the hunters carried back to their caves only fragments from their great kills.

All this was accompanied by magical practices. Before the hunt began, the pursuit and death of the prey was acted, a sure means of securing success in the expedition. By a sort of incantation the bear or the horse was invited to let itself be caught and apologies were addressed to it after the kill, for its soul could return and inspire the survivors of its species to bloody reprisals. It is probable that the pictures of fish, oxen, and bison on the walls of the caverns were meant as a charm to paralyse the living animal into a

---

[1] *V.* the articles of M. Bégouen in the *Journal des Débats*, 26th September, 1926, and the communication of M. Absolon, the director of the excavations in Moravia, to the Ecole d'Anthropologie (Nov., 1926).

similar state of immobility. To have them in stone was equivalent to securing their actual capture. An animal thus depicted was already as good as caught, and the design was further pierced with numerous holes as an added guarantee of a kill.[1]

It is hardly profitable to enumerate all the stratagems to which hunting gave rise. It was certainly one of the greatest factors in the education of early man. It was hunting which led him to invent weapons. I have already said that the first weapons were sticks and stones, which is why the stick has always remained an emblem of power as is seen, besides the instances given earlier, by the rod of Moses, the wand of the fairies, the *lituus* of the Roman augurs, the ivory cane of the consuls, the cane of the drum major, the maces which the beadles and the ushers carry and even the baton of the conductor and the baton of the policeman. What was originally a thick stick became a mace ; what was a sharp stick a spear ; what was a long stick a lance. All these were used for striking at short range. But with the monkey man shares the power of striking at long range by throwing missiles. The stone, which at first is only a hard and pointed prolongation of the hand in the shape of a knuckle-duster or a dagger, later in the shape of an axe fitted into a handle of stag's horn or in the shape of a point fixed to the end of a club, became a missile weapon. The arm which coiled like a spring could make it carry a long distance ; then it was hung from two cords which were swung round and round and so gave the missile greater speed and greater force. The sling has been invented. The stick in its turn became a missile weapon. Man invented the boomerang, a crescent-shaped piece of wood the ends of which have a skew in imitation of certain leaves, a treacherous and deceptive weapon which glides into the air and descends in a zigzag flight, striking to right and to left, reaching the bird which is behind cover believed secure, and returning if the thrower is expert, to the hand of its owner. It is found in the oldest Egyptian civilizations and among the Australians of to-day. Then the stick was fitted with a point in bone or flint and became a javelin, an assegai, and propelled by a leather thong or a crooked stick will have longer range.

[1] *V.* the drawings in the cave of Montespan (Haute-Garonne).

Place now a lighter stick on a piece of gut stretched between the two ends of a bent piece of wood, and there is the arrow, feathered, winged, fitted with a stone point, and often poisoned, and the bow which for centuries will remain the king of missile weapons and will expand into the arbalest and the arquebus, the bow which will also become later an instrument of music, the prototype of the lyre, the guitar, and the violin. Suppose that after a still smaller arrow which can be fired by blowing through a tube, a hollow reed or bamboo, and you have the blowpipe, still in use on the Amazon and in Malaya, the ancestor of the rifle and the projectile ejected by gas, and, at the same time, the ancestor of wind instruments, the shepherd's pipe, the trumpet, the flute made from the tibia of an animal or a man or a bit of boxwood.

Returning to the stone and the sling which was known to the inhabitants of the lacustran villages and which won David his triumph over Goliath, which in antiquity was the fame of the Balearic islanders, and which was still used by the Tartars in the middle of the nineteenth century at the siege of Sebastopol, we find it soon becoming complicated. Imagine several stones attached together by cords and turned at the end of a flexible handle and you have the *bola* which easily trips an animal and was used generally in South America. To it one may add the lasso which was a most useful weapon in the hunting of the horse, the bull, or the ostrich. We have no means of telling accurately at what moment in man's development this or that weapon was invented. But it is certain that well before his knowledge of metal he had invented a great number of weapons whose possession enabled him to struggle on a footing of equality against animals much bigger and stronger than himself. Their invention was no doubt the work of many centuries, but in the end man was able to defend himself against the other carnivora and live on the herbivora which became his usual food.

But it was not only animals that primitive man attacked. At no times more than these was the saying truer : " Man is a wolf to man." The Cannibal Islanders are not the only people who fed on human flesh. Everything goes to show that cannibalism existed everywhere and that it

existed for a variety of reasons for a very long time.[1] The
most imperative reason was hunger. At certain crises it
was necessary to get rid of useless mouths. The old were
superfluous and were sacrificed. The frail ran the same risk,
and women and children fell victims in their turn. Then
war which broke out whenever neighbouring clans fell out
over land abounding in game, often was a chase after human
prey.[2] Raids were made on one's neighbours. Prisoners
were made and eaten. If they were lean they were carefully
fattened. In Fiji man was nicknamed "the long pig".
The remembrance of this early cannibalism has been
perpetuated in legend and tradition. We need recall only
the ogre with the seven-leagued boots and the legend of
St. Nicholas restoring to life the three children killed by
a butcher and preserved in his salting tub. Time and time
again this ferocious practice recurs. Ugolino imprisoned
in the tower devours his children. In famous sieges,
Numantia in Roman times, Paris in the time of the League,
in shipwrecks like that of the *Medusa*, in famines which
decimate a whole population as happened in Russia in
1922, recourse is had to this bloody practice.[3]

Necessity knows no law : that is the excuse of the starving.
It is not always urged as excuse. Among the Fuegans
old women are a choicer food than dogs. "The dogs taste
of otter," they say to explain their preference. At Brazza-
ville, some Yakoma rifleman in the French service learned
that a wounded comrade had lost a leg in an operation.
"You can do nothing with that meat," they said to the
surgeon. "Give it to us to eat." "But it is rotten, it
smells," said the horrified doctor. "That is all right,"
was the reply, "we don't eat the smell," and to prevent
them satisfying their appetite for human flesh the doctor

---

[1] L. Bourdeau points out its existence among the Scythians, the
inhabitants of the Black Sea coasts, the Galatians, the Irish, the Picts, the
Iberians, and shows that it was still surviving among the Danes in the eleventh
century of our era.

[2] Lubbock, *Prehistoric Man*, ii, 136.

[3] *V.* the picture given of the famine areas in Daudé-Bancel, *Le Réforme
agraire en Russie*, p. 92. In the governments where the famine raged it was
the abomination of desolation : beings with human faces, with fleshless bodies
but swollen stomachs as a result of having eaten the most extraordinary
foods, dogs, cats, grass, clay, the leather of shoes and harness, the wood
of household furniture, the carcases of domestic animals and even of human
beings.

D

had to spray the gangrened limb with poison.[1] In the Congo a Belgian officer playfully pinched the cheek of a negro boy. The child was terror-struck and the neighbours pleasurably excited. All of them believed that the officer had pinched the boy's cheek as he might have felt a chicken with the intention of having him roasted whenever he was in prime condition.[2]

Therein one can see a second motive for turning man into food. Gluttony is added to necessity. Human flesh has, it appears, a delicate savour. So at least have told us those who are best fitted to have an opinion. In Tahiti an old Polynesian chief said to Pierre Loti : " The white man well roasted tastes like a ripe banana " (v. *The Marriage of Loti*). The savages of Fiji,[3] however, averred that the flesh of whites was on the whole poor, that it was salt, and that the sailor, when he is old, is hard, tough, and scarcely fit to eat ; the Polynesian made a much better dish. The eyes, the cheeks, and the brain were considered the choice morsels ; the calf and the rump were also appreciated, but the rest was left to the dogs. The Australian savages, to complete the feast, steeped and smoked the carcases.

But perhaps the main reason for the long survival of the practice was the idea that man could absorb man. In eating a dead man the eater believed that he could acquire his virtues : it was a sort of funeral communion. One became brave by eating the heart of a brave man. A famous poem by a troubadour is inspired by a similar thought. By eating the brain one increased one's intelligence, by eating a leg one became more agile. The fat and the blood possessed marvellous properties as cures and, as old belief has an incalculably long life, medicine kept among its remedies fat from the body of a man who had been hanged, or scrapings from skulls, which were believed sovereign cures for epilepsy.

In virtue of this faith in the transfusion of the dead into the living it was permissible and even laudable to consume one's relatives so that their high qualities might not go out of the family, and so the monstrous paradox arose that to

[1] *V.* article by M. Challaye in the *Tribune de Lausanne* of 5th Nov., 1905.
[2] Mandat-Grancey, p. 114.
[3] *V.* article in *L'Illustration*, July, 1902.

eat one's mother was an act of filial piety. At the end of
the nineteenth century an African explorer [1] could relate
that one day a native came to claim the corpse of another
who had been killed. Asked what he wanted it for, he said
that he wanted to eat it because he was the brother of the
dead man.

These bloody customs which existed in our own times in
Africa and Oceania were certainly held in honour as long
as man had no cattle and was ignorant of agriculture.
Cannibalism appears to have been universal. If demonstra-
tion is necessary one can point to the traces which it has
left in most religions, traces which become fainter as the
nations become civilized. There was a ritual anthropophagy
which for long preserved the character of a meal.[2] The
victims which were sacrificed as food for the gods were eaten
by the sacrificers. That is seen in Aztec customs for, in
ancient Mexico, they thus sacrificed children, prisoners,
slaves and albinos according as they wished to obtain a fine
harvest, fruitful showers or the return of the sun from eclipse.
In Greece, in order to cause rain, a child was sacrificed to
Zeus on Mount Lykæus and the sacrificers ate the flesh.
Then gradually it was held sufficient to slay the victim
without eating him. Among the Gauls who made drinking
cups from the skulls of their enemies the druids burned
human victims in cages of wicker. At Carthage, when
misfortune threatened the city, children were consumed
in the fiery belly of Baal-Moloch. Among the Hebrews
the first-born were sacrificed as the first-fruits of a generation.
As time went on, here and there beasts took the place of
human victims. Iphigeneia who was to be sacrificed to
obtain for the Achæans a favouring wind was saved by the
intervention of Artemis who substituted a deer. Abraham
at the moment when he raised the knife to slaughter Isaac
saw a ram take the boy's place. As evolution went on
the sacrifice became symbolic. At Rome puppets of rushes
are flung into the Tiber and in Egypt a doll is flung to the
Nile. Elsewhere in Java, in Siam, in Guiana, clay figures
replace the living victim and in the Roman religion when

---

[1] Mandat-Grancey, p. 172.
[2] V. A. Loisy, *Essai historique sur le sacrifice*, and Malvert, *Science et
religion*.

the believer eats his god really present in the Host, can one fail to see a memory of that mysterious assimilation which gave to a partaker in the homicidal feast the virtues of the man whose flesh he ate ? Can one fail to see in Christ dying on the cross, an expiatory victim and in the Mass the daily acting of human sacrifice ?

Let us leave, however, the unexpected and mysterious results which in the course of centuries the cruel necessity of preserving one's life by eating one's like has produced. To finish with this study of primitive food let us say that it was not long before man invented condiments. One of these, salt, is indispensable to men who live on a vegetable diet and it is equally indispensable to the hunter who cannot be sure of fresh meat. Salt, as we shall see, was one of the most important objects of exchange among the peoples. In certain countries Senegal, Persia, Java, Bolivia, it was possible to make shift with licking certain kinds of clay. In Tahiti a little sea water was drunk with the meal. It is probable that aromatic plants, thyme, mint, hyssop, and rosemary, were early known and sought after. In Polynesia the natives infused or chewed the root, stems, and leaves of a sort of pepper tree. The same qualities, savour and strong smell, led the American Indians to smoke and chew tobacco, a practice destined to have a very brilliant future. In it the natives found a sort of intoxication and forgetfulness. In Australia the *pitouri* was the plant preferred. It was sucked, smoked, and snuffed, and served as a stimulant before battle much as does in modern war the glass of rum given the soldiers before an attack. In parts of Asia a mixture was used of pepper, quicklime, and areca nut which was called by the name of betel, which blackened the teeth and agreeably burned the palate.

Thus in different countries and at different times man discovered tea, coffee, maté, cocoa, and the kola nut, all plants which were used by uncivilized peoples before being adopted by the civilized. One must also mention the poppy from which opium comes, hemp which produces hashish and the coca which produces cocaine. Man seems to have discovered the properties of these very early, a knowledge which remained the property of priests, sorcerers, and medicine-men. They supplied man's need of something to deaden pain, to obtain escape to a dreamworld from the realities of life, from its daily anxieties. It is a pity that these products, creators of peace and illusion, have become dangerous destroyers of nerve and brain, of the whole human machine. Potion and poison are derived from the same word.

A few words are necessary on the ways in which man quenched his thirst, a need as imperious as hunger. The water in the pools and streams was the first supply of drink. But in dry countries, in warm seasons, natural drink was often lacking, which is the reason why incantations to cause rain have so important a place in ancient rites. But the water from heaven, when preserved in the open air, quickly became putrid and nauseous. To keep it fresh men used honey or the juices of plants. Experience quickly taught them that water in which fruit or grain is steeped acquires a piquant taste, produces a pleasurable excitement, and becomes a philtre to produce mirth and jollity. The lacustran peoples knew how to make fermented liquors with raspberries, cherries, and mulberries. Wine and cider go very far back into the past. In other countries sugar-cane or rice, as in Japan, served as intoxicants. Among the Tartars it was barley or milk or the sap of the palm or the birch which was used. India had the soma which intoxicated men. The Aztecs at the time of the Spanish invasion used the sweet and lively pulp of the agave. Thus always refining his methods of satisfying his needs, man invented drinks of which just a sip could bring jollity but which, taken in excess, produced anger and madness. From its beginning, humanity had faults and vices which have never disappeared.

Yet man's experiments in food which I have tried to summarize helped to carry him very far along the road of progress on which he toiled so painfully. Cookery which became a possible art whenever man discovered fire, furnished him with a diet more easily assimilated and was one of the most useful and oldest of industries, while the *gathering* of food necessarily led to agriculture ; *fishing* to navigation, and *hunting* to the pastoral life and to war.

BIBLIOGRAPHY

BOURDEAU (Louis), *Histoire d'alimentation* (Paris, 1894) ; *La conquête du monde animal* (Paris, 1895).

HOUSSAY (Frédéric), " Le régime frugivore. et nos idées originelles," (*La Revue du mois*, 10th March, 1906).

LOISY (Alfred), *Essai historique sur le sacrifice* (Paris, 1920).

LUBBOCK (Sir John), *Prehistoric Man.*

MALVERT, *Science et religion* (Paris, 1895).

MANDAT-GRANCEY (Baron de), *Au Congo* (Paris, 1900).

MORTILLET (Gabriel de), *Origines de la pêche et de la chasse* (Paris).

RECLUS (Élie), *Le primitif d'Australie* (Paris).

CHAPTER II

Two Great Discoveries : Fire and Language

A RUSSIAN scientist, M. Boris Weinberg, has estimated that, during the ancient prehistoric period which ends at the moment when writing appears, man made sixty discoveries.[1] Here one may ask the question—are inventions the result of genius or of luck ? It seems to me that they can be the result of either. The intellect of a man more far-seeing than his fellows can find something new by intuition and sometimes in his amusements, for amusement—which is a spontaneous activity of the mind—is fertile in curious discoveries. But centuries have often to pass before application is made of the new idea. How long did it take for the discovery that amber, when rubbed, has the power to attract light substances, to give birth to the marvels of electricity ? Chance again every now and then reveals some of nature's secrets, but the discovery is put to use only by those whose attention has already been directed to it ; chance is only the unexpected ally of the seeker. A commonplace circumstance strikes him and becomes the starting point for thought and creative activity. Newton sees an apple fall and conceives the idea of gravitation. Edison, feeling the crown of his tall hat vibrate while someone is talking to him, discovers the principle of the telephone.

Be that as it may, among the discoveries of man there is one which by its extreme importance, must be placed in the first rank. That is his discovery of fire, the vanquisher of cold, of night, of matter, a powerful and docile instrument, a weapon terrible and dangerous even for him who makes use of it. That discovery was truly a great event whose consequences were infinite.

When and where it was discovered it is impossible to know. Perhaps it was discovered independently in many places. All that we know is that it already had been found at the beginning of the quaternary epoch. As is the case

[1] *Revue générale des sciences appliquées*, 31st Jan., 1926.

with all discoveries of great antiquity, man forgets his own achievements and ascribes them to the gods. Among the Greeks fire was a treasure which the Immortals reserved to themselves and, when Prometheus stole a spark of it, he was crucified by the angry gods thus robbed of their privilege. Elsewhere fire is itself a god : the word " god " at the beginning means shining. It is a benevolent yet awe-inspiring god, the representative of the sun upon the earth. By the Hindus the god is called Agni. He is sprinkled with soma to nourish him. There are ceremonies and hymns in his honour. Among the Persians his worship has lasted until our own day. Ormuzd is the genius of good, of light, of warmth ; Ahriman, that of evil, darkness, and cold. The Greeks worshipped fire under the guise of Zeus who hurled the thunderbolt, of Hephæstus who ruled subterranean fires.[1] They had relay races of torches which were symbols of life and which must not be allowed to go out. The Romans adored fire under the name of Vulcan whose name is perpetuated in the word " volcano ", or under that of Vesta who is the fire of the domestic hearth. Perhaps it is the legend of a firegod that survives in the tale of Bluebeard and in that of the Ass's Skin.[2] At any rate it is in honour of fire that the yule log is lit and the logs of St. John.

Fire did, in fact, come from heaven, but there was no miracle. The lightning, daughter of the clouds, no doubt set ablaze more than one forest. Fire also came out of the earth in the form of lava, solfatara, or burning gas. It appeared also in terrifying form amid the crash of thunder or the rocking of the earthquake, and there is more than one proof that it was regarded with panic fear. In Rome the spot where the thunderbolt fell was sacred, that is to say, accursed, and the caves whence issued fiery gases were held to be the sad gateways to lower regions where flowed rivers of fire.

It is easy to explain how fire was discovered. It was feared and worshipped before it was tamed. Bold indeed was he who first made that strange force a captive which had to be nourished and protected against wind, cold, and thieves. To preserve it was no light problem. The task preferably

---

[1] André Lefèvre, *La Grèce antique*, p. 44.
[2] Anatole France, *Le livre de mon ami*, pp. 287–301 (edition of 1896).

was entrusted to the more stay-at-home women who were better fitted to watch over it. Woe to those who let it die for want of nourishment! We know how a Roman Vestal was punished for such a crime. In Australia when a tribe migrates, the women carry the embers which they feed with care. Emblem of the hearth, fire represents the everlastingness of the family and later will represent that of the city. When Greeks sailed to found a colony they took with them a part of the sacred fire from the altar of the mother-city. In ancient days to possess fire was for a tribe a very considerable advantage and to restore it, when it had died or had been stolen, was a matter of life and death. It quickly became a cause of war and stratagem between tribes, as J. H. Rosny has well shown in his novel *La guerre du feu*.

It seems that even in modern times there have been peoples who did not know fire. Magellan met some in the Marianne Islands. There are others who have not got beyond the stage of keeping it without knowing how to relight it if it goes out. What a giant step toward a better existence did man take when he understood how to cause fire at will! To possess a sun of which one was lord, to create whenever he pleased light and heat—the step carried him at once above beasts and other men. The solution of the problem was undoubtedly the object of passionate research and many experiments were made. The most widely used method was that of rubbing wood on wood. Experience soon taught men that rapid rubbing developed heat, and then various methods of rubbing were adopted in various countries. The method which seems to be the oldest and which is still used in Oceania,[1] consists in placing on the ground between one's knees a piece of soft wood on which is rubbed quickly a wand of hard wood which is held in both hands and slightly at an angle. It gradually works out a hollow which is filled with wood dust, the spark leaps out and dry grass is placed on it which catches fire. Elsewhere, in Australia, in India, in Malaya, two pieces of bamboo whose whole length has been cut are taken. One piece is sawed by the other; the part which is sawed becomes hot and finally alight. The two pieces which take the shape of a cross have given rise to that mystic cross which is called the *swastika* and which

---

[1] Deniker, op. cit., p. 179.

was the emblem of the cult of fire and the sun. The Spaniards were astonished to find it in Mexico, but long before Christianity it was common in Assyria and Egypt. A third method of producing fire by friction is found among the Zulus, the Eskimos, and also in America. By this method the firemaker puts both feet on a plank of soft wood, then he turns rapidly between his hands in both directions a wand of hard wood. Then the procedure is improved by hollowing out a groove in the plank and by fitting a cord to the rubbing wand in order to quicken the circular motion. Later still the apparatus is made yet more complicated by the introduction of a sort of bow-drill.[1]

It is worth noting how one invention leads to another. To increase the rapidity of motion and the force of penetration of the rubbing wand, man soon learned to diminish or increase its diameter and to fit to it a disc thick enough to hold the cord which set the apparatus in motion. This was the origin of the pulley which later still leads to the invention of the wheel.[2] From it again are derived the windlass and the wimble, the turner's lathe, and the bow used by the draper, the bow-drill still used by the watchmaker or the joiner to make holes in plates of metal or wood.

We must not imagine that these methods of obtaining fire went out of use long ago. The old methods are preserved, as is always the case, in religious ceremonies. At Rome, if the fire of the Vestals had the misfortune to go out, it had to be rekindled by the rubbing of two pieces of wood and Pliny mentions the mulberry, the ivy, and the laurel as particularly appropriate. The Redskins still use the old method in their sacred feasts and even in Europe—in Britain, Sweden, and Poland—it was thus that, at the beginning of the nineteenth century, in certain rites intended to ward off contagious diseases, the sacred flame was kindled.

Another method, probably not so old, was sometimes considered as impious for it was a new invention. It consisted in striking a spark by hitting one stone with another, a flint, for instance, with ironstone. The spark was caught on dry leaves or on tinder made of dried toadstool. The task of making fire became an easier one once iron had been

[1] Deniker, p. 82.
[2] Charles Frémont, *Origine de la poulie, etc.*

discovered [1] and that is why iron was the most used and the most widely spread metal in Western Europe. The flintlock and the tinderbox were not forgotten and they made of the task of producing fire an art demanding a certain degree of skill, until the day when chemical matches placed fire, sometimes to their injury, within the reach of the smallest children.

It is possible that in very early times a third method was known, that which consists in concentrating the sun's rays by means of crystal but this method was wrapped in mystery and its secret jealously guarded by the priests.

Let us return to primitive man. Fire is now in existence. It is submitted to the will of man. At once light and heat, it is to render him invaluable service in this double capacity. It is light. In the night it lights many tiny suns ; it scatters the horrors of the darkness where hover ghosts and terrors and evil thoughts ; it guides the hunter lost in the night ; during a night of storm it comforts the family as they wait in anguish for sign of dawn ; in the long winter nights it lengthens the hours of work in the depth of the caves. It is security ; it is a living barrier against wild beasts for all fear the fire with its flames and red glow. Within the fiery circle of his bivouac to the sound of the crackling of dry wood burning, man can rest from his labours and woman tranquilly sleep beside her children. The beasts fly from it in vain. Fire or smoke pursues them into their lairs, reaches them in the depths of the earth or at the tops of the trees. If man has become the king-beast, it is largely because he learned to master fire.

Nature recoils before fire's red tentacles, even the bear and the leopard. The wood of the forests, the prairies, the mountains, disappears in ashes when fire penetrates into its thickets : nothing can refuse it passage. It is health : it warms and makes flow again the blood chilled by snow and ice ; it gives hope and strength to the sick. It is cleanliness : it is the great purifier clearing the air of the miasmas that poison it and make it deadly ; it destroys all vegetable or animal debris, all the refuse of life which holds seeds of death. It is the hearth, the centre of the family, the tribe, the city. Not foolishly does our speech retain

---

[1] Bourdeau, *Les forces de l'industrie*, p. 206.

the phrase : " This village has so many fires." Round the blackened hearthstone rose prayers as naive as this [1] : " O thou who art eternal, magnificent, always young, health-giving and abounding in wealth, receive with kindly heart these our offerings and give us in return good fortune and sweet health."

In the hut or in the depths of the dark cave, the hearth is at once refuge and sanctuary, the scene of family joys and sorrows, a warm and inviolable place of rest, peopled with memories and dreams, lightened by the joyous flame, ringing with the laughter of children and the shrill chirping of the cricket.

Outside the house fire means fertility. It is the great clearer of land, the pioneer of agriculture. It rids the soil of its masses of briars and weeds and on the land thus cleansed and improved the useful plants grow more vigorously and more abundantly. It is also the magician which transforms matter. For fresh bleeding meat, acorns, and herbs eaten just as they are, it substitutes dishes made tender and pure by cooking. It begins with the roasting of the game or by cooking in the ashes the tubers which have been dug up. Then it advances to the boiling of food in a hollow stone which is filled with water and into which other stones are dropped red-hot. Here is the beginning of an art capable of infinite perfection and which acted as a refining agent on the instincts of those ferocious eaters of raw flesh. Surely as a writer has said,[2] " when gaily gathered round the fire and rejoicing in the smell of a savoury grill, men tasted for the first time roast pork cooked in flour, they must have saluted with thunderous acclamation the fire that created cookery, the fire that warmed their limbs and renewed their strength."

Fire was also a capable worker. It hardened the stake which was to become pile or weapon ; it hollowed out the tree-trunk which was to become a canoe : it hardened the earth that was to be vessel or brick ; it will reveal metal which is first found as brilliant particles among the ashes ; it will be the father of industry giving birth to blacksmiths, goldsmiths, glassworkers ; it is the indefatigable toiler which will go on to make bread, cloth, mirrors, statues, cannon, which will set in motion engines, machines,

[1] André Lefèvre, p. 47. [2] Ibid., p. 49.

aeroplanes. It is the invaluable servant of man in spite of its formidable revolts when it devours a city, a forest, a prairie, or overwhelms a country in a volcanic eruption. Yet with all its revolts it is still one of the great natural forces which has been captured and tamed by man.

Fire discovered, man busied himself increasing the materials which gave him heat and light. For firewood leaves and dried grass, dead wood and ashes left on the hearth, were first used. Where vegetable matter was lacking, recourse was had to the dung of animals, of the camel in Tibet, of the ox in Egypt, Russia, and even in the Vendée. Then oil-bearing plants were used or the fat of animals, or, at need, the fat of men.[1] In some countries, in China and in Persia, the gas that escapes from the earth was used or the mineral oil that flows underground. The old historians knew wells or pools where petroleum was obtainable. Herodotus mentions its presence at Zacynthus, Plutarch at Ecbatana, Dioscorides at Agrigentum. But these were exceptions. Petroleum like coal, peat, and sulphur was reserved for future generations and for a very long time the forest was the great, and practically the only, replenisher of the fire.

What were the hearths of early man like ? At first they were in the open air. Then they were removed to the hut, from which the smoke escaped as it liked through a hole in the roof. Only later was the chimney invented which forced it to go straight outside. The nourishment of the fire was an important task. Butter, soma, and fermented liquor were used, but wind was recognized to be the most effective agent in rousing fire. Human lungs were soon aided by a fan made of feathers or a lotus leaf or a pine branch. Then man devised a sort of blow-pipe which is found in Japan and even in Picardy, but soon the tube is attached to a leather bag which is slowly deflated and inflated.[2] Not without justification did the poets show the winds of heaven confined in the bags of Æolus. Made of goatskin, pigskin, or oxhide, the bags were reservoirs of air and, when one squeezed them, the air was driven violently out. A hole which could be alternately opened

[1] L. Bourdeau, *Les forces de l'industrie*, pp. 277–323.
[2] Cf. C. Frémont, *Origine et evolution de la soufflerie*.

and shut, the origin of the valve, allowed the bags to be filled and kept full after being emptied. Then the skins were fitted to a sort of double handle of wood to which the exit tube was connected and the bellows was invented, practically as it is to-day, small and easily worked by hand for domestic use, huge and worked by rope or chain in the forge which its powerful draught keeps ever glowing.

To lighten his darkness man used as his first instrument a torch of resinous wood. Its light was requisitioned at marriages, banquets, and funerals. Then the branch of pine or cedar was replaced by cords dipped in resin, pitch, fat, or tallow and the candle is invented, while, from the wax of bees are made wax candles whose light is more brilliant and purer, and, as they are more costly, they are reserved for religious rites.

Naturally utensils developed concurrently. Chandeliers and candlebra made their appearance when the torch was hung to a beam or even when, in still earlier days, it was thrust into a hole in the rock. Then to shelter the flame from the draughts, the lantern, made of oiled paper by the Chinese and of transparent bone or horn by the Greeks, was invented. Even bladders were used as covers for the light.

The obtaining of light by the use of solid materials was specially suited to hunter and shepherd peoples. The farmer peoples preferred to use liquid material. Animal fat was the link to this fresh development. In the frozen regions the penguin is so full of fat that if kindled tinder is placed in its mouth it forms as it were a natural lamp. Elsewhere it was noticed that certain plants furnished a liquid which would give light ; in our regions they were the walnut, the olive, the beech, and the colza ; in the tropics, the palm and the peanut. That again led to the making of new implements ; the lamp in all its forms made of a shell or a hollow stone, then of baked clay, and later of metal, becomes a part of the ordinary furniture of the house, the temple, and the tomb.

There is no need to pursue the subject farther. It is easy to see how a single invention, that of fire, leads to a thousand others. And in the realm of mind there was simultaneously another invention no less productive than that of fire in

the material world. Man invented speech. Language, that
is a system of sounds which express things and ideas and the
various relations which the mind establishes between them,
is a work so complicated, so full of art that when men first
began to consider the question of its origin, it seemed
impossible to believe that it could have been the creation
of mortals. Men thought that a god had come down from
heaven for no other purpose than to teach man this marvellous
thing. Others gave the honour of the discovery to some
marvellous genius who shared it with his ignorant fellows.
Others again believed that language was the result of an
agreement between individuals or allied groups.

We do not need to refute those who always explain
difficulties by calling in divinity, and Lucretius long ago
dealt faithfully with the other hypotheses. It is madness,
he declares,[1] to believe that a sort of Prometheus could have
endowed man with speech which he had invented. How
did he receive from nature ability so far above that of his
fellows ? Even if we admit that he had more brains than
all the rest of humanity, and that alone and unaided he
constructed a language, how could he have made it com-
prehensible to others ? How could he have persuaded
others to apply the same sound to the same things, to teach
them how to produce the sounds ? What perseverance,
what misspent energy on both sides ! He might as well
have revealed his invention to the deaf.

The argument is a strong one, and it bears heavily against
the partisans of what they call a convention. The truth is
that the invention of speech which communicates thought
from one mind to another, came into existence by degrees,
by a series of natural stages. The language of look and
gesture was the first that nature taught. Need we quote
Lucretius again ? He remarks that the child, before learning
to speak, indicates with its finger the objects which attract
it and which it desires. He adds : " Every being has the
consciousness of faculties of which he can make use ; the
young bull in its anger butts before horns have begun to
make their appearance ; the young of panthers and lions
fight with claws and fangs before they have either, and
young birds launch themselves into the air demanding support

[1] *De rerum natura*, lib. v.

from immature wings." So among men, gesture was, we may say, the primary and universal language. Everywhere the man who carried his hand to his mouth was understood to be conveying the fact that he was hungry; when, in addition, he flung back his head, it was understood that he was thirsty. Everywhere to throw oneself flat or to kneel was understood as a sign of submission. The clenched fist and an accompanying scowl invited others to assume a posture of defence. Even to-day man uses this sign language when he is among people whose language he does not understand. What traveller has not had to employ it at some time or other?

This sign language is still in use among certain tribes. Widows in Australia are condemned to use it and no other. It exists among the American Indians and is complicated by so many abbreviations and conventional signs that one can almost draw up a dictionary for it.[1] It exists in Naples to-day, and was in use among the Greeks and the Romans— among whom it was actually taught.[2] But it is only a stage. Man speedily advances to articulate speech. Here, too, did he have the animals as teachers? Did he, as Lucretius says, imitate the limpid voice of the birds?[3] Did he who later was to teach parrots to speak, learn speech from the thrush and the nightingale? One is almost tempted to believe it when one finds that in Tunisia and in the Canaries he has invented a whistling language to enable him to converse at a distance. At any rate he exercised and developed a faculty which he shares with his inferior kin. Perhaps he was a singing, before he became a talking, animal.

When one knows that the beasts who cannot speak are able by various sounds to express joy, fear, and pain, is it astonishing that man gradually evolved a speech which could express his feelings and his thoughts? Again I quote Lucretius: "When Molossian hounds are irritated and their great flabby jaws first begin to growl, baring the hard teeth, they threaten with a far different sound drawn back in rage than when, at last, they bark out and fill the plain

---

[1] Lubbock, *The Origins of Civilization*, p. 409; Deniker, p. 158.
[2] *V*. Rich's *Dictionary of Antiquities*: art. "Chironomia".
[3] Six different notes have been noted among them: Letourneau, *L'évolution de l'education*, p. 24.

with their bellowings. And when they set about to lick their whelps affectionately with their tongue and snapping at them make as though to swallow them gently with teeth ready to close, they mouth them with yelpings of quite another sort than when they howl in some deserted house or when, whimpering, they cringe away from a blow." [1]

Other proofs of the aptitude of animals to make themselves understood by their like are easy to collect. The fowl utters quite different sounds when it defies a rival from those it uses when it summons its chickens to share a worm or warns them of the approach of a bird of prey. One may mention the experience of the American Professor Garner, who spent several years studying the speech of the apes and who succeeded in understanding the sense of the various cries. Similarly, man, accompanying the language of look and gesture with hoarse or soft cries according as he wished to express anger or satisfaction, welcome or fear, easily made him himself understood by those who approached him. Now a sound constantly used to express the same sentiment ends by indicating permanently in the group in which it is uttered consent, desire, refusal, threat.[2] The most backward peoples know how to say " yes " and " no ". By an analogous procedure a certain sound means a person, an object, a tree. Then the name which was at first reserved to these gradually is extended to their like ; the proper noun becomes a common noun. It is probable although this cannot be said of many words that a natural noise like that of thunder, a cry of an animal like that of the crow was the origin of this or that imitative sound in speech.

How then did words which at the beginning were probably all monosyllabic later become attached to one another to indicate by modification of form or by change in position the connection which thought established between them ? How did it happen that they were combined and arranged so as to express the whole course of thought ? " It is mankind that has made language," said Diderot. This collective and unconscious work went on for centuries. A race amply endowed with intellect made a brilliant success of it. Others

---

[1] *V*. 1362-72 (Rouse's translation).
[2] The mother having daily the need and the opportunity to communicate with her children, certainly played a great part in the creation of language ; cf. R. Briffault, *The Mothers*.

E

obtained only feeble results. To investigate under what conditions one people was able to progress and another not, is a fine subject for research by historians, geographers, sociologists, philosophers, and philologists, but it does not belong to a work like this to follow the wonderful efflorescence of language over all the world. All that concerns us is to state the fact that the discovery of language by man was a prodigious forward step in civilization.

It was not merely an instrument which made daily life easier, permitting complete comprehension between the members of a family or between the workers occupied at one or at several tasks. It created a solid bond between members of the tribe, the clan, the city. The habit of casting thought and feeling in the same moulds was a bond of union as strong and perhaps stronger, than the fact that the same blood flowed in their veins. Admittedly a common language was no guarantee of perfect concord between those who spoke it, but it involved a certain common way of looking at things, of conceiving things and expressing things that in spite of themselves and their quarrels brought them together. To be able to understand each other is for individuals and nations the first step towards the possibility of mutual sympathy. Then too it was a bond between the generations. The experience of the generation that was passing could now be saved for that which was to take its place. It could be transmitted orally from the old to the young; it could accumulate and become a treasure, a heritage which would increase as time went on.

Having thus obtained fire and language as helpers, man raised himself more and more above the beasts. He was like a diamond which emerges from the clay in which it was hidden. Vigorously he stepped out on the long road on which there were to be no halts towards the new discoveries of which the next chapter will tell.

BIBLIOGRAPHY

BOURDEAU (Louis), *Les forces de l'industrie.*
BRIFFAULT (R.), *The Mothers.*
DENIKER, *Les peuples et les races de la terre.*
FRANCE (Anatole), *Le livre de mon ami.*
FRÉMONT (Charles), *Origine de la poulie du treuil, de l'engrenage, de la roue de voiture ; Origine et évolution de la soufflerie.*
LEFÈVRE (André), *La Grèce antique.*
LETOURNEAU, *L'evolution de l'education.*
REINACH (Salomon), *Cultes, mythes et religions* (vol. v).
LÉVY-BRÜHL, *Les fonctions mentales dans les sociétés inférieures.*
LUCRETIUS, *De rerum natura* (bk. v).
RENARD (Georges), *La nature et l'humanité.*
VENDRYES (J.), *Le langage.*

CHAPTER III

The First Industries

IT is correct to place at the head of man's needs food and drink, for he must under penalty of quick death satisfy his need for these daily. But when one comes to discuss housing, dress, and the first industries, it is impossible to place in order of priority these needs which different forms of human activity supplied. Country, climate, and environment must all be taken into consideration, and it is only right to warn the reader that, in this study of those different forms of each which underwent an evolution whose stages can be approximately dated, I do not imply that the order of discussion is the true chronological one. It is quite likely that all developed in a measure together. At the same time, it seems to me logical to begin with the study of the various tools which, one after the other, aided man, the *homo faber*, to make what he needed, adding thereto the study of the more or less rudimentary utensils which he made with them.

They can be grouped according to the material employed. Man used seven materials—*wood*, *shell*, *stone* (with bone and horn as subdivisions), *clay*, *copper*, *bronze*, and *iron*. Vegetable materials were at first of great service to him. The trees gave him pointed sticks suitable for use in digging the soil, dry leaves for his bed, branches as material for his hut, planks for furniture, bark for clothing, thorns to serve as fasteners for his clothing, handles for tools, maces and clubs for attack and defence, and, in America, some trees with particularly hard wood gave him cutting weapons and tools.

When he began to take thought for the morrow and turned to preserving food against the day of hunger and water against the day of thirst, he used the receptacles which nature had placed in his way, gourds, calabashes, bamboos, and coconuts. Then the idea came to him to manufacture containers in their image. He made cups and ladles of wood, baskets and hampers from rushes, straw, or osier. Grass-plaiting and wickerwork have certainly a history that goes back to dim antiquity, but, owing to the fragile nature of these industries' products, examples could scarcely survive. But we know that the use of wooden tools has lasted throughout the centuries : witness the lath wand which is not only the badge of Harlequin, but is used by masons and upholsterers ; the flails and winnowing fans used on farms and in mills ; the pestles with which for so long grain was crushed and the mallets which the potters and the coopers still use.

When, however, man desired to work on the objects that surrounded him something was needed harder and more solid than wood. First of all man used shell. Shell, before stone was used, played a part in human development which has not been sufficiently emphasized, save in the works of M. C. Frémont, an engineer, who studied the origin and evolution of prehistoric tools so as to teach the workers of to-day to know better and to perfect the tools which they use now. Shell gave early man not merely ornaments and, later, a currency, but also scoops, vases, ladles, knives, razors, hooks, and, in America, even tomahawks. It was used to dig up the ground and to fell trees, and in a measure its use survives, for the stone tools faithfully reproduced the characteristics of the natural tools, oystershells, mussel-shells, and the rest. A number of tribes in North America, in Brazil, in Tierra del Fuego, and in Oceania still use tools of shell,[1] and the screw which the Latins called *cochlea*, that is to say, shell work, seems to have been modelled on the spiral shell of the whelk, which, like the conch, gave birth to a music instrument used in the armies of Rome.

Stone, however, was much more commonly, one may say universally, used and is a much more lasting material. It renders such services that in many places it was regarded as divine. This was certainly the case with stones that fell from the sky. Regarded as sacred and sometimes carefully wrapped up, they were worshipped at Delphi and in Arabia, as well as by the savages in Siberia and Dakota. They are connected with the most ancient beliefs and in particular with beliefs on fecundity.

[1] Frémont, pp. 7–10.

First, of all, man, in order to defend himself or attack another, to crack a nut or bring down a fruit, armed himself with the pebble he found at his hand. It is not impossible that in tertiary times certain flakes of flint found in our day were in use as tools and bear traces upon them which proves them to be tools used by an intelligent being. But I have already dealt with the controversy over the so-called *eoliths*. On the other hand, it is certain that to the beginning of the quaternary epoch belong flints which were artificially flaked off. These flakes are still very roughly trimmed, but man had learned that with the aid of another stone as hammer he could flake off from a block of flint—known as the *nucleus* —oval, pointed, or circular flakes. The oldest of them which at one end have a sort of heel easy to grip and at the other a cutting edge have been named *coups de poing* by Gabriel de Mortillet. The name seems to convey that they were used to strike an enemy at close range and it is possible that on occasion they were used thus. But they were far more tools than weapons. They seem to be a sort of rasp used in the cutting of wood.

In them we see plain imitation of the shell. By the side of *coups de poings* which, although found in a great many countries, are called *Chellean* or *Acheulean*—the latter are simply a little lighter and longer than the former—*scrapers* used to clean pelts have been found which have the triangular shape of the shell called *pecten* and which by a series of slow transformations will become the shovel, the mattock, and the pick. A sort of scratching knife also has been found, for use on hard material such as bone, ivory, and the horn of stag or reindeer, and this is the prototype of the file. It is possible that the turning movement needed to get the whelk out of its shell, and which was done by the aid of tiny and very sharp tools suggested the screw far more than did the tendrils of the vine or the creeper.

As man progressed, a new method of using flint appeared. By the pressure of a bone or a stick it was split into blades more or less thick, which, according to their destined use, were touched up on one face or on both. So another stage of chipped stone work was reached which is called *Mousterian*, from the station at Mouster. Tools of the earlier stage have been found there, especially the scrapers for pelts. They are accompanied by borers for making holes in the skins, chisels and unpointed knives, toothed instruments which served as saws, hollowed scratchers which could be used to make a rounded stick or to cut a branch circularly.

Another step forward—and the steps of pre-history are giant's steps, for each covers a dozen centuries—and we come to the civilization called Aurignacian. In this it is the rule for the stone to be touched up and worked on both faces. The engraving tools which had already appeared are present in great quantities : the scratchers are of several types, curved, angular, etc. Another step and we are at Solutré with its finds of pointed tools in appearance like the leaf of a willow or a laurel, and which are not arrow or javelin tips, but a sort of file sometimes handled laterally, sometimes constructed in the shape of a parrot's beak and, along with these, scratchers, borers, notched blades, for working on bone or ivory and also eyed needles of bone.

What was the origin of the needle which rendered and still renders so many services ? It is a development of the bodkin which was at first of flint, then a shred of bone. Thin bodkins pierced the pelts and through the holes were passed the leather or fibre thongs that were to hold them together. This was already a rough kind of sewing. Then the holes became smaller and closer together and at the same time the bodkin became smaller and thinner. Thread gradually replaced fibre and leather. To get it into the holes it was first of all rolled round the head of the bodkin which had a grove in it for the purpose ; then it passed across a hollow made in the head of the bodkin and then, when it was made of linen or cotton, it was made thinner and passed through a gauge. Pebbles and shells which have been found pierced by conical holes were probably used in calibrating the thread.

When we pass from Solutré to the stage represented by the station of the Madeleine we seem to notice that there has been a halt or even retrogression in flintwork, but on the other hand there is clearly considerable improvement in the working of bone and ivory. Cups, lamps, clay models of bisons and coloured frescoes make their appearance. No more is only the useful sought ; we have reached a stage when art appears and serves beauty alone. Then we come to an epoch of transition which is called *Tardenoisian*. Of this period have been found a great quantity of tiny tools in flint the purpose of which is not very clear. Some points which are very fine and very brittle appear to have been used in tattooing. Then at Campigny we find the pick and the spade beginning to make their appearance. And so we arrive at the neolithic period whose characteristic is *polished stone.*

Polish was at first applied only to the less hard materials —wood, bone, horn, ivory. It is at this stage applied not to all tools but to a few, and also, in Egypt for instance, to bracelets which were used as ornaments. The rubbing was done on a block of sandstone and sometimes a block of granite. In the Aube such a block has been found which is called " the block of ten fingers " from the appearance of the hollows formed in its surface. Damp sand was usually used in the work. Thus rubbed, perhaps for weeks, chisels, spades, lance- and javelin-points, arrow-points, pedunculate or barbed, acquired a polish and a finish which distinguishes them from all the earlier tools. Sometimes too, by the aid of water, sand, and a turning stick, a hole was pierced through an oblong stone sharpened on both sides and through the hole was passed a handle of wood or horn and there was a mace or a hammer. Sometimes the handle was of stag horn. Again with horsehair, leather thongs, fibres, resin, and bitumen a cutting and brilliantly polished head was fitted on to a stout shaft of rounded wood, and there was the axe, a powerful weapon in war and a splendid tool for felling and cutting up a tree. In certain lands the axe was an object of worship : among the axes discovered—they are of every shape—some have been found with holes pierced in their heads which seems to show that they were meant to be hung up as dedicated offerings.

Flint was the stone most in use because it is the commonest and the most easily worked. In what is to-day Belgium, at Mur-de-Barrez in the Cantal and in the Upper Nile valley there were flint mines sometimes on the surface sometimes underground. At Grand Pressigny, near Loches in the Indre-et-Loire department, workshops have been found which have an area of hundreds of square yards where were manufactured weapons and tools in light coloured flint, the finds being especially large blades and nuclei which the people of the neighbourhood nicknamed from their shape " pounds of butter ". At Girolles in the Loiret, again, the axe was the speciality. But in places where the precious stone could not be got, it was replaced by quartz, hardened sandstone, serpentine, jasper, jadeite and even volcanic obsidian which, if more brilliant, is more fragile. When such polished stones are discovered very far away from the places where they were quarried, it is not too rash to believe that they travelled as objects of exchange of considerable value from one people to another.

Stone, even when very hard, is capable of still greater transformation. In Egypt, vases of quartz, agate, and rock crystal have been found and it is certain that the softer stones, like alabaster and limestone, were worked with chisel and saw by the earliest sculptors of the bas-relief work which has survived in many a prehistoric cave.

In America, on the Pacific coast, where volcanoes are numerous, obsidian was in common use and not only was made into very sharp lance and arrow points but into circular mirrors from which light was intensely reflected and into that Mexican weapon which is called *maquahuitl*, and is a club of wood both sides of which are fitted with sharp blades of obsidian.[1]

While stone was thus developing in importance, bone was having a similar fortune. At first man thought only of smashing the bone to get the marrow from it. But he soon discovered that it could be put to various uses. In some countries bodkins, hooks, and harpoons in bone and needles of fish-bone were in use. Later, when cold forced the men of our regions to take refuge in the caves, instruments made of horn or staghorn were used, and also those astonishing carved horns adorned with representations of the reindeer, the goat, the ibex, or the horse, the handles of poignards or what are called the *bâtons de commandement*.

Another material which early was pressed into the service of early industry was earth and, in particular, clay. It was dried in the sun, then hardened by fire. Receptacles of wood were good for preserving fruit, grain, and nuts, and even for liquids, but had the great inconvenience that

---

[1] To be seen in the Musée d'Ethnographie at the Trocadero.

they could not be placed on the fire. The finding of a stone which had been naturally hollowed out—what is technically called a *geode*—is a very rare occurrence, so, with a little clay, an edge was added to a hollow stone which was not quite deep enough, or the clay served to stop up cracks in a wooden receptacle, cracks which the deposit from dirty water had already half closed. From now on, a liquid could not merely be kept, but in the first case, it could be heated without danger, and in the second case the wooden receptacle became the starting point of a new industry. The idea of the basket produces the art of pottery.

There were two essential methods. In the first the basket of rushes, the saucer of woven grass—as they can be seen to-day among the savages of Africa and America [1]—were constructed and served as models. Lumps of clay were rolled over them and pressed in and then hardened in the heat either of the sun or of a fire. But the basket could also be used as mould. Inside the basket at the bottom and on the sides a layer of clay was placed; then it was placed on the fire. The vegetable matter was burned away, and there remained a vase of baked earth of the same shape as the burned mould with the same design and keeping the marks of the interweaving which had been destroyed. The fragments of pottery found in some neolithic stations still bear the marks of the wooden mould. Here and there, gourds were reproduced in baked clay. Later the moulding process was able to dispense with this primitive method and the circular bit of wood which the potter used to make equal the sides of the vessel which he was making on a movable stand, gave birth to the potter's wheel which, if the Chinese annals are to be credited, was invented 2,700 years before our era begins. On the other hand, the brick, at first unfired and then fired, was used to make walls and in Babylon to make books.

It is not difficult to see how one invention is connected with another. Pottery placed in the kiln gave a clue to new discoveries. Certain fusible matter was deposited on the surface of the baking vessels. Sometimes it was a sort of shining and solid varnish and so enamel was discovered,

[1] Deniker, p. 184.

or it was a sort of sand which liquefied and we have the origin of glass.[1]

The first pottery—which as far as Western Europe is concerned, dates from the neolithic period—is gross in composition, badly baked in the sun and often has the mark of the cord which surrounded the mould. Then it becomes more artistic—for it is a universal tendency to try to embellish objects in daily use—and has geometric designs made on it by incision in the unbaked clay, and often the incisions are filled with white or red clay. It is possible that other colours were used, but being of vegetable origin time has obliterated them.

There is at first no originality of shape. All are modelled on baskets, on leather vessels, and often on gourds or calabashes. The verse of Ronsard is well known wherein he speaks of the dissolution of living bodies. " Matter remains : form perishes." In the evolution of tools and utensils the contrary is true. Material changes : form remains. Then, gradually, vessels heavy in form gave place to others more delicate, with polished exteriors and with decoration in relief and painting, sometimes put on in a coating which was baked with the clay, sometimes put on after the baked clay had become cold. Figures of animals and plants, vague reproductions of the human head, mystic marks like the *swastika* vary the decoration which, as we have seen, is due to enamel, to the insertion of bright stones, to vitrifaction, which at a later date will transform earthenware into porcelain and finally give birth to glass.

In various parts of the globe, in China as in Mexico and Peru, in Chaldæa, in Egypt, in Persia, as in the Ægean Islands and in Alsace, schools of pottery developed, of which some certainly influenced others and which seem to have advanced from imitation of nature to a stereotyped style, which is sometimes of a religious character. But the documents which we possess do not permit us to establish the exact connection between them ; they show us only what has been the general development of the ceramic art.

In Elam of which Susa was the capital, a remarkable

---

[1] Beads of glass have been found in tombs which were brought to Western Europe in the neolithic period.

development which disappeared before the historic period, has been observed. It has been asked and still is asked, if the technique of the painted vases did not come from Crete or Egypt or Western Asia. We know only that as far as the red and black vessels are concerned, both types are widespread ; the black were baked in the open air, the red by firing inside the house.

In any case, it is possible that pottery which by its use of models led to sculpture, led also to metalwork, that minerals were mixed in the clay, that, in the ashes of the kiln, the potters noticed hard and shining matter which, when heated, became fluid like water and when cooled again took the shape of the place where they lay, and that thus men learned to separate the metal which so far had been known to them only under the form of particles of gold or silver or copper.

It is also possible, although all these questions of origin are doubtful, that the working of metals began in the eastern steppes among the nomads who were urgently in need of them for, in their wandering life, they could not carry about with them as household utensils fragile vessels of baked clay and they had to seek unbreakable substitutes for vessels of wood and leather. It is possible that these nomads were the first blacksmiths, the first to invent and profit by an industry which the wandering gypsies of to-day work at with tireless energy and undeniable mastery.

However that may be, metals endowed humanity with new power. In the beginning they were a luxury. They served as ornaments before they were made into useful objects. The metals, called precious, competed with precious stones. Just as rock crystal, sapphires, emeralds, and amber were promoted to the dignity of jewels, because of their sparkle or their colour, so silver, gold, and copper attracted man by their brightness and particles found in a pure state were used on collars and pendants. Gold, especially, which has the colour of the sun, under the form of nuggets or extracted from the sand of certain rivers, was known and valued in remote antiquity. We know how famous Pactolus was among the Hellenes, we know the legends of Danæ yielding to a shower of gold and of Jason sailing to win the Golden Fleece, the gold masks which lay on the faces of the mummified kings of Mycenæ and, in a very different civilization, the German, we know the tragic story of the Rheingold. At the period of the European invasion of America, gold was in common use there; the natives were entirely ignorant of iron, although, as compensation, they knew platinum. For long the name of Peru was synonymous with fabulous wealth of gold and popular fancy lingered over the legend of El Dorado where the pebbles on the roads were gold. In Mexico, gold was regarded as something quasi-divine and sacred and the theft of it was punished by death.

Lucretius who saw so clearly into prehistory, ascribed the discovery of metal to the accidental firing of a forest by lightning and the consequent appearance of runnels of molten lead and copper and he tells us that when man tried to turn gold and silver to common use they were found to be too soft for lasting work. Thus, he says, copper won the day over gold which was despised as a useless metal in violent contrast to the supreme position it was later to enjoy. Here it seems to me Lucretius has gone wrong. Gold was never despised. It remained what it was at the beginning a luxury, a choice metal which was reserved for adornment, jewellery, palaces, and temples.

But it is certainly true that the common metals had a greater importance if not a greater value. They were in daily use, but, according to the country and nature of the ground, and according as they were more or less mixed with less useful metals, they appeared in different order in different regions. In Asia, in Europe, and in America, copper seems to have been for long the king of metals. Weapons, tools, and household utensils were made of it. It was worked by a hammer and poured into moulds. At the dawn of history, in the Mediterranean area, it predominates in the tombs. The smith in the Homeric poems calls himself the worker in copper (*chalkeus*). In copper were forged by the Cyclops, the bucklers and shields of the heroes. How did the first smelters and smiths work? We may get an idea of their methods from the Malays. " To make filagree work they melt the gold in a ricepot, blowing the fire with their mouths. If the mass to be melted is too big, three or four men sit round the pot, transformed into a melting-pot, and breathe together as each can, thus producing a continuous effect." [1]

But soon, just as among the Malays, bellows replaced human lungs and rudimentary ovens were built with pipes [2] to carry the wind to the fire. Types have been found in Silesia and Hungary, and that still in use in Catalonia does not differ much from the primitive sort. It is possible, too, that by a procedure which to-day is used in charcoal making a sort of grindstone was constructed with alternate layers of minerals and burning material, with an external covering of clay. This is what is used by the negroes of Equatorial Africa who are good metalworkers.

Metalwork implies mining, an art which had begun in the days of flint. In the beginning, man used such minerals as he found mingled in the sand, the debris of the rocks which had contained it or which had been carried into the beds of rivers. Then surface veins were followed up, sometimes underground, although the mines could never have been deep, since man was ignorant of the arts of draining and ventilation. It was a painful toil, this work in the quarries whence stone was obtained, and no less hard that in the mines whence metal was obtained. Later it will be the fate and the punishment of slaves and criminals. From these holes from which wealth emerged came the groan of human suffering, the sad accompaniment of industrial development.

In the course of the processes to which metal was submitted it was noticed that copper blended with another metal acquired a hardness and a power of resistance which it had not in isolation. Between metals there were mystic and magical marriages. Chance and much experiment revealed the qualities of the various alloys, copper with tin, copper with zinc, etc.

The first alloy was the most widely spread. This was bronze. In the East, that is, in China, in Malaya, and in other regions there were large deposits of tin : in the West, that is, in Spain, in Auvergne, in the Cassiterides (near Britain), it was found in smaller quantities. In America, that is, on

---

[1] W. Marsden, *History of Sumatra*, i, 270–5, quoted by Letourneau, p. 239.
[2] Morgan, p. 140.

the Pacific coast, it occurs in places. In these widely separated regions the bronze industry developed, sometimes self-contained in that all the necessary elements were present on the spot, sometimes requiring certain elements to be brought by exchange.

Bronze supplanted stone but, as is usual, in religious rites, the asylums and citadels of tradition, the use of the latter survived for centuries. It was a stone knife which was used in Egypt to disembowel the body that was to become a mummy, which among the Hebrews was the agent of circumcision, which in Rome slew the sacrificial victim and which in Mexico cut out the heart of the human sacrifice. In France, in Auvergne, stone shares were fitted to wooden ploughs as late as fifty years ago (Franchet). Its use persisted not only alongside that of the new metals but if one may say so, within the metal instruments themselves. For, as I have already said, contrary to what happens in nature, in art material changes, but form remains. Only gradually did the worker in bronze become original and produce those vessels, jewellery, weapons, bits, brooches, pins, and axes with recurved edges which have been recovered in hundreds from the tombs of Egypt and Assyria as well as from those of Europe and from the debris of the lacustrian cities.[1]

But here and there in Europe and in Asia, objects of iron are mingled with objects of bronze. The iron which fell from heaven in the aeroliths was no doubt the earliest to be exploited, for it is found there practically pure. But such finds were rare and, although iron, in the form of oxides, enters into the composition of many rocks, it is so mixed with other matter that only long experiment could succeed in isolating it. But, even so, those who succeeded in producing

---

[1] The facts related above concern especially the old world. The first industries in America similarly included wickerwork, grass-weaving, and shellwork. In the *sambaquis* of Brazil and the *paraderos* of Patagonia there are numerous remains of flaked and polished flints. When the Europeans landed in the New World the most advanced peoples of America, the Mexicans and Peruvians, had scarcely emerged from the neolithic stage. They had just reached the stage when metal is beginning to compete with stone, when bronze appears, but when iron is still unknown. They possessed sun-dried bricks, pottery, cloths made from cotton, agave fibre products, the wool of llamas and vicunas, the skin of bats, and the feathers of birds. They had goldsmiths who made jewels in wax by methods which I need not describe because they have been fully dealt with by M. Capitan in a volume in this series. Generally speaking, their development seems to have been like that of Europe and Asia. Cf. *Le travail en Amérique avant et après Colomb*, pp. 90–1.

it in some bulk were richly rewarded. They now possessed an incontestable superiority over their neighbours. Whether it was a matter of felling trees, of weaving clothes, or making war, they had the use of tools and weapons which feared no rival, and which could be used without regard for economy, for iron was sufficiently common to be easily replaced.

In Western Europe, the iron industry is of two types. The older is revealed to us by the excavations at Hallstatt in Bavaria, and seems related by its products to the products of Asia Minor on the coasts of the Black Sea which were carried westward by the Russian steppes and the Danube valley. The other, that of La Tène, a valley in the canton of Neuchâtel in Switzerland, derives on the contrary from the Mediterranean culture and came north by the Ægean Islands, Greece, and Italy.

For the work of the smith, whether in copper or bronze or iron, new tools were necessary : these imitated and replaced those of earlier ages. There is the anvil, originally a block of stone before being a mass of metal ; there is the vice which keeps motionless the article on which one is at work and substitutes for the grip of hands or feet, rigid iron bars, which are brought together by a screw ; there are the pincers whose origin is a piece of wood cleft in two and kept together by a ring to let one seize the glowing metal without taking hurt ; there is the gouge, a sort of groove which worked into the thick part of a flint-chisel can hollow out a piece of wood and which, when it is made of metal, is the ancestor of the punch and of the cutter for making coins ; there is the pestle, the mallet for driving in piles, the beetle which are fitted with handles, so that they can be used with a downward stroke ; there is the hammer of all dimensions and forms handled so as to be used laterally. It is used to hammer flat the iron drawn red from the fire as well as pieces of gold and silver ; it is used, to notch stone or stick, upon the cutting chisel ; it is used to drive in a nail once a bone tool but now made of more solid material and with greater penetrating power. Saws, rasps, files, etc., they all gain a power of action which they had not had before.

Only much later was the art of soldering learned. It was with bolts, plugs, and rivets that man first made secure the various pieces of metal. But when the art of tempering was discovered, although we do not know how or when, there was none of the old materials, wood, bone, ivory, stone, copper, bronze, lead, zinc, which had not been vanquished by the hardness and durability of the instruments man owed to iron. If it never took the place of gold or silver for jewellery from which such beautiful filagree work was made, for everything else, arrowheads, lances, swords daggers, shields, as well as vessels, cooking utensils, pins and brooches, its use meant not merely the introduction of something at once stronger and more durable but also the possibility of quickening the pace of man's progress towards a better state. In our own time do we not estimate the place of a people in the scale of civilization by the amount of iron which it uses?

Without going so far as that, however, let us try to estimate the distance which separates man, armed with a cudgel and a stone which he had picked up, from man who had now at his service a metal so malleable and so resisting, and we cannot but conclude that man has conquered a formidable section of the rocky road up which he travels.

F

BIBLIOGRAPHY

BARTUEL and RULLIÈRE, *La mine et les mineurs.*
BEUCHAT, *Manuel d'archéologie americaine.*
DENIKER, Work already cited.
DERULLE, *La sidérurgie.*
FRÉMONY (C.), *Origine et évolution des outils préhistoriques.*
GRENIER, " La plus ancienne poterie d'Alsace," in *La Vie en Alsace,* June, 1926.
LETOURNEAU, *L'évolution du commerce dans les différentes races.*
MACALISTER, work cited (on the " bâtons de commandement ").
MONTAIGNE, *Essais* (c. xxx : The Cannibals).
MORGAN (J. de), *L'humanité préhistorique.*
RIBOT (Théodule), *L'imagination créatrice.*

CHAPTER IV

The Dwelling-place

SLEEP is one of man's primary needs and to sleep in security one of his most legitimate desires. Consequently for refuge against inclement weather, against wild beasts and other men, he seeks a shelter where he can rest undisturbed. According to his environment, these shelters are of different kinds, and it is impossible to say which kind was used first. The kind depends principally on the climate and the surroundings. If we try to classify the habitations which man has used, we must consider in turn those which nature offered him, and then those which he himself constructed, and then among the latter distinguish between those which were fixed and those which could be transported.

The shelters which nature put at his service were the trunks of hollow trees and thick foliage wherein he could hide. The Chinese say that man lived in the tree-tops for many a day, and in this home in the air mocked at the endeavours of tigers and lions to reach him. In Brazil natives have been found who sleep suspended from the trees in a sort of hammock made of interwoven branches. In the Sudan there are whole villages perched on great cotton trees.

When man had to sleep on the ground, the skin of an animal hung on four stakes protected him from the dew, the rain, and the frost : in some places, as in the Pampas, he sheltered himself under the shell of a giant turtle. But his favourite refuges were overhanging rocks and caves which the movements of the earth or the violence of water had opened. They were not absolutely peaceful shelters. Sometimes man had to risk his life to reach them in the sheer precipice in which their entrance gaped ; sometimes he had to dispute their ownership with hyenas, bears, or panthers ; like strongholds they were taken, besieged, and retaken in battle. In the glacial period when a defence against cold was imperative they were the scene of bloody conflicts. In certain cold countries, as still happens in Lappland, man made a hole in the ground and slept under a white coverlet of frost and snow. I borrow from Étienne Richet's *Les Esquimaux de l'Alaska* [1] a detailed description of these dwellings which have scarcely changed their form since a remote past and which can stand as the predominant type of hut in regions near the pole.

" The Eskimos of Alaska have two sorts of dwellings, one for summer and one for winter. The winter dwelling has for base a hole dug in the ground to the depth of a little over a yard. At the four corners are placed posts made of stripped tree-trunks about eight to ten feet high. Other trunks stretched between the posts form the walls. The ceiling also is made of trunks or branches placed neatly one beside the other ; in the middle a square hole of two to three feet is left to let light enter. The better to protect the inmates against cold a second wall is built outside the first either of stones or of trunks whose intervals are filled either with stones made round by the action of water or with earth. The whole building including the roof is covered over with turf, clay, and layers of moss ; snow and ice complete it. Frost acts at once as plaster and plasterer, and hermetically seals all the gaps and cracks. The house is entered by a subterranean passage four to six yards in length, low and narrow, so that one has to go on hands and knees and looks like a rabbit creeping into its hole. The passage ends in a circular opening, within the outer wall ; the sides are made secure with stones or great pieces of ice and a bearskin or the skin of a reindeer or porpoise is hung over the sloping entrance which admits one to the interior."

Inside the house and, here I summarize M. Richet, the nearer part where the passage ends is sloped, and here the domestic utensils are stored ; the further part contains the hearth placed below the opening in the roof which can be closed with a piece of sealskin and benches of wood on which are stretched skins and mats and which are used as beds. Lamps give light and heat. M. Richet thus ends his description : " This ingenious bit of construction is in the shape of a Greek cross, the subterranean passage representing

[1] Paris, 1921, p. 82.

the nave. Seen from outside the hut with its round squat dome covered with earth and snow looks very like a natural mound."

The winter house within which man defied the frost was replaced in summer by a similar hut which was built on the surface of the ground and had no hole in the roof because the cooking was done in the open air. In many of the less cold countries at the neolithic period the huts were sunk in the earth or the sand. This was the case, for instance, in Alsace and Auvergne.

Sometimes whole tribes sheltered in the caves. The old writers have handed down to us the story of troglodytes who lived underground in Arabia and Africa.[1] But indeed there are few countries where one will not find subterranean dwelling-places. They are common in China, in Tunisia, in Spain, in Egypt. In France, in the valleys of the Loire, the Loir and the Cher, they have survived to our own day. Alfred de Vigny in the early pages of *Cinq-Mars* shows us them in Touraine where the peasants, as it were, carry their fields on their heads. " If you climb a hillside covered with vines a little trail of smoke warns you that a chimney is at your feet. The rock is inhabited and families of vintners live in its subterranean depths, sheltered at night by the earth whose surface they cultivate laboriously in the daytime." The chalk of Champagne like the tufa of Touraine is very suitable for such artificial caves. The precious evidence on prehistory which the caverns afford us is well known.

We now come naturally to the habitations built entirely by the hand of man. The most important are those that are fixed and were made by peoples which were completely or half sedentary. The most simple of all is the hut, such as we find it to-day, among savages such as it is represented on antique vessels in the shape of cabins, such as it was in the Siberian tundra, where the frozen soil is poor in vegetable life. The course of development appears to have been something like this. To protect himself from the cold winds man first of all built a curtain of branches interlaced with straw or of woven rushes. These still survive in the screens

---

[1] In his *Persian Letters* (xi to xv), Montesquieu places among the Troglodytes the utopia which he, like so many other writers, amused himself by creating.

which the roadmen use to shelter themselves when they have to work exposed in all weathers. Then he made the screen so that it would completely surround him, either in circular shape or by setting his screens in two parallel lines and closing the ends of this sort of corridor. But protection was still needed against the sun, the rain and the dew, and so man invented the roof. Where the screen hut was circular the roof was conical if stiff branches were used, cupolar if the branches were flexible. The quadrangular hut had a roof formed of two sloping sides if the climate was rainy, a flat roof that formed a terrace, if rain was rare. If it was very rare, man got rid entirely of a useless covering and slept in the open air.

The shape of the hut is determined by the climate and the materials used. We may note, for instance, that the use of flexible branches bent in the middle and curving upward at both ends seems to have determined the form of the roofs in the Far East and given to the Chinese and Japanese pagodas that peculiar twist which recalls the slanting eyes of the yellow races.

The hut with a single opening to serve as entrance still exists in Australia and in Tierra del Fuego ; with a gable and of hive shape, that is, of hexagonal shape, it is common in South Africa.

How did these rudimentary dwellings become the houses that we know ? In mountainous countries, in Auvergne, for instance, or the highlands of Scotland—is there a reminiscence of the cave life there ?—rectangular or round houses were built underground, the earthen sides of which were some three to four yards deep and were buttressed by stonework : the floor was composed of a mixture of clay and broken stone ; the roof of beams covered with turf, which was all that could be seen from outside ; for entrance there was a sort of narrow, low corridor along which one had to crawl. The resemblance to the Eskimo hut is striking.

When the hut was erected on the surface the gaps in the structure were filled with mud, reeds, and bits of turf, and so a sort of wall was obtained very easily in the regions of the grassy steppe. The mud wall which is still common in Russia, existed in Gaul and Spain in the time of Vitruvius, and it exists to-day in the Sudan, in Turkestan, and in Mexico.

Later pitch and cement were used. In alluvial regions, such as the Delta of the Nile, squares of dried mud were used, a form of wall that had durability only because rain was almost unknown. Thus were built the walls of the houses and the cities of Elam, of Assyria, and of Media, of sand, pitch, layers of rushes, and sun-dried bricks, which have been called *adobes*. This method meant that the walls had to be of enormous thickness for they disintegrated fairly easily and with time so completely that buildings crumbled into dust and their ruins were nothing but a heap of earth. But the procedure led to the invention of fired bricks which were first made, most probably, in the East, which took the place of the book in Babylon and were gathered into libraries. But the invention does not seem to have reached Western Europe till the Roman conquest.

Now take the contrary type of country, the country where the woods are dense and leafy. Wood becomes the predominant material in house building. Houses are made with tree trunks sometimes squared, sometimes not, with roofs covered with *tavillons* which are like scales. The tree trunk is the first model for the column which is later to play so important a rôle in architecture and in Mexico façades in stone are found which are clearly copied from the façade of wood.

In the primitive dwelling-places little attention was paid either to lighting or to ventilation. For long the windows, if there were any, were only narrow skylights. At first the door was only a bundle of branches ; then it became a wicker screen hung between two stakes. Then came the notion of attaching it by cord of hide or fibre to one of the stakes so that it could swing. Then the interwoven branches gave place to a solid plank as is found in the lacustran houses ; then this panel was hung on pivots at top and bottom to make opening and shutting easy. Man had invented the hinge. At the same time care had to be taken so that the door would shut tightly. A piece of wood or bone was attached to it which passed behind the other stake opposite the one on which the door swung, or which passed into a hole in the wall, if there was a wall instead of the earlier stake. The door could thus be closed from without. To close it from within another piece of wood served the same purpose on the inside of the door. Sometimes to facilitate entry from without a hook was worked through a hole which enabled the bolt to be moved or raised. This is the origin of the lock and key and of the latch.[1]

All this could easily be done in wood but stone began to be used sometimes to make the frame of the house more solid, sometimes, in the form of slates, to protect the roofing from the storm. This form of house is common in semi-mountainous countries. In Phœnicia monolithic houses have been found cut out of the rock with holes made in them to serve as door and windows. Elsewhere, on the heights

FIG. 2.—Houses on piles at Manila (*Voyage pittoresque de Dumont d'Urville*).

where trees did not grow or there was only shrubbery, temporary homes for men and cattle were built of plain stones and this was done in Upper Egypt. The stone house was the prevalent type all over the Mediterranean area, a region where rock and cliff and shingle abound. Occasionally even fallen boulders furnished the wall and a light lean-to served as shelter.

The methods of the early masons varied. Sometimes stones cut to fit were placed one on top of the other; sometimes stones of unequal sizes were fitted into each other

[1] Frémont, *La serrure.*

and joined with cement; sometimes as in Peru walls were made with a mould of mortar composed of sand and pebbles. Here and there the art of building arches was known.

If we turn to a country much subject to earthquakes like Japan we find that the house is reduced to very low walls which support a movable framework of wood scarcely shut in by matting or paper. Easily broken up or burned it is quickly rebuilt. At any rate there is no chance of the inmates being crushed if it collapses. It need scarcely be said that in warm climates where it is pleasant to live in the open air the house is low and small because it is very little lived in, that in cold climates it is surrounded with thick walls and takes up far more space because long winters have to be passed inside it. Similarly its roof will slope more or less according to the quantity of snow that it is likely to have to support and in the mountain lands where it may receive far too much, it is almost buried under a cape-shaped roof which nearly touches the ground.

If we turn to a damp country which abounds in swamps and bogs, we find that the house also goes on stilts, that is to say, it is built on piles so that it never comes in contact with the damp surface of the ground. In Sumatra, where torrents pour over the plains in the rainy season the houses are thus suspended between earth and sky. In Madagascar and in the Valais the barns are similarly placed. At the corners they rest on logs which flat round stones of some size cover and protect so that the barn floor is to some extent guarded against the invasion of rats and mice as well as against damp. Later the cellar will have a similar function to fulfil.

Let us turn now to mobile houses. These belong to the nomad peoples like the hunter peoples, or semi-nomads like the shepherd peoples. We may call them portable huts. They are of similar shape, conical or square. When, as occurs in America, they are round they are often surrounded with a ring of earth which serves to keep off water. Among the Assyrians and the Hebrews they were rectangular and topped with canopies to ward off the sun. But everywhere they are built of materials which are at once strong and light, for, when the family that inhabits them moves, the whole structure has to be carried with them by men, women, and

children. Only later will man have the aid of beasts of
burden. In any case the apparatus of the movable house
is very simple,—some pegs, some ropes, and for covering
skins sewn together. In some countries the use of bark
or plaited straw makes the burden lighter but only in the
summer, until cloth woven of wool or hair will be large enough
and strong enough to defy sun, rain, and wind. The tent
thus made up has remained practically unchanged until
to-day, although its dimensions and its workmanship have
increased and improved.

We have no means of knowing what was the furniture
in the primitive home, but we can make a good guess at it,
by what we see in the poorest homes that we know. At
the beginning there were bundles of dry leaves, straw, fern
or seaweed to sleep on : some heaps of stone or earth to
sit on, a block of wood or stone to serve as chopping block ;
later the squared log to serve as bench ; still later a stool
and a table of wood. That is practically all that there was
in the hut. Later, very much later, among the nomads,
will appear the chest in which the family wealth is stored.
Then man begins to lay a mat on the floor of trodden
earth. In Japan and in warm countries, this is still what is
done. The straw is shut up in a covering and the two become
the mattress. Suspended on a framework of wood it becomes
the bed, the bed where man is born and dies, the bed which
for long the head of the house will think it an honour to
build, as we see in the *Odyssey* [1] : " It was I that built it
and none other," says Odysseus. " A bush of long-leafed
olive was growing within the court, strong and vigorous and
in girth it was like a pillar ; round about this I built my
chamber till I had finished it with close-set stones and I
roofed it over well and added to it jointed doors close-fitting.
Thereafter I cut away the leafy branches of the long-leafed
olive and trimming the trunk from the root I smoothed
it round with the adze, well and cunningly, and made it
straight to the line, thus fashioning the bedpost and I bored
it all with the augur. Beginning with this I hewed out my

[1] *Odyssey*, xxiii, 189 (Murray's translation).

bed till I had finished it, inlaying it with gold and silver and ivory and I stretched on it a thong of oxhide bright with purple."

In the house there was another thing that was essential, the hearth; slightly raised above the level of the floor it was built up with fire-blackened bricks; above it there was a hole by which the smoke went out and the rain came in. Later, when it was placed against the farther wall of the house and sheltered by a screen the hearth was gradually transformed to a fireplace with mantelshelf. Sometimes it was placed to one side or removed to a neighbouring room which became the kitchen. Sometimes, and this was the case in warm countries, it was replaced by a brazier in which charcoal and perfumes burned. Perhaps there was added to this scanty furniture a bored stone or a bored piece of wood, which could hold a torch and a few utensils, tools, and amulettes leaned against or hung from the walls. That gives us a fairly adequate description of a dwelling-place whose like is still seen in poor countries. I have seen some not dissimilar in Lower Brittany. And yet modest and rudimentary as they were, they were sacred places; they can be looked upon as the first temples. The cult of the domestic fire was born within them, a cult as strong as it has been lasting.

I have said nothing about the siting of huts, cabins, and houses. They were sited differently in the different countries, to obtain coolness and shade in warm countries, to get all the sun that was possible in cold countries or were buried deeply in the ground to obtain heat otherwise. The wind played a principal part here. In the neighbourhood of the sea, instead of being built on a height where they ran the risk of being wrecked by a hurricane, the houses were built in the shelter of a valley, and it was the same on the mountains —where the houses were built out of the path of the prevailing wind and with forests protecting them against the avalanche. In Provence the farm seeks the protection of a rampart of pine or cypress against the fury of the *mistral*.

But whether hid in a depression or perched on the side of a hill the houses could not for ever remain isolated. They felt the need to come together, whether because of the social instinct existing among members of a family or a clan or a desire to come together in face of danger. The houses then turned either their fronts or their backs to what was now a street, sometimes grouped themselves in a circle round a central place or straggled out along a road. Some had subsidiary buildings, barn, court, or stable, which made one building with them. In others, the secondary buildings were separate and clustered round the parent one. Little agglomerations were thus formed, hamlets which became villages. The choice of a site was the result of more than one motive. First of all, the resources of the site in the matter of food and water had to be calculated. A favourite site was the neighbourhood of a spring, a well, a pool, a lake. The marshes and the banks of the river were justly feared because of their liability to flood and fever. But the shore of the sea had its merits, since fish and shellfish were to be had in abundance. The site chosen was a sloping beach protected from the waves by a dyke and certain areas of water were marked out as possessions from which competitors were excluded. Even to-day the nations partition the waters of sea and lake. Another favourite site was near a forest, since there wood, game and fruit could be had in plenty. Certain African tribes, the Fang for example, proceed through the land eating and destroying the forest that feeds them. Other tribes of less restless disposition settled near flint quarries and later near metal mines, just as in our days the oil prospectors founded towns in California and Georgia whose only reason for existence was the profit they drew from productive territory.

Another motive, too, aided powerfully in determining the choice of a site—the desire for security. Man had to defend himself from beasts and other men. So if he lived in the plain he surrounded the huts with a circular palisade protected by a ditch in which sharp stakes were ready to receive and impale the assailant. The South African *kraal* [1] is built on this model. Sometimes turrets, look-out posts, or *miradors* which permitted a survey of the surroundings completed the ramparts.

Elsewhere the villages were sited on rising ground or

[1] Deniker, p. 98.

built on a mountain terrace. Here too ditches, palisades, and then walls were constructed to protect the inhabitants. The camp at Chassey (Saône-et-Loire) is a type of these large fortifications covering about twenty-five acres. In every country where such high ground was to be found it was occupied in this way. Athens was not the only city that had an acropolis ; many towns were divided into the upper and the lower town. The summit of the mountain where were built temple and palace and citadel, was the protector of the cities when it was not the stronghold of their oppressors. In the Middle Ages a village earned the name of town when it was fortified.

In North and Central America it was in the steep cliffs which edged the rivers that flowed far below (the Colorado river and the Rio Mancos) that men quarried out habitations which hung over steep precipices (*cliff-dwellings*). But also, and very frequently, the caciques built their houses, or the priests built their temples, on artificial mounds. Sometimes it seemed that the earth like the opossum which hides her young from danger in her pouch, took into its entrails its threatened children. In Mexico, for instance in the middle of a plain, there is often found a natural hollow in the ground in which water lies and forms a pool, but in the so-called cave of Montezuma which takes its name from the story that the Mexican king and some of his subjects hid themselves in it from the Spanish conquerors, a large village of refuge was established.[1]

In America, too, we must mention the *mounds*, artificial hillocks which are often real fortresses with turrets, case-mates, several concentric enclosures and entrances very difficult to penetrate (Ohio and Wisconsin). In Sardinia are found peculiar cone-shaped structures which are called *nouraghe*. Their walls are very thick ; entrance can be obtained only by crawling through a doorway so low that a big stone is enough to close it completely. Inside is a large room egg-shaped and a stairway hidden in the thick wall by which access is obtained to the upper storeys which end in a terraced roof. As far as we can judge by appearances these were refuges to which the population fled in case of danger and analogous buildings are found in southern Italy,

[1] A facsimile can be seen in the Musée d'Ethnographie at the Trocadero.

the Balearic Islands and in Shetland. We may also mention as a further type of the place of refuge what the Italians call *terramare*. These are found on the banks of the Po and consist of embankments of earth enclosing a swamp upon which a whole town is erected on piles.

In other places the same desire for security caused the islands whether in rivers or in the sea to be inhabited. Not without reason was Tyre built on a rocky island in the sea or Lutetia on an island in the Seine. We may recall too the *crannogs* of Scotland or the lagoons of Venice where islands carefully built up and made solid afforded a practically inviolable sanctuary.

The lacustran cities are examples of these settlements on or in the water. What better ditch could one find to put between one's village and its attackers than a sheet of water—sometimes as broad as 5,000 feet, as was the case at Robenhausen on Lake Pfæffkon in Switzerland? There is no need to wonder at the number of them. There are more than 200 examples in Switzerland, many in France, in the Jura and the Alps, a good many in North Italy, Scotland, Russia, North America, India, etc. Some of them must have had several thousand inhabitants. They perished in the flames destroyed by invaders or, just as many towns and castles have come down from the heights to the plains in proportion as the sense of security increased, so these left the sites which were in truth not very convenient whenever it was no longer necessary to take such precautions. Yet some of them still exist in Sumatra and New Zealand.

On a par with these villages where the crowded population managed somehow to retain the inviolability of the family hut, are the curious dwelling-places found in Mexico.[1] Entire towns have been constructed inside the cliff with several storeys of caves and subterranean halls or are built in the form of hives which are called *pueblos* and whose cells are built on to the hillside in such a way that one supports the other, that the flat roof of one serves as a building ground for the next. They were entered by means of ladders stretching from the ground floor to the top storey of this composite building. Here the family and the collective

[1] Capitan, *L'Amérique précolombienne*, p. 9.

habitation both existed. While the married couples had each their own home, the unmarried occupied common houses, which served also as places for social intercourse and pleasure. The whole of Oceania and certain districts of Indo-China [1] have experienced this division of social structure, which is reflected in the house, and which seems to go back to the remote past.

Whatever its nature, hut or cave, house or tent, the dwelling-place of man had profound influence on his evolution. It fashioned him as much as he fashioned it. The head of a household by the simple fact of having a house of his own, a little personal kingdom, learned order, foresight, and the habit of caring for the morrow. His character became less rude, less savage. It was softened by the presence of wife and children. The wife, master and guardian of the home, while the man was away hunting, fishing, or at war, became conscious of the importance of her part as manager, as queen of the inside of the home. Then when the family became a clan, and the hut became a village, there came into existence social organization, shadowy at first, but with every generation becoming more definite and complete.

Architecture developed equally. To summarize its history we can say that the palace, the temple, the tomb, and the fortress have been the essential forms which its development has taken.

One of the minor marvels of history is the transport and employment of those immense blocks of stone which some-times stand aligned like Titans, sometimes stand isolated like steeples, or form what are called cyclopean buildings and serve as ramparts to the cities of antiquity. How in their lack of the machines and devices of to-day without any other instruments than rollers, ropes, levers, and capstans, did the men of old hew and put in place obelisks, columns, pyramids, and menhirs which were common in every country at a very early date ? We shall meet this question again later on, and it may serve as a conclusion to this chapter in which we have tried to show the first attempts and the first achievements of man as builder. In this sphere, too, he has made many inventions, and I do not hesitate to repeat these words of

[1] Deniker, p. 199.

a philosopher who sought to defend the practical inventor against the depreciation of certain intellectuals : " If, in the distant ages when man faced nature naked and without weapons we trace the road he has travelled up to the civilization of to-day, in which the machine is king, we stand amazed at the amount of imaginative power which he has produced, used, and often simply wasted and ask ourselves how such achievement can be denied or lightly valued."

BIBLIOGRAPHY

BEUCHAT, *Manuel d'archéologie américaine.*
BRUNHES (Jean), *La géographie humaine.*
CAPITAN, *Le travail dans l'Amérique précolombienne.*
FRÉMONT (Charles), *La serrure (origine et évolution).*
GARNIER (Charles) and AMMANN, *L'habitation humaine.*
HOMER, *Odyssey,* bk. xxiii.
RICHET (Étienne), *Les Esquimaux de l'Alaska.*
VIGNY (Alfred de), *Cinq-Mars.*

G

CHAPTER V

CLOTHING AND WEAPONS OF DEFENCE

MAN is not born with his house on his back like the tortoise or the snail. Nor is he covered with woolly fur like the bear or the sheep, nor yet with a thick hide like the ox or the horse. Even if in his very early days he was much shaggier than he is now, yet his skin was not proof against the bite of the north wind, the teeth of animals, the sharp points of thorns or of insects, or the hard surfaces of the rocks. Hence was born the need of clothing.

It is a mistake to think that the feeling of modesty is the origin of clothing. On the contrary, it is probable that clothing is the cause of the sense of shame.[1] Primitive man has not any idea of decency or indecency : he sees nothing about the human body which there is any reason to hide. A negro king considers himself adequately dressed in a pair of boots, a top hat, and a red jacket. Montaigne [2] quotes the answer of a tatterdemalion to those who sought to make him feel ashamed of his nudity : " You have your face bare : Well, I am all face." According to a phrase which comes from the Indies, a savage sees nothing wrong in " being clothed in air ".

Man's adoption of clothing comes from three causes. There is, first of all, the regular seasonal changes from heat to cold, as a result of the succession of day and night, of summer and winter : there is rain, tempest, wind, frost. The need to protect himself against the severities of climate was felt especially in the changing climates of the regions round the poles ; in the tropics the custom of going about without clothing continues to this day. Secondly, there was the presence of briars and thorns, insects with poison stings, animals with sharp teeth, stones with sharp corners and edges—all hostile things against which he had to find

[1] It is possible that the apron of the woman was intended to conceal at the menstrual period an issue held to be impure, and that the sense of shame arose out of this concealment.

[2] *Essays* : On the custom of clothing oneself.

protection. Finally, there was the desire for self adornment, to be remarked upon for one's personal decoration, the wish to cause fear or arouse jealousy—these feelings must have influenced strongly the childish and impulsive mind of early man.

The practice of painting the body was a beginning. Chalk, charcoal, ochre, the juice of certain plants, were the agents, and each colour had no doubt a symbolic significance. Red indicated life, and that is perhaps the reason why the dead in skeleton state were often painted a colour which promised resurrection.[1] In some countries white, like black elsewhere, was a colour of mourning. Besides, painting was a method of embellishment, as is seen in the case of several statuettes,[2] and is not that the motive of the very civilized ladies of to-day, who use rouge and powder, blacken their eyelids with pencil, use kohl below their eyes, and henna on their fingers as the Koran enjoins Moslem women to do.

When Captain Cook landed for the first time in New Zealand, he noticed that his sailors often returned from excursions on land with their noses stained with red or yellow. The native women, to make themselves beautiful, had redecorated themselves, and there was no notice " wet paint " to give the unfortunate mariners warning.

The Bible tells us that the patriarch Job called a daughter of his Keren Happuch, which means " horn of eye-paint ", and that an angel called Azaliel came down from Heaven on purpose to teach the art of rouging to the daughters of men. Is there any likelihood that the said daughters waited for any angelic or diabolic instruction ? The historians tell us that among the ancient Germans certain tribes painted themselves black to enable them to surprise and terrify their enemies. Others preferred bright colours, and I imagine that in the motley and gilded and embroidered uniform of the great ones of the earth and their armed escorts we have a continuance and modification of this custom.[3]

---

[1] *V. Les primitifs d'Australie*, p. 70.
[2] Morgan.
[3] Generally speaking, dark-skinned people prefer light colours, and vice versa.

From this many coloured adornment which rapidly wore off, man soon passed to something more durable, tattooing.[1] Certain flints, very small and very sharp, which have been found at Fère-en-Tardenois and in North Africa, seem to be tattooing instruments. Sometimes by means of a shape in wood or in clay figures were imprinted on the back or the chest of the individual, which had probably magical significance. This was the case in Mexico and Peru. There were two distinct methods of tattooing—*incision* so that the design stood out in scars and *puncture* by the use of a needle which introduced under the skin black or blue powder. The Congo supplies us with an example of the first manner.[2] Here the dandies have a cut made which runs from the root of the hairs to the end of the nose. The juice of a certain plant is then squeezed into it to prevent it from closing, and a scar is thus formed which looks like a cock's comb. Among the Kaffirs a line of artificial warts from the forehead to the neck is considered beautifying. The women do not fall behind the men in their efforts.[3] In Tibet, having previously covered their faces with starch, they inlay them with tiny pebbles, forming geometric designs. Among the Ainus the women tattoo moustaches on their faces as if they envied the males their beards. Elsewhere their backs, their breasts, their temples, their thighs, are covered with a medley of intricate lines and their skins are damasked with flowers and stars. There a little doubt that these or similar practices were held in honour by our remote ancestors. Sometimes there was a religious motive : certain marks placed on the correct spot had the property of amulets. Sometimes the motive was utilitarian : the American aborigines maintained that tattooing protected them from sunstroke, and that certain dyes mixed with fat kept off mosquitoes.[4] But most of all the motive was simply that of making oneself beautiful.

There is more than one strange survival.[5] Passing over the Roman ladies, who, like their German sisters, dyed their hair red with a dye produced from the beech, and, omitting

[1] Deniker, p. 206.
[2] Mandat-Grancey, *Au Congo*, p. 80.
[3] Deniker.
[4] The Hottentots rub themselves with fat and ashes to keep out the cold.
[5] Duelling scars have not yet ceased to be fashionable among the youth of Germany.

Fig. 8.—Natives of Nouka-Hiva (*Voyage pittoresque*).

the contemporary practice of getting rid of grey hair, tattooing itself has not yet disappeared. It exists among sailors and prostitutes : it flourishes in prisons, and it is the pride and joy of many criminals. In Japan porters make themselves what they call a " shirt of flesh " by using flesh-tints which take the place of clothing. A master of the art tattooed a fantastic dragon on the left arm of the last of the Czars when as Tzarevitch he visited Japan and a swan on the chest of King George V while he was a young officer in the Navy. In 1898 Baron de Mandat Grancey declared that it was the correct thing among the English nobility to have the coat of arms of the house tattooed on the calf or a design on the wrist, and that ladies of the highest social standing had a fine lace pattern tattooed on their legs, an original method of having holeproof hose. There was also an American lady who went so far as to have the " Last Supper " of Leonardo da Vinci tattooed on her shoulders, the Christ on her back-bone and the Apostles on her shoulder-blades. It is also well known that Bernadotte, who became king of Sweden, always refused to allow himself to be bled, because he had on his arm a design dating from his Republican days, with a motto hardly suitable for an autocratic monarch, " Liberty or Death ! "

We can say, therefore, that, although at the present time tattooing is exceptional, neither man nor woman has changed very much in the matter of adornment. Nowadays, we embroider not the skin but the coat. Figured silks and wondrous uniforms are the visible proof that the spirit of tattooing lives.

Fashions and beliefs whose reason we do not know caused primitive man to submit to and inflict painful mutilations and deformations. To increase manly beauty he stuck through his nostrils a feather, a branch of coral, or a stick of metal. Among the Eskimos a piece of bone or horn or agate is stuck into the lower lip, an ornament known by the name of *labret*. It was a mark of royalty among the Incas. In Australia youths undergoing the rites of initiation to the rank of manhood have several teeth torn out. Among the negroes fashion ordains the breaking, filing, and sharpening of the teeth to a point. Elsewhere the ears are artificially lengthened, so that they fall on to the shoulders, a practice that is found in Easter Island and among the Kanakas. " Long ears " was the name given to the Peruvian nobles by the Spaniards.[1] In default of better methods, the ears were pierced and buckles, rings, and weights suspended from them, a custom that still exists among the ladies in civilized countries and even among sailors. Circumcision, a religious rite among the Israelites and many other peoples, is another case of this propensity to improve on the human body.

Deformations of the skull constitute still another. In the Punjab the skull of the child is worked upon from birth. The aim is to flatten the rear surface, which is done by letting the head rest on a hard surface, by massaging it with the hands, or by enclosing it in an earthen vessel of the desired shape. Similarly, there is the custom of causing a deep cleft in the chin by pressing each day with a piece of polished wood the place where the cleft is desired. Certain customs have a hygienic value [2]; the custom, for instance, of avoiding bandy legs and knock-knees by means of tightly rolled bandages. In France the scientists have been able to study the form of cranial deformation called Tolosan,[3] which consists in lengthening the head to the shape of a sugar-loaf, and in Bolivia, as well as in Asia Minor and North America, this method of producing doliocephalics has been in favour. We cannot explain why, unless doliocephaly was perhaps a characteristic of a dominant race. Are further examples necessary ? Everyone knows of the deformation of the feet submitted to by Chinese women. The practice, it is said, does not go back to a date earlier than some twelve centuries ago, but it is connected with ideas which are far earlier. A traveller [4] saw the practice still existing at the beginning of the twentieth century in an orphanage run by a European sisterhood, and describes it thus : " From the time the child is three or four years old the feet are tied tightly in such a way as to bring all the toes and even the heel under the sole of the foot so thoroughly that thenceforward only the big toe thrust into a tiny slipper rests on the ground. It is a torture which causes the children to utter cries of agony. Many of them die under it, and those who

[1] Lubbock, ii, pp. 182, 265.
[2] Article by M. de Parville.
[3] Deniker, Broca, Gosse, Topinard, etc.
[4] G. Weulersee, *Chine ancienne et moderne*, p. 230.

survive, even if they are not made hopeless cripples, suffer all their lives." Perhaps it is the result of an idea that it is necessary to suffer to be beautiful, and of a barbarous conception of beauty, but the practice is clearly related to that obtaining among the natives of New South Wales of cutting off the little finger, to those that caused the mutilations of the hands recorded on prehistoric caverns, and to those which cause modern women to risk pain and ill-health through tight lacing and tight shoes, or, to be less tragic, to wear false hips, bustles, crinolines, and other devices intended to modify the form and proportions of the body which nature gave them.

From modern customs let us return to the origin of clothing. At the beginning it appears that man wore on his body three or four strips of hide which developed into the various articles of clothing. Let us begin with the head. It was always considered the supreme part of the body, and it is actually the seat of sight, hearing, taste, and smell. It is not without reason that the words " head " and " chief " are synonymous. The leather strip that surrounded the forehead served to hold back the hair and prevent it blinding those who wore it long. Among certain peoples it served as a quiver and arrows were stuck in it. But it was easily transformed into a circlet of leaves, of flowers, or of feathers. It became a mitre, a diadem, a royal crown, the emblem of greatness and of power, or religious adornment. Among ordinary mortals it was the origin of an enormous variety of bonnets, hats, and caps, whose substance differs according to climates and seasons, and whose appearance often betrays precisely what rank in the social scale its wearer occupies. As to the hair, it lent itself to every fantasy. In one place the women shave the head and the eyebrows completely. Elsewhere the hair is cropped in places. Long, as in the case of the Merovingian kings, short as in the case of the revolutionaries cropped *à la* Titus, partially cropped as in the case of the Roman priesthood, it possesses various symbolic significance. In Japan it is arranged in slabs, which are pressed down on the temples ; in China it is woven into a pig tail. Sometimes it is reduced almost to nothing, sometimes it is built up in an imposing edifice. Feathers are stuck in it, and pins, horsehair, or the tail of some animal—a prelude to the days of the perruque and the vast constructions that great ladies bore on their heads in the days of Louis XVI.

The strip which surrounded the neck quickly became a collar, from which was suspended flowers, as in Tahiti, but, especially, hard and coloured seeds, shells, bright stones, pearls, bits of amber, coral or ivory, and amulets of all kinds. Soon the skin of a beast was attached to it, which was worn before or behind, on the back or on the breast, according as the wind blew, and here is the ancestor of the corset, which in later times will cover the bust. The collar in the age of bronze will be adorned with glass beads, and will change into a collar of hard metal which has been named *torques*, and which resembles the high stiff collar so long worn by officers.

The strip which served as a belt and which was used to compress the stomach, a useful function in days of famine, also developed. All sorts of things were hung from it : the scalp of a slain enemy, the teeth of men or of animals which were trophies of war, or of the chase, knives and hatchets. Sometimes the tail of a lion or a horse hung from it. But, chiefly among women, it was increased by the addition of a narrow piece of skin or bark, a frail rampart of chastity which the least movement displaced, so frail, indeed, that some scientists have debated whether its function really was to conceal or to draw the attention to what was hidden.[1] This waist cloth of very restricted dimensions will gradually lengthen, and become the apron, the petticoat, and the prodigious development which that article of female clothing has undergone is known to everyone.

While the belt became a metal one among men, rings, which were perhaps signs of servitude before they became ornaments, began to be worn by women on the arms and the legs. They were made of flint, of ivory, of mother of pearl, of alabaster, of metal, and they are the heralds of the sleeves and the hose that will appear later and of ornamental rings generally.[2]

Then it became necessary to tie and join together the various articles of clothing. In the beginning thorns fulfilled this function, and still fulfil it in some places, and it was on their model that bone-pins and then metal ones were

[1] Cf. in Ernest Gross's *Les débuts de l'art*, a long discussion on the point.
[2] Morgan, p. 196.

made. Then came the brooches of which our safety-pins are a revival, and which from the age of bronze had a decorative as well as a utilitarian function to perform. They are often really works of art, like the modern brooches, which are their descendants, and the button of bone or of metal (the latter appearing in the age of bronze) is also an ornament as well as a fastener. The clasp appears only at a later day.

But there were other sorts of fasteners. Through holes pierced in the skins of animals strips of hide were passed or vegetable fibres which were then drawn tight and tied. The system still survives in the corset, and the lacing boot. This was the beginning of sewing. Thread began to be substituted for the thick cords, and instead of the large holes made in leather or cloth came the tiny holes made very close together. To spin and to sew thenceforward was the favourite occupation of women. The distaff and the spindle with the needle were their ordinary tools, and from the quantity of stone or metal spindle-rings found in neolithic tombs and in the lacustran stations, we can estimate the importance to which this feminine and domestic industry had attained.

The clothing thus manufactured was adapted to sex, to climate, and to the social status of those who wore it. Practically everywhere a sort of sack, with a hole through which the head could pass, served as blouse and tunic and took the place of the shirt, until the shirt was invented. But in warm countries floating garments are preferred : they are often so everywhere by women and for priests and they are so still by the upper classes of effeminate Asia. On the contrary, simple, tight-fitting, and unembarrassing garments are preferred by workers, or soldiers, and by the Spartan maidens who underwent the same training as the Spartan youths. In cold countries they did not merely cover the trunk ; they protected the legs, and so among the Gauls, the Germans, and the northern peoples breeches, the ancestors of our trousers, were worn, things unknown to the Greeks and the peoples of the South.

Footwear was long in making its appearance. Our ancestors went with their feet bare. The skin of their big toes and their heels was hard as horn. At a much later date after some battle between Arabs and Europeans the corpses of the Europeans were recognized, although they had been despoiled, by the corns and callouses due to their shoes. Gradually men made themselves wattle sandals, wooden shoes, and mocassins of pliant leather. For horsemen boots were simply the skin from the legs of horses, barely dressed, and being transferred almost untouched from the animal to the man.

To supply this need of clothing and adornment, which grew ever greater (for mothers take pleasure in dressing and adorning their children) man utilized all sorts of material. He first of all used the skins of beasts. In the old legend Hercules wears a lion's skin, Bacchus a panther's, and Pallas Athene a goat's skin, which covers her back and breast. Animals which nature had provided with a downy or shining fur like the mole, the marten, the ermine, the fox, were the first to be deprived of their defence against the cold. In all the stations where stone tools have been found there were quantities of tools for piercing, scraping, rubbing, and polishing these spoils of the chase. Among the Eskimos it falls to the men to prepare the skins of the larger animals—wolves, bears, walrusses, seals—while the women dealt with those of the smaller animals—muskrats, hares, marmots—and of sea-birds, using thimbles of sealskin and needles of bone. Coats and gloves were made from skins, both being inventions of cold countries. Probably things proceeded very much in the same way elsewhere. The skins cleared of hair and softened in urine or in water mixed with ashes, were turned into leather, which was then softened with oil and fat and made into impermeable clothing. Currying thus seems to have preceded tanning.

To finish with leather one has only to state that other peoples used it to make drinking vessels and vessels in which to store water, wine, oil, or air, the last in bags which were the ancestors of the bellows and of forcing pumps, thongs to hold garments together or to attach a stone dagger to a handle, cuirasses, whose name betrays their origin, wallets in which were carried food and tools, and then, as we have seen, shoes and later still saddles, panniers, bridles, and harness which could be used on asses and horses.

From the quadrupeds man borrowed also hair, the wool

which the sheep left on the bushes and from which he made felt hats by a process still in vogue among the Mongols. " The method of making these hats is a simple domestic matter.[1] First of all a layer of wool and of hair is placed on an old piece of felt : the edges are trimmed, it is soaked in boiling water, and then the felt is rolled up inside the wool. It only remains to tie the roll up firmly, trample it underfoot, throw it in the air sufficiently often, and the task is finished. The roll is undone, and there is the wool matted, the felt complete." A barbarous method, no doubt, but one which doubtless was already a refinement on a simpler method used by certain savages in Australia and New Zealand, who simply make an elastic and coherent substance of hair, human or animal, or wool, by rolling the material either between the hands or with the hand on the thigh.[2]

The time came later when men knew how to shear regularly sheep, goats, camels, llamas, and vicunas. Their borrowings were greatest from their cousins the vertebrates. From the birds they took mainly down from geese and swans and coloured feathers to serve as ceremonial adornment. Seneca, however, speaks somewhere of people who clothe themselves with feathers and in Hawaii, Mexico, and Peru there existed an art of feather work,[3] whereby were made, by fixing feathers on wood or on cloth, plumes, mantles, and mosaics representing a butterfly, a rose, a carpet of flowering plants. The workers who professed this art did wonderful work, but the costly and delicate clothing which they produced was used only by the greatest in the land and at solemn ceremonies ; it was never in daily popular use. Only the feather fan has survived.

From marine animals the peoples dwelling on the sea-coast, especially in cold countries,[4] made clothing from the skin of the salmon, and impermeable garments from the skin of the seal or the walrus. They used whalebone, too, while in warmer seas fishers and divers have brought into use coral, mother of pearl, pearls, and tortoise shell.

Vegetable matter has equally served to clothe man. Wood was material for shoes : the bark of the mulberry was

[1] Letourneau, *L'évolution du commerce*, p. 225, quoting Huc.
[2] Deniker, p. 215.
[3] Capitan, *L'Amérique précolombienne*, p. 85.
[4] Deniker, p. 14.

beaten into a sort of petticoat which in Tahiti, for example, was coloured and was equivalent to cloth. At an early date man learned to weave grass, rushes, and straw, and then the fibres of certain plants. Linen was one of the earliest and was used before hemp. Cotton produced by the wool-bearing tree, as the Greeks called it, did not pass unnoticed in the East. From the bits which were gathered thread was made by a rolling process. Then it was observed that a weight hung to the thread and made to turn aided the process. This was the invention of the spindle. In the neolithic tombs have been found quantities of spindle rings in stone, which were used by spinners in those distant days. To-day the spindle is becoming something to be preserved in a museum : only in remote places is it ever seen in use. But for centuries this invention, one of the earliest made by man, was the peculiar property of woman, the sceptre of the mistress of the house. Even yet it has not quite disappeared : it survives in the spinning mills worked by steam or electricity.

Rightly did Lucretius [1] say that the art of plaiting preceded the art of weaving. Weaving is indeed an extension of plaiting with a finer element, i.e. thread, than straw or rushes. Weaving takes the place of the slower and less practical work of the needle. The weaver's loom has been added to the line of inventions, vertical at first, as it still is at the Gobelins. The weaver worked standing at first, and his was a trade therefore reserved to man, but it fell into the sphere of woman when the loom became horizontal and could be worked by a person seated. The material thus produced was, as is usual with anything new, a luxury reserved for chiefs, kings, and priests, but it quickly became popular. One result of the invention was the development of dyeing, which had begun with tattooing. Now the juice of certain plants, like woad, madder, saffron, and indigo, certain earths like ochre, and minerals like china clay and alum, or colours taken from insects like cochineal, formed a palette which could rival the most brilliant plumage. Embellishment and design satisfied the overwhelming desire for adornment, that desire which in the mating season makes the peacock display his resplendent tail and the cock strut up and down before his harem, a desire which is no less powerful among members of the human family.

[1] *De rerum natura* v : " Nexilis ante fuit vestis quam textile tegmen."

For proof one need only refer to the toilet articles found in the neolithic tombs, especially when metal affords more variation of form. There are big pins, combs, mirrors, metal objects for adjusting clothing, brooches to hold them together, and above all an astonishing collection of jewels, collars, pendants, eardrops, and spirals in brass, and filagree work which appeared in Egypt and Chaldea thirty centuries before our era ; open work in gold or silver made of rolled and soldered metal threads. The art of the goldsmith added to that of the lapidary was one of the oldest and, at the same time, one of the most honoured in the New World as in the Old. There is no cause for astonishment here. To-day luxury trades are better remunerated and more esteemed than those which are merely useful.

The materials are fragile enough by nature, and one can easily understand why they have come down to us in a torn and discoloured state. Yet the bandages in which the Egyptian mummies were wrapped remind us that the linen in the land of the Pharaohs was renowned for its whiteness and its delicacy. In Mexico and Peru, thanks to their late appearance in history, have been found superb examples of the ceremonial garments which chiefs and priests wore on solemn occasions—mantles of butterfly wings with border ornaments with eyes like the tail of a peacock, embroidered jerkins, painted cloth woven from many-coloured feathers, which imitate the display of parrakeets and birds of paradise. The luxury of fine dresses has been faithfully handed down from age to age. Its origin goes back to a remote past.

As to the technique of manufacture of the various materials, this varied from country to country. In Peru methods are found which recall the tapestries which are made at the Gobelins or Beauvais. Elsewhere, in Carmania, for instance, the ruling type is a complicated pointwork, with borders and alternations of colour. Elsewhere, again, it is embroidery superimposed on woven stuff. The possession of the art of embroidery was one that was highly appreciated in the royal ladies of Homer's day : Argive Helen was a famous exponent of it.

To this brief study of clothing, it is necessary to add a word on weapons of defence which were also designed to protect the body, but in this case against wounds and blows.

SAVAGES IN BATTLE.

FIG. 4.—Burial of a Chief. André Thevet, *Les singularités de la France antarctique autrement nommé Amérique* (1556), after the volume of John Grand Carteret entitled *L'histoire, la vie, les mœurs et la curiosité* (Paris, 1927). Note the instruments for kindling fire that are being placed in the grave.

In this sphere, too, the desire to attract attention ended in producing articles of utility. Men wore terrifying masks or an imposing plume or the head of a bear, a bull, or a boar, of the talons of a bird of prey, or the antlers of a stag, or the horns of an ox. Then what had been designed to adorn the warrior or terrify the enemy became a means of avoiding wounds or making them less serious. The bracelet protected the arm, the collar blunted or turned a weapon. The garment of animal skin, especially if it was thick as is the hide of a bull, naturally developed into a cuirass. It was completed by the invention of what is a mobile cuirass, the shield, which, in its beginnings, is only a plain staff designed to parry a stroke, which was lengthened and widened and became a plank of wood or of woven osier equipped with a catch by which it was held. Sometimes round, sometimes long and rectangular, slightly convex, padded with cotton or hair, covered with leather or felt and later with metal, it was practically impenetrable by missile weapons hurled by hand. Finally the helmet with the horns which crowned it, and the horse-hair which adorned it, became more than just something to scare the enemy. It broke the blows of the club which threatened the head. The cuirass, which soon was made of metal, imitated the scales of the fish or the serpent or the plumage of the bird, and so paved the way for the armour which will end by shutting up the warrior in a fortress of steel.

No longer does man go blindly into the danger which comes from nature or animals or other men. The faculty of providing against it has developed. He knows how to adapt the material in his possession so as to make it serve to preserve his life. He has tried more than one method of survival. He is on his way to possess the earth.

BIBLIOGRAPHY

BOURDEAU (Louis), *Histoire de l'habillement et de la parure* (Alcan, Paris, 1904).

BOUVIER (Jeanne), *La lingerie.*

CAPITAN, " A horn ornament on the head of a Red Indian : Comparison with the pierced horns of the Magdelenian period " (*Décade*, Capitan, 1907) : *Le travail dans l'Amerique precolombienne.*

GRATEROL (Maurice), *Du costume et de la toilette dans l'antiquité.*

GROSS (Ernest), *The Beginnings of Art.*

MORTILLET (A. de), *Les armes* (course of lectures at the Ecole d'Anthropologie, 1926-27).

PARAF (Mathilde), *La dentelle et la broderie.*

QUICHERAT, *Histoire de costume.*

RACINET, *Le costume historique.*

H

CHAPTER VI

Man and the Animals

PRIMITIVE man is not merely neighbour, he is also kin of the beasts and even of the plants which surround him. To the animals especially he was related by ties of origin and he had no shame in acknowledging the relationship as his descendants have to-day. He knew that they were his companions in life whom he ate or who ate him, but he respected them, admired them, imitated them, and went even so far as to deify them as mysterious beings who had faculties and knowledge which he himself did not possess. Among their numbers he early distinguished, in relation to himself, two classes. On the one hand there were the malignant animals to be dreaded; on the other the inoffensive, feeble animals whom he could master and mould. The former inspired respect and fear; the latter sympathy and gratitude, two reasons, opposed, indeed, but equally convincing, to make him revere them and try to conciliate them.

In many countries—for it is not proved that the custom has been in force everywhere—a growing family, a clan, allied itself to one of the animals which bulked most largely in its life. The animal was a friend, a protector, an ancestor; it gave its name to the clan which adopted it; it became its *totem*.[1] As such it is protected as much as it protects; it cannot be killed and eaten except in exceptional circumstances when at a religious rite one " communicates with it " by feasting on its flesh and blood. The Iroquois, who have the tortoise for totem, declared that they had knowledge of the moment when the ancestral tortoise changed himself into human shape. Totemism flourished in America, in Australia, in Egypt, probably among the Celts and elsewhere. The beaver, the hawk, the kangaroo, the eagle, the parrot, are found among the animals who are fathers of this

---

[1] The word comes from the American Indians.

or that tribe, and it is possible that the obligation to spare the species to which a clan believed itself related led sometimes to its domestication.

In other countries, India, for example, the belief in the transmigration of souls into the bodies of beasts, in the rebirth of the drunkard in a pig, of the wicked in a tiger or a snake, is another way of recognizing the original relationship between beings which life was to carry farther and farther apart. Is this the reason why we meet in the most ancient civilizations with goddesses with the head of a panther, sphinxes which have the head and shoulders of a woman on a lioness's body, gods with the heads of rams or jackals, such as one finds in Egypt or bulls with wings and the faces of men, as one finds in Assyria? Among the Greeks we find everywhere this alliance of the beast nature and the human—satyrs with goats' feet, centaurs half men half horses, myrmidons who claim descent from the ant, sirens with the head and shoulders of a woman and the tail of fish, Pallas Athene with the face of an owl, Hera with the eyes of an ox. Between the Athenians and the grasshoppers there existed fraternal ties. How many cities and peoples have had an animal for emblem? Rome had the wolf as Siena had later, the Lydians the fox, the Gauls the wolf or the cock, the English the leopard. The arms of our noble families are survivals of these ancient relations between a human clan and an animal species.

Be that as it may, the crocodile and the lordly tiger have both been sacred beings, a sort of mortal god; the serpent which almost everywhere was feared and adored and still as a result of that fear had temples and worshippers in the days when Lucian, the Voltaire of paganism, was poking fun at the so-called Immortals of Hades and Olympus. Similarly the ibis, a wading bird and enemy of all that crawls, the ichneumon, eater of serpents and destroyer of their eggs, and even the labouring ox and the ram, the reproducer, have obtained out of gratitude quasi-divine honours. The reverence of man for these enigmatic beings which surrounded him was so great that he projected them, as it were, into the heavens, the Great Bear, the Great Dog, which left its name to the dogstar, the Scorpion, shone in the zodiac or among the constellations.

But man had not merely these mystical relations with

the animals. He recognized quickly that there were certain animals to whom he was game, and there were others who could become either his prey or his allies. With the former, the larger wild animals, he was in a state of perpetual war. He had either to kill or be killed. He was forced to hunt and snare them, and he did so so successfully that he stamped out certain species in certain countries; the wolf and the bear in Britain, for instance, while elsewhere the great carnivora, retreating steadily before him had to hide themselves in the forests or the deserts. Once the lion, the hyena, the cave-bear were common in Western Europe. Change of climate and the hostility of man combined to drive them out.

Fig. 5.—Mammoth reconstructed (Museum of Petrograd), as it was found in the frozen lands of Siberia (*Petit catalogue illustré du Museé de Saint-Germain*).

But with the smaller carnivora and especially with the less wild herbivorous animals he was on a different footing. His action towards these took three forms.[1] Against some of them he used force and skill. He subdued them and sometimes *parked* them round his dwelling. He succeeded in reducing them to impotence, in retaining them to be disposed of at will, but he did not go further. Others, still using skill but also kindness and good treatment, and, perhaps, even a sort of magnetic force, he succeeded in *taming*, that is to say, making them familiar companions who could aid him to

[1] Letourneau, *L'évolution de l'éducation.*

capture and tame others. Tame elephants are used to capture those that are still at large, and the bull, still reeking from its struggle, is placed in the herd of oxen which have been tamed earlier. When it came to animals whom he did not need to fear, taming became an amusement. It was amusing to catch a bird, a cat, or a dog and to conquer their wild nature by sheer patience. Man probably made many attempts. Many failed, some succeeded and a third stage was reached. Several species were *domesticated*, that is to say, they became man's servants and helpers and were fed, protected, and ruled by him.

The services which he demanded of them can be grouped under four heads. First of all they were a reserve of food. He fed them in order to be fed by them, to eat their milk, their eggs, their flesh, and also to clothe or adorn himself with their skins. Then he made of them slaves and condemned them to hard labour; he took them as helpers in his difficult tasks, he turned their strength to his profit; he treated them as living machines in order to spare himself effort; he taught them to carry heavy weights, to drag vehicles, to plough the land. Then he made of them allies in hunting and fishing or companions in war. Finally he made them instruments of his pleasure; he asked them to please his ear or his eye; he kept in cages the singing birds, whistling thrushes, and speaking parrots; he bred peacocks and pheasants because of their brilliant plumage; sometimes he turned monkeys and bears into buffoons to make him laugh.

The animal species which have in this way been humanized are few in number. Among them are nineteen mammifera— the gazelle and antelope which figure on the monuments of old Egypt are included—thirteen birds, two insects, the bee and the silkworm, out of the eight hundred thousand species that have been catalogued, two fish, the carp and the goldfish, which know the hours when they are fed and seem to recognize the person who feeds them. One can omit the legendary dolphin which bore Arion on its back. There is thus a total of thirty-six species to which may be added the oyster which man looks after with interested solicitude, and certain parasitic insects which he breeds to destroy other insects destructive of his harvests.

We cannot follow the evolution of all the species which man turned to his use. We can only deal with the most important. The dog, it seems, was the first animal to be domesticated. At the beginning of the quaternary epoch it is still wild, a kinsman of the wolf. Then it divides into innumerable varieties from the Egyptian jackal to the Australian dingo which does not know how to bark. Very probably the dog voluntarily joined the bands of hunters. He pursued the game in their company and in this tacit association the prey was shared as if a contract had been signed ; the quarry was the possession of all who had assisted in bringing it down. Thus regular and constant relations were established between men and dogs. The dog accepted as master a being whom he felt to be his superior and man finding this worshipper and servant extremely docile, employed him on all sorts of tasks. The dog which has the instinct of property became the guardian of the dwelling-place, which he made to ring with fierce bayings. Then he protected and shepherded the cattle ; the sheep dog and the hunting dog are met with in the age of polished stone. Among the peoples of the Arctic he drew the sledges on the snow and ice. The Molossian dogs trained to fight were a formidable section of the Gaulish and Germanic armies. It is probable that a long heredity of servitude made the dog more easy to train as time went on and post dogs, salvage dogs, and police dogs represent the last stages of an education which has been going on for over forty centuries. Yet it is noteworthy that not all the peoples succeeded in using the dog. The friend of man was in several countries simply a slaughter-animal. In China, in Mexico, in Tahiti, in Australia, it was highly esteemed as a dish. In many a siege this demi-anthropophagy, as Bernardin de Saint Pierre calls it, was resorted to by the desperate ; in Paris, in 1870, people ate Newfoundland dogs and poodles.

The domestication of the dog rendered possible other achievements of a similar kind. One of the first of these was no doubt that of horned beasts. The sheep and the goat, both in Europe and Asia must have been easily vanquished. Then it was the turn of the ox which demanded greater effort as might be expected in view of the strength and temper of the bull. It is possible that the oxen which were reserved at first as sacrifices were captured in the first place for religious reasons. All these furnished milk, wool, leather, flesh, fat, bone, horn, all very useful things. They were precious, therefore, living or dead. How did man discover that the removal of the genital organs from the males was a sure way of fattening them and rendering them less wild ? . Perhaps because he noticed that prisoners who suffered a similar loss lost their manhood and grew fat. At any rate, the sheep, the bullock, and the capon go back to a very respectable antiquity. Flocks and herds were forms of riches which grew of themselves and one can understand that the word *capital* meant originally the possession of a number of heads of beasts.

It is worth noting that, in certain divisions of animals, some species became civilized, others remained wild. Thus the aurochs and the bison remained wild and free in the forests, while members of the same family, the yak in Tibet, the zebu in India, and even the buffalo let themselves be tamed. The pig was established in the sty while the wild boar wandered as it pleased in the woods. Thus the chamois and ibex, true Highlanders, were able to keep their independence, while the goat accepted slavery. In lands where there were no representatives of either the ovine or the bovine race, man tamed the lama, the vicuna, and the guinea pig. From this domestication sprang the whole of the pastoral civilization and, as in evolution one advance always leads to another, it rendered far more fruitful agricultural civilization to which the manure and labour provided by the beasts was a most important reinforcement.

In how many a legend do cattle play an important rôle ? Among the Greeks the Argonauts go out on the quest of the Golden Fleece ; Io changed into a heifer is worthy of the love of Zeus and the same god changes himself into a bull to carry off Europa ; Phaedra is the daughter of Minos and Pasiphae, and Minos is the Minotaur. In Egypt the bull Apis is honoured as a divine being and it is forbidden to kill an ox. Among the Hindus the cow is a sacred animal demanding gratitude and respect. In many countries it is a crime to kill one.

Man employed on varied tasks the beasts which he had, or thought he had, tamed. Rams and boars were harnessed to the plough. Oxen worked in the fields or drew wagons. These peaceful and slow-moving animals are rarely represented as trained for hunting or war. Yet in Ceylon they were used as a living screen to hide the approach of the hunter. Among the Hottentots they were guardians of the herds and their brothers the bulls, if one may believe Lucretius, were launched against the enemy. Lions led by their trainers marched in the hosts of Parthia, and it is true that the Egyptian monuments show us the Pharaoh charging with a lion by his side. But, says the poet, these were dangerous and unprofitable experiments. These allies, once flung into the battle, made no nice distinction between friend and foe; they ran here and there striking and wounding. Man had finally to renounce their use, as he renounced the use of leopards and cheetahs which were employed in hunting in old Egypt, because their trainers never succeeded in teaching them to share with man the prey they had pulled down. Man had better success with other animals.

Hindu legends speak of an army of monkeys obeying a human commander, and history tells us of the panic fear that mastered the Romans when they first had to face the elephants, those living fortresses whose skin was a cuirass that protected them from the Roman arrows. It took the Romans several years to discover the vulnerable spot under their bellies. The submission of these giant beasts and the training of them in Africa and especially in India, to raise logs with their trunks and to carry on their backs a howdah and several hunters who are rocked therein as gently as a babe is rocked in its cradle, can be considered a fine achievement of the human intellect.

Another conquest which seemed to Buffon the noblest ever made by man, was that of the horse. It is probable that the first step thereto was the conquest of the ass, a weaker and more manageable animal. It has been noticed that the Bible which tells one not to covet one's neighbour's ass or his ox, says nothing about the horse, and we may conclude that it was then a rarity. In our lands, while the stone age lasted, it was pursued and killed for food; its head and its whole body pierced with holes or transfixed with arrows is a common subject among the pictures in the caverns which man drew in the belief that an animal was the more easily captured if one caught its likeness and fixed it on the rock. Here and there are traces of a cord. That means that man knew how to capture the horse, but it does not prove that the horse was then domesticated. Asia appears to have been the place where the horse was enslaved. In Greece, it was sacred to Poseidon, god of the sea, a fact which leads one to believe that the horse came to Greece from over sea. To tame it was a work of some difficulty and required that extreme skill which is displayed by the cowboy of to-day ; the bridle and the bit had to be invented to master the fiery steed. It is most probable that at first the horse was only ridden ; the rider, without saddle or stirrup, kept on its back by the grip of the knees. Thus joined as it were to one another, the horse and his rider seemed to be but one animal and animated by a single will. The impression which such a sight made on those who saw it for the first time is represented by the legend of the Centaurs. Two thousand years later when the Spaniards invaded Mexico, the natives were under the same delusion, and could not believe their eyes when they saw the mysterious animal come in two. The horses themselves they believed to be divine beings and the first time they secured a dead one, they cut it up and sent a quarter to the most important towns to prove to the people that these monsters were not immortal. When later the horse was harnessed it was at first to war- or royal chariots.[1] Its speed, its pride, its beauty for a long time saved it from being put to painful work. It was a luxury animal which was kept for war, racing, and ceremonial processions. To own a horse was the privilege of the noble or the rich. In Rome as in Athens the knights belonged to the upper middle class. The word *chevalier* has kept to our own day its aristocratic significance and even in our modern democracies the sons of old families when they go into the army prefer to serve in the cavalry.

Among certain peoples, the Arabs for instance, the horse is petted, caressed, admired. " Do not call him my horse," cries a poet, " call him my son. He runs more swiftly than the tempest, quicker than a glance. He overtakes the gazelle. He says to the eagle, ' I fly like you.' He is so

[1] L. Bourdeau, *La conquête du monde animal*, p. 83.

light that he could dance on the breast of your mistress and she would take no hurt. He understands as if he were man. All that he lacks is speech." The Koran calls the horse the supreme possession and another poet says, " Who are they who will weep for me when I am dead ? My sword, my lance, and my chestnut steed. Tall and graceful he will trail the reins as he goes to the well having now no rider who will water him." Alas for the decline and fall of a race ! Much later in history the day comes when the proud charger is reduced to be a beast of burden on a level with the ass and the mule. It will be sent to work in the fields and taught to draw the harrow, the plough, the roller, and the reaping machine. For centuries it will feel the lash of brutal drivers. According to an old saying the great cities of Europe were the paradise of women and the hell of horses. Then by one of those strange turns of fortune's wheel, it is to-day replaced by the automobile and tends to become what it was at the beginning of its history, a luxury animal which is kept for sport and a slaughter animal for which special establishments have been opened.

What the horse was to the peoples of Asia and southern Europe the reindeer was to the Lapps, the elephant to the Hindus, the camel and the dromedary to the nomads of the desert. Among the Arabs the *mehari*,[1] or running camel, is like the colt brought up in the tent with the children. It is part of the family and receives a complicated education. It is taught to stand motionless at first by the hobble and then merely at the sound of a command ; an iron ring is attached to its right nostril through which runs the rein by which it is controlled ; a saddle is placed on its back for the rider ; it is taught to kneel at a call which it is taught to recognize by blows from a stick on its knees and in the end it becomes that rapid and docile animal which well deserves the name of ship of the desert. The ordinary camel [2] with the two humps may not have all the qualities

---

[1] Chauvet, *Le chameau*, Paris, 1926.

[2] M. de Varigny in the *Journal des Débats* for 29th July, 1926, gives some interesting details quoted from Commandant Cauvet's book : " On what does the camel feed ? On the few rough plants which it finds here and there, and which the other domestic animals have no use for, not even the ass, which unlike the camel cannot do without drink. That does not mean that the camel will refuse a really satisfying and appetising meal if it gets the chance of one. Its stomach, that of a ruminant, has a capacity of eighty litres ; it can store

of the *mehari* but it is none the less a valuable beast. It carries everything its owner possesses, provisions, women, and children. It fears neither heat nor thirst nor weariness; it carries with it reserves of water and fat such as enable it to go for several days without food or drink. Dead, it renders as many services as when it was alive. Of its hair, tents and mantles are made; its flesh is eaten, the humps being choice morsels, the skin is transformed into footwear, while with its milk the female camel feeds the family and the young horses.

For the reindeer, one may refer to the narrative of Regnard, the writer of comedy, who made a journey to Lapland in 1681. "Lapland has no other domestic animals than the reindeer, but in it alone there are as many things of use as in all the animals which we maintain. Not a fragment of it is thrown away; the Lapps use its hair, its skin, its flesh, its bones, its marrow, its blood, and its nerves. Nothing is wasted. The skin protects them from the inclemencies of the weather. In winter they wear skins with the hair still on; in summer skins from which the hair has been removed. The flesh is juicy, fat, and very nourishing, and the Lapps eat no other meat. The bones are extraordinarily useful. From them are made arbalests and bows, arrow tips and spoons, and everything they make

there an abundant supply of provisions, and never misses an opportunity to do so. But in the desert there are few chances. It eats, therefore, what grows in the desert, plants without leaves, and juicy plants which accumulate water and scarcely ever become dry, living on intermittently, for with their long roots they resist drought and begin to sprout again whenever any rain falls, and survive, even if none has fallen, for they can live on the dew which falls in the frosty nights.

"It is therefore somewhat meagre fare that the camel has in the desert. It finds it with difficulty, and in small quantities, and yet out of this miserable income it can economize and build up reserves. Its savings accumulate in its hump, which is a fatty mass formed of a peculiar type of fibrous tissue forming a reservoir in the empty cells of which fat accumulates. On this fat the camel lives when its vegetable food is obtained in even smaller quantities than usual. The hump grows smaller and becomes flaccid when its owner has suffered too great privations, and becomes hard and fat again when the camel has found good feeding. Consequently, when the Arab is about to set out on a long and difficult journey he chooses the camel with the biggest hump. The camel has also reserves of water. Since it is by no means certain when it will be watered, it stores up reserves in a series of cells situated in the lobes of the stomach. They are about one hundred in number, and each can hold 200–300 centilitres of water. This exposes the camel to a new danger, for travellers dying of thirst do not hesitate to kill it for the water it contains. In a work, the camel is a primary condition for the exploitation of land from which otherwise no profit could be drawn."

is ornamented with bone. The tongue and the marrow are considered the most delicate morsels and lovers present these portions to their mistress as a choice gift to which they usually add bear or beaver flesh. The Lapps often drink the blood, but as a general rule they keep it in the animal's bladder which is left out in the frost and when they wish to make soup they cut off what they need and boil it with fish. They have no thread except what they make from the nerves of the head of the reindeer, and these they spin. They use the finer to make clothes and the coarser to sew together the planks of their canoes." Add to all that the fact that the reindeer supplies them with their ordinary drink, milk, and that it carries loads and drags the sledges over the ice at a great speed and with a strength that makes it a formidable enemy when it revolts against ill-treatment. Even to-day it is only half-domesticated and is still half savage.

To come down now to smaller animals, man was able to tame the cat, the great foe to rats and mice, and therefore protector of the harvest and the family stores, the independent cat which never gives but merely lends, which is attached to the house where it is accustomed to live as much as to the people who feed it and pet it. He also succeeded in using the hawk for hunting—one finds it represented in iron in ancient Armenia—and the ferret which hunts the rabbits in their holes. In China and in ancient Egypt he also made use of the talent of a fishing bird, the cormorant, which wore a ring on its neck, a sign of slavery and a necessary measure to prevent it swallowing the catch. Ancient Egypt also seems to have domesticated the crane and the ibis, and there has always been a sort of alliance between the people of Alsace and the storks. In Mexico it is still a bird, the *agami*, which guards and controls the herds like a sheep-dog.

By the side of these we must find a place of honour for the many-coloured, harmless, and noisy inhabitants of the courtyard, for all the species that we include under the term poultry. They provided man with feathers, down, eggs, and meat. Hens, guinea-fowls, ducks, pigeons, all so easily tamed, geese are his and this feathered world increased by storks and flamingos with the long bills which devour frogs and reptiles, is in some countries made complete by the rabbit whose proverbial fertility can become a danger as has been the case in Australia and by the guinea pig which came from America and is in so many laboratories the privileged martyr of science. All these have become inseparable from man to such an extent that one cannot imagine a farm or a village which does not house these familiar and noisy guests.

Among the animals domesticated by man it is noteworthy that there are no monkeys. It is true that some have been trained to carry water and use the pestle and mortar, but nothing very much has ever been obtained by using their imitative talent. Man has refrained from doing more than using their long hair for women's coats and their glands for rejuvenating worn-out old men. They are also seen, occasionally, disguised as clowns and acrobats. But no effort has ever been made to train them in bulk for useful work. Perhaps in man's eyes they committed the sin of being much too like him, of being a caricature of him and reminding him ever of his own animal origin.

We may also pass over without discussion the animals whom the skill and caprice of a trainer have rendered temporarily docile—caged lions and tigers which finish their career sometimes by taking a bloody revenge for captivity, boxing seals and kangaroos, and a number of animals which are more or less trained, from the squirrels running round their prison, white mice drawing a tiny cart, fleas firing a cannon, to spiders and lizards which have brought consolation to prisoners and magpies, jackdaws, jays, and starlings which hop about the village cobbler's shop. Their taming is among man's most successful efforts, but it is without meaning. Man in their case sought merely amusement.

One must be chary about guessing the time and the place when and where the species of which man has made use were domesticated. But, without being too rash, we can say that the camel was domesticated in Arabia, that the elephant was tamed in India after the cold had driven it from the northern regions, that the pheasant came from the banks of the Phasis, as its name shows. We can also fix with certainty the date when the turkey was brought from America to Europe and when Europe brought the horse to America, the merino sheep and the rabbit to Australia. But for all the others we have no exact knowledge at all.

What is worth noticing, however, is that man seems to have halted on a road on which he had made very great progress. As far as the domestication of animals is concerned he has lived for centuries on the heritage transmitted to him by remote ancestors. He has carried his inventive genius to other spheres. He seems to have ended by despising the conquest of animal force and to have turned to the task of conquering other and more powerful forces, those of inanimate nature. What does he do to-day? For gain he rears ostrichs in Cape Colony, silver foxes in Canada and in the northern United States. But for the most part he is simply a destroyer. Humming birds and birds of paradise have fallen victims to woman's passion for finery. Seals and penguins are slaughtered by tens and hundreds of thousands annually. The whale is pursued remorselessly even to the Polar seas, where it has taken refuge. One would think that man was striving to empty the planet of all its adornment of living things and was killing for killing's sake. No doubt in compensation he has perfected the rearing of certain species. He has improved the breeds of his cattle by intelligent selection. In this sphere he has collaborated with nature ; with her he has produced life.

If to-day he tends more than ever to substitute for his living machines those with arms of iron and steel, that should not prevent us, however, from recognizing what the conquest of these first allies meant to the race. It has been calculated that on an average an ass represents in labour power two men, an ox five, and a horse seven. Even if such an estimate is by no means certain, still there is no doubt that, thanks to the aid brought by these servants which he made, the work of man was lightened, made easier, and made less. It was an unexpected relief for the feeble, for women, and for slaves. It meant the possibility of undertaking tasks which human weakness had till then made it impossible to tackle. It meant that agriculture on a large scale was possible, and long journeys for men and goods. There is no exaggeration in saying that the conditions of human existence were completely changed when man had no longer simply his own strength to call upon. If he succeeded in conquering the earth he owes his victory in very great part to his friends and allies, the animals.

BIBLIOGRAPHY

BOURDEAU (Louis), *La conquête du monde animal.*
CAUVET (Commandant), *Le chameau.*
DAUMAS (General), *Mœurs et coutumes de l'Algerie.*
DENIKER, Work already cited, pp. 227–30.
LETOURNEAU, *Evolution de l'éducation.*
REGNARD, *Voyage de Laponie.*
VARIGNY (Henri de), Article in the *Journal des Débats* of 29th July, 1926.

CHAPTER VII

THE BEGINNINGS OF AGRICULTURE

AT the same time as he sought to domesticate animals, man sought to domesticate plants. On other territory he pursued the same course. Agriculture, indeed, is intimately connected with the raising of cattle, not only because cattle are necessary for heavy work and for the manure which they supply, but because it pursues a similar aim. Again it is a case of taming what is wild, of modifying and multiplying for the advantage of man that which grows of itself from the earth. Again it is a case of creating life, of choosing between plants, of reproducing and perfecting those which are of service to him and of destroying those which are not. Here too, man is obliged to contend against forces which he cannot control. When he placed the grain in the soil he had to wait till a mysterious process was accomplished beneath it. He had to make frost and heat, rain, snow, and sun his allies. He had to show great patience and see far ahead. He had to observe the periodicity of the seasons and fit his work to it. That explains why agriculture was a late development in countries with a special climate. It originated probably on sun-bathed plateaux, while the valleys were still swamps, then in countries where the soil was light, fertile, and well-watered, that is, in plains intersected by streams and in alluvial land.

It requires no great effort of imagination to understand how miraculous it must have been for man to be able to take regular nourishment from the land. It meant the permanent leaving of a mode of life which was always precarious, the escape from the perpetual recurrence of famine, from desperate expedients in the struggle for food. Agriculture was an inestimable boon to man, and its first result was to make him sedentary.

As is usual a divine origin was attributed to agriculture. In Chaldæa the god Oannes was its discoverer; in Egypt, the goddess Isis; in Greece the kindly Demeter, the legend of whose daughter, condemned to pass six months of the year below the surface of the earth, might be a poetical rendering of the history of a grain of corn. In Italy Saturn had lorded it over an age of gold in which the goats came of their own accord to offer their udders swollen with milk, in which lions lived peaceably beside the herds, in which serpents and poisonous plants did not exist. In Mexico, Quetzalcoatl, a divine being, white of skin, black-haired, and bearded, perhaps a refugee from Atlantis, brought from the East the art of cultivating the soil, the art of working metals, and so deep a love of peace that he stopped his ears whenever he heard war mentioned.[1] " In his reign the earth was covered with flowers and fruits ; one ear of maize was big enough to be of itself a man's load ; the cotton displayed itself on the trees dyed in the richest colours ; the air was full of sweet odours and birds in gorgeous plumage sang ceaselessly the sweetest of songs." Thereafter he went back into the east whence he came. In Peru it was the legendary hero Manco Capac ; in Persia it was Zoroaster who introduced agriculture, and among the Iroquois and in India it was also the work of a divinity or a superman.

But these mysterious benefactors, the legendary heroes, were not alone in being the objects of worship. Trees and plants had a sacred character. There was assuredly a vegetable totemism. Among the Egyptians the flower of the lotus was held in mystic respect and Taine [2] found amusement in demonstrating how the onion which so scandalized Bossuet became a divinity on the banks of the Nile. " Begin by transporting yourself to Egypt before the warriors and the priests were born, to the mud of the Nile among savages half-naked in the mud, half-drowned in the water, half-burned by the sun. How strange indeed is the picture presented by that black expanse smoking under the heat where crocodiles and fish which crawl splash in the water. A year ago there was nothing to be seen but mud. Now what a change. There has arisen out of it a tall straight reed, with shining stem, its body filled with juice deep in the mud. Every day it grows and changes. At first green, it becomes red like the sun in mist. Then

[1] M. Chevalier, *Le Mexique ancien et moderne*, p. 84.
[2] *Voyage aux Pyrénées*, p. 121.

I

it raises itself now half, now wholly, from the mud and warms in the sun its scaly belly full of bitter sap. The sap flows out breaking even the triple skin and drips from the wound. What a strange life ! And by what miracle does the top of the stem become a plume and a parasol ? The first men who gathered it wept as if some poison had burned their eyes. But in winter when no fish was to be had, it rejoiced the heart of him who met it. These enormous globes, did they not resemble the hundred breasts of our mother the earth ? More appeared as the water retired. Some divine power surely was concealed beneath the hard, scaly skin. May it never cease to be born anew ! The crocodile is god because it devours us, the ichneumon is god because it protects us, the onion is god because it feeds us."

There is nothing to be astonished at in this deification. In our own days in Mexico the *peyhotl*, the plant which amazes the eyes, as Dr. Bouhler who has studied its strange effects, calls it, is still the object of worship among the natives and has ceremonies in its honour. It is a sort of cactus with a round head which grows in the barren places on the high plateaux, and slices of it dried and infused give to him who partakes of them wonderful visions of marvellous richness of colour. The missionaries in vain preach against this magic plant. It goes on being adored as an incarnation of the divine.

Among the ancient Greeks, the oak which also nourishes man with its acorns, gave oracles at Dodona. The laurel was sacred to Apollo, the poplar to Heracles, the vine to Dionysos ; the olive, emblem of peace, arose from the earth at the bidding of Pallas Athene. Many a divinity of the countryside among Greeks and Romans like nymphs, dryads, fawns, silvani, lived under the bark of the trees or hid themselves in the caves or in sacred woods.

But in vain has man in a burst of humility robbed himself of the credit of having invented agriculture in favour of divinities of his own creation. The truth is that agriculture was a slow growth which arose from man's repeated efforts to satisfy his craving for food.[1] It is directly connected with the stage when man gathered his food. Among modern primitives man hunts, fishes, or goes to war, while woman

---

[1] Karl Bücher, *Etudes d'histoire economique*, pp. 31–3.

gathers fruits, roots, and tubers. The first invented the cooking of meat. He it was who first roasted the game. The second invented the cooking of vegetables. This division of labour throws light on what happened at the beginning of the formation of human societies. Woman, sedentary because she had to look after the children and tend the hearth, gathered and brought in grain. Nothing more was needed than that she should let fall a grain or two near the hut, near the cradle of the children. Accustomed by her own nature to the mysteries of fecundity she marvelled to see coming from the womb of the soil a young and fragile stalk which at first had to be cared for like a child, then grew strong and fat, and ended, a miracle indeed, in reproducing exactly the plant which at some distant spot had supplied her with grain.[1]

Woman, then, can rightly be called the mother of agriculture. Whether one appeals to the North American Indians, to the tribes of Guiana, Brazil, Australia, Polynesia, New Zealand, or to the customs of Celts and Scythians, as related by Strabo, or to those of the Peruvians described by Garcilasso de la Vega, everywhere agriculture at its beginnings appears as woman's work.

At these beginnings it was certainly no complicated task. The pointed stick which grubbed up the roots served to dig the holes in which the seeds were buried. This digger is found in many countries. In Madagascar forty years ago the visitor could see a squad of women armed with their pointed sticks range themselves in line like soldiers at drill. At a given signal they dug the stick into the soil, turned it over, traced a furrow, threw in the seeds and stamped the earth flat to bury them. This was their way of tilling. A first refinement was to add to the pointed stick to increase its penetrative power either a weight or a crossbar on which the foot was placed. This was the origin of the spade; the *vanga* in Italy is still of this type.

This rudimentary agriculture did not yield much produce. It was only a supplement to hunting and fishing. It would have been insufficient to count on as the sole means of obtaining food. The necessity to till the ground more

---

[1] Salvioli, "Gli esordi dell' agricoltura," in the *Rivista di Sociologia*, Sept.–Oct., 1899.

thoroughly was quickly felt. The hoe was invented which was perhaps only an adaptation of the flint scraper which is found in the Mousterian epoch and which had a handle. Perhaps it was just a plain piece of wood in which the junction of two branches formed an acute angle, the longer being held in the hand while the other moved the earth. It can be seen on very ancient monuments from Egypt in the Louvre and, according to legend, it was with a hoe that Romulus killed Remus. The mattock at first worked by hand was then dragged at the end of a rope pulled by beasts of burden. In certain countries the digging animals, the mole and the rabbit, were imitated.[1] Among the Caribs of Guiana, the claws of a great armadillo tied by twos took the place of the hoe. But where the earth was very easily moved as in the mud of Egypt, it of itself sufficed to grow harvests. The seeds sown broadcast on the slightly scratched surface were trampled into the soil by the flocks, goats, pigs, or sheep, or, if a little more care was required, placed one by one in holes expressly dug for them, a method still practised in China and which has been re-adopted but regularized by the mechanical sowing machine.

This cultivation by the hoe which is still connected with garden work also yielded no very brilliant results. Yet in some countries it lasted a long time. It was the only sort of cultivation known in Mexico when the Europeans landed. But two facts produced a distinct improvement in method. The first was the domestication of draught animals which made man's task lighter as he had to use less muscular force and was mainly occupied in guiding his team. The second was the invention of the ploughshare. In its origin it was only the hoe made longer and drawn by beasts. It was made out of a branch of elm and oak bent naturally or artificially into the shape of a pointed hook which served as the share and later was covered with metal. Another branch, jutting out from the major branch in the opposite direction to the share, served as handle.[2] The worker, by leaning on the handle, drove the share into the ground.

This machine, which seems to us simple in the extreme,

---

[1] Deniker, p. 648.

[2] *V.* Rich, *Dictionary of Greek and Roman Antiquities*, arts. " Aratrum " and " Stiva ".

appeared so wonderful to early man that it, too, was given divine origin. In Egypt Osiris made a present of it to humanity. In Greece it was Triptolemus. The Scythians believed that the first fell from heaven. In Peru, when ploughing with beasts began, the procedure was thought so marvellous that the three beasts who dragged the plough were regarded with no less awe and wonder than the most dazzling of Roman triumphs. The historians took especial care to transmit their names to posterity.

From that hour a great transition was made. Agriculture passed from the hand of the women to that of the stronger men. From being simply a protector, man became a producer. When it came to grinding the grain, woman still was master of the handmill and her aid was demanded at haytime, harvest, and the vintage season. The kitchen garden, too, was still her concern. But the family became at once sedentary and patriarchal, that is to say, under control of the father, while agriculture became a serious and important occupation and took the first place among the means of livelihood. Everywhere where nature lent itself to the change, there was a veritable revolution in customs and ways of life.

The plough was gradually improved. Instead of being made of a single piece of wood, it was made of several pieces joined together. The share is made of bronze and then of iron. It includes a blade to cut the turf and a breast to turn it. Such it will remain practically unchanged till the nineteenth century, when there will be new inventions in this sphere of human activity.

Then other implements appear—the harrow, which is at first only a bundle of thorns before becoming a line of metal bars fitted with sharp teeth, the roller, in the beginning merely a tree trunk which was used to flatten the soil. Then will come the harvest instruments—the rake which moves on the soil among the grass and the sheaves as a comb moves on the human head, the forks to turn the hay, the wooden sickles [1] fitted with a toothed flint fixed on with pitch; later without changing its shape the sickle will be made of bronze and then of iron and will be lengthened into the scythe.

[1] Morgan, p. 184.

The grains used—corn, rye, meslin, barley—appear in Nearer Asia, Egypt, and Europe before the age of polished stone. The harvest seems to have been a double operation, as it was in ancient Italy, as it is in some places in Touraine, and as I have myself seen it outside Antibes. The ears were cut first and then the straw. To get the grain out of the ears, use was made either of the instrument which the Romans called *tribulum*, a plank which bristled with flint flakes, or of horses which stamped out the grain on the thrashing floor, or by the rhythmic use of flails. Then to separate the nutritious grain from the light shell that protects it, it was winnowed, the fan being either of skin or of willow and to turn the grain into flour it was ground. At first the grinding operation was merely one of crushing the grain on a flat stone with the aid of another stone flat on one side ; then the one was hollowed and fixed while the other moved round the hollow which it fitted. Then both were pierced so that they could be turned with a handle. It was slow and painful work, one of the hardest that had to be done and it was left to the women, and later to the slaves who were muzzled in case they should be tempted to make a meal of the fine white flour. It was a labour which caused long and bitter complaining, but those upon whom it fell had to wait for centuries to be relieved of it by the substitution of water and wind power for that of the human arm. It was in this toilsome fashion that the lacustran peoples succeeded in making a sort of unleavened bread not unlike the buckwheat cakes which can still be found in Brittany.

The invention of agriculture compelled man to be more prudent and to take longer views. He had to take account of the times when he could work, and when he could not ; of bad seasons and to learn how to store up for bad times the harvests of good times. For the grain he built barns and granaries which sheltered it from damp, if not from rats, ants, and weevils. In very dry countries he built silos underground. Then for each plant from which man derived food and drink, special apparatus was created. For nuts, olives, beech nuts, apples and grapes, the last originally trampled by the feet in the vat, were constructed presses and a whole series of new utensils, leather bottles, jars and casks of all kinds. Similar apparatus was devised to turn milk into butter and cheese.

But to follow out the transformation of agricultural implements would take us too far afield. Our time will be more profitably spent in examining how man arrived at the selection of plants which he judged were worth cultivating. Out of some 140,000 species it is estimated (Candolle) that he selected about 300, but we have practically no information where or when he did so.

As examples let us take two plants which won his favour, corn and rice. Corn which was the conquering grain in Nearer Asia, in Egypt, and all over Europe, seems to be a native of the first-named country. It has been found in a wild state near Mount Hermon in the north of Palestine. How was it cultivated ? We do not know. We find it in the oldest Egyptian tombs. We find it in the ruins of the lacustran cities beside rye, barley, buckwheat, and millet, the last of which perhaps disputed with it for sovereignty for a considerable time. Let one try to imagine the effort of thought which was necessary to enable man to choose it from so many grains and the centuries which it must have needed to become the predominant vegetable food. Rice, which needs damp lands and warm climates, originated in the Far East. It has always been the preferred food in India, China, and Japan.

Asia thus appears to us as the great nursing mother whence came to our world the most important of our foods. The vine had been successfully grown in Palestine before it reached the Mediterranean world, although we do not need to credit the story of the giant grapes of Canaan. Dionysos, the god of the grape, lands in Greece as a stranger from the Asiatic coast, and at a much later date the Romans very similarly introduced the vine into Provence. The olive seems to have travelled the same road brought by the Greeks to the same country. The peach (*persica*) bears witness by its name that it came from Persia, although perhaps, like the mandarin, it came originally from China. The Roman general Lucullus, a famous gourmet in his day, had the distinction of bringing from Cerasos on the shores of the Black Sea the fruit which is still called the cherry. Vergil [1] speaks of " the Pelusiac bean ", the lentil, which came from Pelusium in the Nile Delta, and which played an important

---

[1] In the *Georgics*.

rôle in Hebrew life in the days of the patriarchs. From Asia, too, we got the fig, the quince, the pomegranate, the citron, the majority of the spices, peppers, cinnamon, nutmeg, cloves, and a crowd of aromatic plants like frankincense, myrrh, and benjamin. For we must not simply regard plants as food providers. They serve many another use. I have already mentioned the implements, weapons, vases, and baskets that men made from trees, never to speak of the fact that plants determine the fauna of a country— what would become of the reindeer if the lichen were not there to feed it and what would become of the Lapp if there were no reindeer ? Trees furnished man with clothing whose first material was flax, hemp, the bark of the lime tree, or straw. They offered him material from which furniture and boats could be made. They gave him dyes to colour his materials and to paint his body and the rocks, woad, indigo, saffron. They had medicinal virtues. The simples as they were called were for ages the most esteemed remedies, and are still the most popular. One cannot possibly over-estimate the services which the botanic world rendered to humanity or the influence which it exercised on its destiny.

A single tree, the coconut, a native of the Indian archi-pelago, gave its giant nuts, its milk, its leaves of which ropes were made, and from it were derived oil for burning, mats, dyes, and fermented liquor. It is not incompre-hensible that certain trees were sacred for primitive men, and that it was an offence to fell them, and we can under-stand, too, that history has preserved the names of those who brought them from their original homes. History did not fail to commemorate Jussieu who brought back to France in his hat three tiny cedars which can be seen to-day, and whose branches more than a century old will go on to shelter the generations of the future. In Mexico the tree with multiple uses was the *maguey*, a species of aloe, which provided fibre for cords and paper, thorns for brooches and pins, and edible roots and, above all, that heady liquor called *pulque* which is still the favourite with the natives.

Nor let us forget the flowers which are nature's smile. There were only a few, and these not very varied, which our remote ancestors knew. But each land had its own flowers and the fact that the word *paradise* means garden, that the happy life conceived of as in either the past or the future was practically everywhere placed by human imagination in a flowered and perfumed Eden, proves that, if not at the very beginnings of humanity, at least at a very early date, violets and roses, jessamine and wistaria, charmed the naive minds of the primitives. Like their admirers, the flowers went on reproducing and perfecting their species. They were gathered as they grew wild by women and girls, and in the form of wreaths and garlands they had their place in religious ceremonies. The hanging gardens of Babylon, the floating gardens of Mexico, that American Venice, which were really floating islands on which grew flowers and vegetables and the gardens at the outskirts of the city in which was displayed all the vegetable wealth of the country and the pleasure parks which around the palaces of princes flaunted their waterfalls and their gigantic statues on the slope of the hills, prove how greatly horti-culture had developed at a very early date.[1] Now flowers,

[1] Michel Chevalier, *Le Mexique ancien et moderne*, pp. 24–8. " The Mexicans have a passion for flowers. In magnificent gardens they bring together those which are remarkable for their perfume or for the brilliance of their colours. They add to them medicinal plants methodically arranged, and those of the native shrubs, which have special claims because of their flowers or their foliage, or the excellence of their fruit or their seed, and trees of majestic or elegant appearance. They delight in placing their flower beds and arbours on the slopes of the hills whereon they are held, as it were, suspended. Thus they rival the celebrated gardens of Semiramis, considered by the ancients whose verdict the moderns have accepted, to be one of the wonders of the world. By means of aqueducts they bring water from afar to their gardens, which they display in waterfalls or fill with it wide ponds in which chosen fish live. Mysterious summer-houses are concealed amid the leaves ; statues rise from amid the flowers. Just as in Europe we collect the most curious animals in our zoological gardens, so the Mexicans call on the animal world to adorn and give attraction to these delightful spots. Birds of gorgeous plumage shut up in cages as big as houses, wild animals and even snakes are to be seen in their gardens."

Then comes a description of the royal gardens which were on the slope of a hill on which had been built a stairway of five hundred and twenty steps, and whose summit was crowned by a pond from which water fell successively into three reservoirs adorned with gigantic statues and M. Chevalier continues : " The humblest individuals shared the taste of their betters for flowers. When, shortly after his landing, Cortes entered the town of Compulla, the inhabitants, men and women, came to meet him and mingled with his men ; they carried bouquets and garlands of flowers, which they threw round the neck of Cortes's charger and passed round his own neck a wreath of roses.

" A further curiosity was the *Chinampas*, or floating gardens, which adorned the lakes. Masses of fibre which floated and rafts which were covered with grasses had no doubt given the Mexicans the idea of them. These artificial islands from 60 to 120 yards in length were devoted to the cultivation of fruit and vegetables for the market of the capital. Some were solid enough

fruit-trees, vegetables, have not remained in their native lands. What migrations, what journeys across rivers, mountains, oceans! Corn and rice have crossed the seas to conquer America. In revenge, America sent to Europe maize which in the beginning, forgetful of its origin, she called Turkish corn, and with the tomato the sweet potato, the vanilla, the banana, the coco-bean, the pepper pod of Cayenne, and the ordinary potato, more precious than the gold of Peru, its original home. Africa, in its turn, gave us oranges, mangoes, and almost certainly coffee.

It is well-known that certain flowers, like the dahlia and the fuchsia, bear the names of those who brought them to Europe. It is known that both tulips and roses have pedigrees. But no one has ever written a general history of the pacific invasions made by plants of one country into another country ; no one has yet traced the exact and complete course of the patient acclimatizations which have covered the surface of the world with fruit trees and useful plants.[1] Nor can we tell how arose the art of grafting, how the miracle of making grow on a wild tree fruit which was not its own became a common practice, or how sweet plums were made to grow on thorns. It was the result of innumerable experiments, of methods kept secret by those who discovered them, then handed down from father to son, gradually being made public and finally becoming a common possession of mankind. What is certain is that for a long time these methods were not very scientific. Agriculture in many parts was semi-nomadic. After the harvest the field was abandoned. Its tillers went intentionally to another, for it was held that the earth had need to lie fallow for a very long time. Little by little was the process discovered of improving and fattening the soil. It was seen that it became more fertile by the combination of several substances to which was added marl or lime. It was noticed that land gave a better harvest if it had been cleared by fire and cows

to permit of shrubs of a considerable size being grown on them, and sometimes even light huts were built. They could be moored, if one wished, to the bank, or could be propelled with a pole on the lake in all their flowery beauty. This spectacle much impressed the Spaniards, and made them say that they had been brought into an enchanted land like to those of which they had read in the romances of chivalry."

[1] See, however, the excellent work by M. de Candolle cited in the bibliography.

and sheep had been left to feed on it ; the fertilizing property of ashes and manure was discovered. It was probably very quickly understood that plants, like animals, were thirsty, that, if one wanted them to live, one had to supply them with water. In other words it was recognized that water is indispensable to fecundity and that if rain which does not bow to human wills, not even to the call of the sorcerer, refuses to fall, the soil which is cracking with the heat must be artificially watered. The inundations taught man much. No one but knows how eagerly they were awaited in Egypt. Elsewhere man invented the art of irrigation which had in the East a very long history. Stage by stage the springs were brought down from the hills, streams and rivers were split into rivulets. In the plains wells and cisterns were made, the water being raised sometimes by means of a pole with another at the end for lever as is still done in Asia, sometimes by means of a rope and pulley as in our own country.

Thanks to all this the face of the world was transformed. The desert and the brushwood were driven back. The cultivated lands were clad in wonderful robes of green, emblazoned with many a colour. In poet fashion Lucretius [1] hails the new appearance which the earth took on before men's eyes. "Day by day they made the forests climb higher up the mountains and yield the place below to their tilth, that they might have meadows, pools, and streams, crops and luxuriant vineyards on hill and plain, and that a grey green belt of olives might run between to mark the boundaries stretching forth over hills and dales and plains, even as you now see the whole place mapped out with charming variety, laid out and intersected with sweet fruit trees and set about with fertile plantations of trees."

But it was not merely the aspect of the soil that had changed. A new civilization arose with the growth of agriculture. The peoples who adopted it, submitted to endure disciplined, regular, daily work accomplished often by a co-operative effort according to the seasons. They had a hearth, a home lit up at night by the oil lamps, surrounded by a stockade. They took root there where they were born, where their dead were buried. Eaters of bread, they had

---

[1] *De rer. nat.*, v, 1370–8 (Rouse's translation).

gentler manners and began to hold cannibalism in detestation. Within their villages there thronged a dense population, which was fundamentally peaceful and formed a whole in which peasants and workers lived amicably side by side. Every change of environment causes a change in habits, ideas, beliefs, and the change that wedded man to the soil, fixed him on the land and for the first time gave him a country, was an enormous one.

BIBLIOGRAPHY

BOUHIER (Dr.), *Le peyhotl, la plante qui fait les yeux émerveillés.*
BOURDEAU (Louis), *La conquête du monde végétal.*
CANDOLLE (A. de), *L'origine des plantes cultivés,* 1912.
CHEVALIER (Michel), *Le Mexique ancien et moderne.*
FEBVRE (Lucien), *La terre et l'évolution humaine.*
RICH, *Dictionary of Greek and Roman Antiquities,* art. " Aratrum ".
SALVIOLI, " Gli esordi dell' agricoltura " (in the *Rivista di sociologia,* Sept.-
   Oct., 1899).
TAINE, *Voyage aux Pyrenées.*
VERGIL, *Georgica.*

CHAPTER VIII

IT would be no paradox to dedicate a history of human endeavour to laziness, the queen of the world. Man works hard from sheer laziness, giving himself any amount of trouble now, to spare himself more trouble later on. Forced to work by imperious need or desire, he makes every effort while working to reduce the amount of necessary effort. He will cut through mountains and isthmuses so as to make his travelling easier and shorter, to cut down distance to lessen fatigue, to gain an hour or two or a day or two. The principal progress which we notice in material things as we pass from one epoch to another, is economy of time or of toil plus an increase in effectiveness or in production.

These remarks on the law of the least possible effort could not fail to occur to anyone who studies the development of locomotion and transport. We see man starting with very simple and laborious methods necessitating a great expenditure of strength and energy, then gradually, at the cost of great exertion of his inventive faculty and by many an experiment, discovering methods which for the future, however, save him from such expenditure of his own strength. It was difficult for him, we may believe, to find easy methods of moving people and objects. It is the evolution of these methods that we will try to study in this chapter.

In the beginning when man desired to go from one place to another on land he had to rely on the strength of his own legs. It was a very long time before he invented instruments to help him—stilts to aid him on marshy ground; skis or snowshoes to enable him to travel on the snow; apparatus of knotted cords to help him to swing along from tree to tree as is done in Spain, in India, in New Caledonia; ladders to enable him to scale a roof or a rock. Had he a load to carry? He had nothing but his own strength to aid him.

If he used his arms, in vain did he multiply handles, grips, and load supporters. He could not escape discomfort and fatigue ; his muscular strength soon gave out. Even if the thing or the person to be carried lay on a rough stretcher and he secured the help of a second carrier, the task was uncomfortable and heavy. Consequently he lost no time in devising ways to carry his load so as to leave his hands free. He threw his basket or his bundle over his shoulder and carried it on his back. It is thus that the negro mother carries her infant which she suckles in this position with her long elastic breasts. In South America a thong which goes round the forehead sustains the load which weighs on the loins, or the shoulders support it with the aid of straps such as luggage porters use for their loads, or soldiers and ramblers for their knapsacks, or the masons for their hods, Atlas for his burden of the world, and the caryatides so beloved of the architect. Most often it is the head which is used as the support for a load ; for instance, among the negro carriers used by African travellers or among the hill peoples whose women are often completely hidden beneath a huge bundle of forage. This was the method adopted by the young Jewish maidens when they drew water from the well and by the young Athenians who are called *Canephorai* and painters and sculptors have long admired the grace of the attitude they adopted. The method is also still in use in Asia where the navvies carry their baskets of earth on their heads following a very old tradition since the men who built those enormous mounds on which the ancient Egyptians raised sphinxes, pyramids, and palaces carried the earth precisely in this fashion. Let one reflect that to erect the higher storeys of a building it was necessary to build up to the same or to a slightly greater height a sloping embankment on to which the stones and bricks were slid, and one can imagine the thousands of workers which such methods made necessary. We find terrifying figures in historical documents. The Bible tells us that in the building of Solomon's temple 70,000 men were employed in transporting materials, while 80,000 men were employed in cutting wood in the mountains for beams and panelling. What enormous labour must have been needed to hew out, transport, and set in place the gigantic blocks of stone of which the pyramids were made, or the obelisks made out of a single stone, or the stone slabs in the cyclopean walls at Mycenae, or the menhirs which are found from Brittany to India. The prisoners and slaves who executed these formidable tasks must have numbered hundreds of thousands.

At a congress held in London, Emile Levasseur said [1] : " Go to the British Museum and see graven on the Assyrian monuments how a millennium before our era were transported these masses of granite whose imposing ruins impress the traveller of to-day. The stone slid with difficulty over the planks which were laid down on its route and advanced

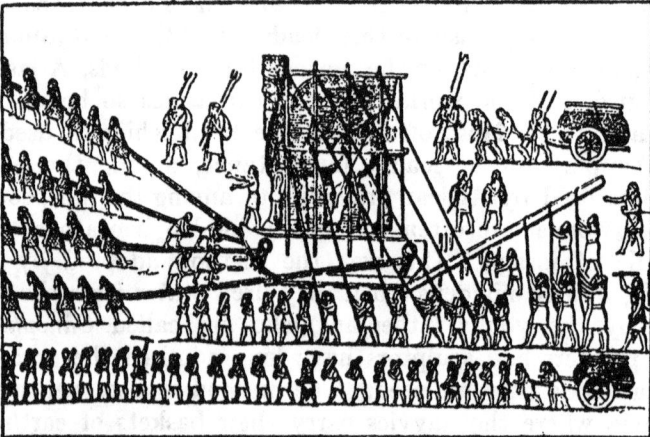

FIG. 6.—Transporting an Assyrian colossus after a bas relief at Kujunjik, after Layard, *Nineveh and its Monuments*.

through forests cut for its passage. Crowds of men were busied taking up the planks behind it and carrying them forward. Others were harnessed to it by hundreds with cords at which they strained. Around them the overseer, lash in hand, drove them to greater efforts and flogged them like beasts of burden. And that, indeed, is all they were, and cheap beasts, at that, whose strength and life was exhausted at the caprice of a master and who were reckoned of very little worth, if one may judge this from the fact that the

[1] *Comparison du travail à la main et du travail à la machine*, p. 73. Paris, *Bulletin de la Société d'encouragement pour l'Industrie nationale*, Feb. and Mar., 1900.

sculptor makes them tiny figures beside whom their leaders are veritable giants."

Nevertheless one sees here the first instruments which were invented to supplement or aid the strength of man's arms,—ropes which were damped to stretch them, levers and rollers. But how many centuries did it take to accomplish this slight progress ?

The Eskimos, when they wish to transport by land the enormous carcase of a moose which they have killed, pass two ropes under the belly of the animal from which two strips of skin have been cut to serve as thongs. Then they drag it on two stakes which, propped up by a big stone, serve as support and then on both sides they pull at ropes to raise the huge beast. Here is the principle of the tackle.

Later, by means of the capstan, the pulley, the windlass, it will be made easier to move a load, but several centuries will be required for these to be developed. Meantime man, and often woman who takes his place, seized eagerly at any chance to drop the rôle of beast of burden which was imposed upon them every time they changed their place of abode, or had to transport game or provisions. That is why whenever certain animals were domesticated, the human pair sought to transfer their burdens to them. The problem then was how to arrange the loads for the beasts to carry. Several ways of solving it were found. The simplest was to tie the load on to the animal's back. The ass first, then the mule, and then the horse, the ox in China and in India, the camel in Arabia, the elephant in southern Asia, the dog in more than one country, had to carry loads proportioned to their size. Their backs were covered with sacks, panniers, baskets, grass, or branches. It is probable that the girth and the packsaddle were early inventions. The palanquin which the elephant carries, and which is a little room in itself, is the product of an advanced civilization.

How did the beast of burden become a drawing, from a carrying, animal ? I have shown in an earlier chapter how it was harnessed to the primitive plough. That was the first step. Suppose then [1]—for in these matters we can proceed only by suppositions—that there were placed on the back of the ass or mule two branches with their leaves trailing

---

[1] The supposition is Deniker's.

K

behind. Suppose further that some bundles were tied on to the branches, then that a man or a child had the notion to sit on the bundles, and then that for comfort he placed a third branch at right angles across the two dragging branches Then we should have in embryo the shafts and driver's seat of the cart.

Such we may believe was the origin of the sledge which is still in use in countries which are not cleared, the Alpine lands, for instance, or Siberia. The sledge slides over the ground or the snow drawn in the plains by horses or mules, in the frozen countries by reindeer and dogs and in mountain lands where the weight itself is a source of energy, it is often drawn by men who need to hold it back rather than drag it forward. The sledge rendered, and is still rendering, many a service. Its importance is shown by the fact that it has survived and also in the fact that in the funeral rites of ancient days it is included among the number of valuable things like the canoe and the horse which have to be buried with the dead man in order that he may use their services in that other world in which he is still alive.

Fresh and very considerable progress was made when from the sledge there developed the chariot and the cart. It is probable that the first step was the placing of rollers under the body of the sledge to lessen friction and jolting; then, to get more lightness and more mobility, two discs were cut off from the roller and tied together by means of an axle. This was the origin of the wheel, a marvellous invention which derives from the pulley and which many peoples, including the American Indians, never discovered. At first it was solid like that which children who in their games unconsciously reproduce the primitive phases of human evolution, make for their toy carts, and also like those which are found in Roman carts and still exist in China and other backward countries.

Then in its turn the wheel was made lighter. It was cut into spokes and later still was covered with metal. At this stage we have the two-wheeled cart which is seen on ancient monuments and models of which have been found in many tombs of the bronze age, a fact which seems to indicate that some religious significance attached to the chariot. This vehicle which almost touched the earth behind, became the war chariot in which the warrior and the driver stood upright, the chariot armed with scythes which is found among the ancient Persians and the Belgae of old Gaul, the racing chariot and the triumphal chariot of Greece and Rome. Sometimes it was drawn by men as in Japan, or in the streets of Paris. Throughout the East it has remained a two-wheeled vehicle, but, at an early date, at the time of the lacustran cities, the four-wheeled chariot, invented perhaps in mountainous districts where greater stability was desirable, began to appear in Europe.

Must we repeat again that one invention inspires another and no sooner is one perfected than its successor is a matter of urgent necessity ? The lighter car which travelled along on its two wheels at some speed made necessary relatively continuous roads. For ages there had existed only wretched footpaths such as are traced by animals to their watering places, simple tracks across forest and prairie. They bristled with stones and thorns, faithfully reproduced every dip and rise in the ground, were easily wiped out by nature always jealous of trespass on her domains. Now flat and durable roads were required and, as the rains changed all the routes into swamps, the idea of metalling arose ; pebbles made smooth by the rivers and slabs of slate were used for this purpose.[1]

Again one invention produced another. To cope with these hard and stony roads it became necessary to harden the feet of the animals, and even of the men who trod them often for long distances. From that hour our barefooted ancestors knew the use of shoes and boots shod in iron. Boots of woven grass were put on horses and mules or of woven broom such as can be seen to-day in Japan. The horses in Homeric Greece are said to have feet of brass ; they wore a sort of boot of leather fitted with a metal sole.[2] They were as truly shod as men. Later the fantasy of princes like Nero caused them to be shod in gold and silver. Later still in the Middle Ages in Europe, iron shoes appear which to-day the racehorse is spared, but the use of which has been extended to other animals, to sheep even, when they have a long road

[1] It is worth noting that quite early (e.g. in Crete) the roads were studded with inns, which supplied relays of steeds and offered travellers lodging.
[2] G. de Mortillet, *Les origines de la chasse*, p. 407.

Fig. 7.—Rope bridge on the Magdalena (Colombia).

to travel, and to the oxen which draw carts. In some villages can be seen a curious combination of beams and ropes whose function it is to keep the animal suspended in the air, and hold it absolutely motionless while it is being shod. The apparatus in France is called *travail* from the Latin *trabaculum,* and as it irks, subdues and fetters, the word is applied to everything that needs effort and brings weariness.

From dry land man had to pass to water. As he advanced across the land, streams and rivers crossed his path. What was he to do confronted by this barrier of water ? He sought a ford by which he could cross without the risk of being drowned. It has been noticed that in Denmark those mounds which contain the kitchen refuse of primitive populations are on a line which links up the fords on the neighbouring rivers (Dechelette). When the river was not too wide, man used a natural bridge made by a fallen tree, which joined one bank to the other, or intertwined creepers which were joined between earth and sky. These natural bridges which are quite common in the Andes served him as models for work of his own. We see that clearly by the suspension bridges made of *maguey* fibre which were used in ancient Peru. On a rope tied to a tree on either bank swung a wicker basket in which the person who wanted to cross placed himself and another rope by which the basket was set in motion set up a regular come and go from one bank to the other. Later, bridges of boats were invented, then bridges in which abutments of masonry supported a wooden platform. The bridge made completely of stone was a much later development which for a long time had a sacred character. In mediaeval times in Europe bridges were still the task of certain monkish orders.

But even before the bridge was invented deep water could not stop our ancestors on their way. The primitives of to-day are excellent swimmers and daring divers. They hunt the shark, catch fish in their hands, and let themselves slide over waterfalls. If the current is too swift or the width of the river too great to make swimming possible, they use, for lack of anything better, inflated skins.

But the river is not merely an obstacle. It is in the consecrated phrase a road which travels. It inspires those who live on its banks to go adventuring with it. A tree trunk

as it drifted past was bestrode by some swimmer who managed
to guide it by the motion of his hands.[1]   This was the
beginning of the canoe which was at first a tree trunk hollowed
out by fire.   Then other devices were tried.   A framework
of willow or bark covered with skin made a passable canoe.
The *kayak* of the Eskimos gives an idea of what this rudimentary skiff was like.[2]   " At least five yards long, about
fifteen inches wide in the middle and about a foot deep,
pointed at both ends like a canoe, it is composed of a frame
of laths of very light wood fastened to one another without
the aid of nails and completely covered with stretched
sealskin.   It is thus completely watertight everywhere.
A single circular opening with a jutting edge allows a person
to get inside it and by a miracle of skill and agility sit down.
Once seated in the *kayak* the Eskimo of whom only the upper
part of the body is visible, fits to this edge a thong of sealskin
which comes up to his armpits.   A hood, also of sealskin,
armlets, and gloves, complete his equipment ; twine of
fishgut shuts everything up hermetically.   The waves can
rage as they please ; they will do no more than wet part of
his face.   Thus soldered as it were to his boat he and it form
one whole."

On calmer waters bundles of reeds tied together, as in
Egypt, or trunks of trees lashed side by side became rafts on
which men and loads could be transported.

To guide these frail barks, were they large or small, man
first used the pole.   But this was not enough when the river
became deep.   Then the oar was invented, and the paddle,
that is to say, a shorter pole but broader, and taking a stronger
grip of the water.   Doubtless it was not long before it was
noticed that an oar placed at the stern had more effect on
the steering of a boat and rendered it more obedient.   This
was the beginning of the helm which was a late invention ;
even among the Phœnicians, the great sailors of the ancient
world, its place was taken by two broader oars placed at
the stern.

The first attempts at navigation were made probably
on rivers whose banks were near enough together to make
the chances of shipwreck very slight.   To go downstream was

---

[1] Australian savages have been seen to use this method for short journeys.
[2] E. Richet, *Les Esquimaux de l'Alaska*, p. 108.

easy. All one had to do was to let the boat be carried by the current. To go upstream presented a difficult problem. In Assyria the boat was taken to pieces when the destination was reached. Only the skins were kept and the journey home was done on foot on the bank. Later the boatmen took ropes and hauled the boats back home singing as they pulled and in this hard work they were aided by oxen and horses. Arrived back whence they had started, if the season was unfavourable for another trip, they drew the boats on to dry land, turned them upside down, and used them as shelters. That is why in many places the huts are of the shape of inverted boats.

Like streams and rivers the smaller lakes tempted these amateur sailors and perhaps it was on them that a new invention was first seen. There, as on land, man sought to get rid of the labour necessary to keep in motion the vehicle on which he was carried. But on the lake it was no use appealing to the strength of animals. The dolphins and tritons which let themselves be harnessed to the sea-chariots of Amphitrite and Aphrodite never condescended to pull ships. The swan which on the ancient monuments draws the bark of the sun, until indeed it became the docile servant of Lohengrin, never allowed itself to be harnessed by man.

The whales which, in Fourier's phrase, will one day draw the ships on the surface of the oceans performed this service only in utopias. So lacking animal force man appealed to a natural force. What he could not find in the water he found in the air. "Wind is nothing more than a certain quantity of air put in motion by a change in atmospheric equilibrium." [1] Thanks to the alternations of heat and cold which are constant in our climates the atmosphere becomes a heaving ocean of air agitated by great waves and powerful currents. The speed of the wind can rise from about one inch and one-half per second to fifty, sixty, and eighty yards, and its force can be great enough to derail and overturn railway trains, to wreck houses and set in motion cannon whose fastenings it has broken. So cyclones and hurricanes have always struck terror into man. From the bags of Æolus, according to Greek legend, raging tempests

---

[1] The definition given by Flammarion in his book, *L'Atmosphère*, pp. 472 and 532 (Paris, 1873).

escaped. The Japanese artists represent in the shape of fantastic dragons the typhoons which lash the sea to fury and wreck the forests. It was a legitimate fear this of our ancestors, especially when such convulsions of nature were accompanied as a rule by thunder and lightning.

Yet it was this savage force, undisciplined and terrible, that man proceeded to subdue and make work for him. He proceeded to imprison it in a shred of bark, of skin, of straw-matting, in a sail. He compelled it to make his boat which seemed to be going of itself,[1] to go across the water. I

Fɪɢ. 8.—Barrow with sail in China (*Voyage Pittoresque*, 1834).

was a singularly important event this capture of an inanimate force, and was the prelude to conquests whose range is incalculable. In his boat, driven by the wind, man could sit practically idle. His rôle changed. He needed no longer to labour ; he had only to rule the boat and guide it. Less muscular work, more brain work—such was the progress which he made, and such is the progress which the human societies are still making to-day.

The sail was early invented in some countries ; in others

[1] Is this the reason why in Homer's time the ship is thought of as a living being, having a face, cheeks, eyes, and ears ?

it was never discovered. While in China it was fitted to barrows, and in Holland to sledges for use on the ice, the American Indians marvelled at the ships which came to their coasts from Europe, and although the ships of Columbus appear to us to have been of singularly meagre dimensions, the natives thought that they were winged castles floating on the water. Were they gigantic birds ? No, but rather dwelling-places where lived the spirits of the air, an explanation the more suitable since from them emerged centaurs and gods armed with thunder and lightning.

FIG. 9.—Double canoe in Oceania (*Voyage Pittoresque*).

But centuries were needed to enable man to build large ships and risk long voyages. In the beginning when he summoned up courage to launch out on what Homer calls the unharvested sea, he went like a prudent sailor from headland to headland. He rarely left harbour in the night-time, for he did not yet know how to guide his course by the stars. He rarely sailed in winter-time, the season of tempests. When he did put out, yielding to the appeal of the siren, he did not go far from the shore. He distrusted treacherous currents and capricious winds. It was doubtless in the inland seas where the tides are almost unnoticeable along the broken coastlines, amid archipelagos where the isles are thickly strewn together sometimes almost touching one another, that the ships with oars and sails grew steadily larger in numbers. Man gradually grew bolder and when he had succeeded in finding some marks of guidance in the heavens, when he made the discovery that certain winds are regular like the trade winds and the monsoon, blowing alternately in one direction and its opposite, he reached a stage when he was reasonably certain that he would not lose his way and that the winds would bear him where he wished. Then he was able to take the resolve to launch out into the deep. Horace marvelled at the courage of the man who, with heart clad in triple oak and brass, dared to brave in a cockleshell of a skiff the fury of the waves and the storms. Yet he knew only the blue Mediterranean which even its most violent passions never goes beyond the limits within which it is confined. But what must have been the fear of these landsmen when they halted before the ocean ? Was it not a monster whose breathing was marked each day in gigantic motions, whose roaring deafened the ear, whose assault demolished cliffs, whose rages overwhelmed the coasts ? There are peoples who live by the ocean, like the negroes of Africa, who have never dared to trust themselves to it, and have remained terror-stricken before this infinity of water losing itself in an infinity of sky. There are other peoples, fisher folk or island tribes, who fought and played with this formidable opponent. But it is easy to understand the superstitious fear which it inspires in those who are not born on its shores. We may cite a Roman witness [1] The legions of Vitellius in what are now the Netherlands were suddenly exposed to a particularly high tide : " Vitellius marched at first without any difficulty over a beach which was quite dry or barely washed by the last effort of the waves. Suddenly under the pressure of the north wind an equinoctial tide arose in which the ocean, raised to its greatest height, assailed and broke our columns. Far and wide the land was inundated ; sea, shore, and countryside presented the same appearance. It was no longer possible to distinguish solid ground from shifting sand, the path from the pool. The soldier was swept off his feet,

[1] Tacitus, *Ann.*, i, 70.

drowned in the depths, battered by horses, baggage, and corpses which floated between the ranks. The lines lost their formation. The men were in water to the breast, sometimes to the neck. Sometimes they were carried out of their depth, and were overwhelmed or scattered." A little later Germanicus lost all his fleet in the same district. The ocean which in the sixteenth century of our era swallowed up the great Armada of Philip of Spain which was sailing to conquer England gave many a lesson to those who thought they had conquered it.

But this takes us too far from the beginnings of navigation. Before becoming the monsters which they are to-day, the ships began to become more solid. They were built higher so as to escape the inrush of the waves. Means were found of keeping them steady on the moving surface on which they were tossed. At rest they were kept from slipping away by means of heavy stones which, in the age of metal, became anchors which bit into the soil or rock on the bottom. They acquired new shapes. Sometimes they were made rounder, sometimes slimmer, and the barks of the Polynesians had added to them an outrigger, which enabled them to brave the storm. To obtain greater speed, more oars were used and then several banks of oars. Keels, masts, sails progressed equally. Man thus conquered an element for which he had not been made.

Master now of means of transport by land and by sea, dreaming even then of the conquest of the air as is shown by the legend of the man-bird, Icarus, he could now easily move from place to place, and this relative, but ever increasing, facility of transport and communication made possible intimate relations between the different countries. It developed a new form of activity, trade, whose origins we shall now examine.

BIBLIOGRAPHY

BEUCHAT, *Manuel d'archéologie américaine.*

DECHELETTE, *Archéologie celtique.*

ESPINAS (Alfred), *Les origines de la technologie.*

FLAMMARION (Camille), *L'atmosphère.*

FREMONT (Charles), *Origine de la poulie, du treuil, de l'engrenage, etc. Etude sur le frottement des cordes et sur les palans.*

DENIKER. Work already cited.

LEVASSEUR (Emile), *Comparison du travail à la main et du travail à la machine* (Paris, 1900).

MORTILLET (G. de), *Les origines de la chasse.*

TACITUS, *Ann.*, lib. i.

CHAPTER IX

THE RELATIONS BETWEEN THE PEOPLES. WAR AND COMMERCE

HUMAN groups belonging according to race and environment to very different civilizations could not fail to come into contact. Now for the most part their customs and interests differed and hence arose a natural antipathy and hostility between them. But they had also common interests. One possessed what another lacked and hence arose the necessity of maintaining peaceful relations and friendships. Hence war and commerce.

War which was much the commonest state of things among the primitive peoples has played an important part. Within each people it made necessary discipline and authority. It made powerful the leaders who were needed to wage it. It welded together in iron bonds groups which had lived in isolation. It created kingdoms and empires. It enriched this or that tribe by the booty in cattle and slaves which successful raiding brought, and by the land which successful invasion took from the enemy. It brought about a mingling of races, of customs, of ideas. It has, as it happened, a not unimportant part in the formation of human culture. And, we may add that it developed in man qualities of courage and endurance, that it compelled him to invent a quantity of implements for attack and defence and so contributed to the progress of industry.

But the services which war undoubtedly rendered were offset by the lamentable destruction of wealth and life, by the ruin of towns and villages, by the enslavement of the conquered, by the succession of massacres and reprisals, by the deterioration of manners and morals, by the exaltation of brute force, by the unchaining of the cruellest instincts which not merely allowed, but ordered, murder, theft, arson, and rape. There was the constant opposition between militarism and liberty and the advance of the human race towards a juster, happier, and kindlier life was terribly delayed.

Fortunately war was more and more counterbalanced by relations less wasteful of life. Alliances, travels into foreign lands, and especially commerce, caused the gradual establishment between the peoples, I will not assert of fraternity, but certainly of a conciliation of opposing interests, a mutual comprehension of the ties which, in spite of all that separates and differentiates, unites members of the same species.

FIG. 10.—First meeting of Capt. Cook with the natives of Oceania.

The beginnings of commerce demand our particular attention. They rest entirely on the free exchange of goods between two individuals or two groups. In the transaction both parties gain. Each finds it an advantage to sacrifice his possession to take that which is offered to him by the other in return. And indeed it could not be otherwise. If it were otherwise, each would hold on to his own and exchange would not be possible.

This conception, which seems to us so extremely simple, was long in being reached. It remained beyond the comprehension of certain tribes if one may credit the words of Moffat who was a missionary to the Bushmen. " A man," he writes, " struck with the difficulty which the women found in nourishing their children after weaning them because they had at their disposal neither milk nor grain of any kind, offered to get them goats if they would give him in exchange ostrich plumes and skins. This offer was received by the bushmen with roars of laughter. They asked him if their ancestors had ever reared cattle. Cattle, they said, were there to feed man not to be fed by him according to the invariable practice of their fathers. The same man gave the same advice to all the Bushmen whom he met, but without result."

FIG. 11.—Death of Capt. Cook.

Similarly, when Cook arrived in Oceania, he could not bring the islanders to sell him what he needed. He got them to accept presents in return for which they gave what they considered an equivalent present, a coconut in return for a piece of hardware, and a sucking pig for a bit of cloth. It was a pledge of friendship, a reciprocation of kindly feeling, but nothing more. It was not exchange, argued and arranged in the regular fashion. Foreign trade seems to have preceded internal trade. It is probable that wherever the communal clan life was the rule, commercial exchange was useless, and seemed contrary to custom. Each individual had what he needed in order to live ; if he lacked anything he borrowed from his neighbour who had the right to borrow in turn. It was exchange, but exchange of services. Even yet among the Eskimos, a man who is the owner of several *kayaks* is expected to place at least one at the service of his neighbours. But between one clan and another things were different. Here there were things which one clan had and the other lacked.

If we examine the information afforded to us by the direct documents of prehistory we find certain objects which must have been objects of exchange, since they are found far, and often very far, from the country of their origin. Thus we know that regular flint works supplied weapons and tools to distant regions. Those of Grand Pressigny (Indre-et-Loire), for instance, were distributed throughout a good part of Europe. Amber, which is found in the Baltic, was carried to the southern shores of the Mediterranean, while in Egypt has been found another sort of amber of a redder hue, and certain amethysts which are African in origin. Obsidian travelled from volcanic regions to many a country where volcanoes were unknown. It is the same with jadeite, deposits of which are found in Switzerland, and in the Far East. I have already mentioned how in order to make bronze, tin had to be brought to Europe from Asia Minor, the British coasts and Malaya. Coral, turquoises, gold nuggets, sea shells, callaïs, and ingots of metal, certainly passed from hand to hand and so were distributed throughout the world.

The objects borrowed from far countries were weapons and tools for the men, jewels for the women. For the latter trade was in its origins luxury trade. The difficulty of communication was very great. How did these precious treasures arrive ? Sometimes a flood of invaders brought them with them from countries where civilization was more advanced. In the ancient world there seem to have been two main currents of invasion besides many secondary ones. The first began from Mesopotamia, reached the shores of the Mediterranean and from there by the isles of the Ægean via Egyptians, Phœnicians, Greeks, and Cretans reached the north of Africa and the south of Europe. The great inland sea was one of the great highways of commerce together with the valleys of the rivers which flowed into it. The second current, slower and intermittent, seems to have come out of northern Asia, from the north of China perhaps, and went on land following the sun to submerge in successive waves the north and centre of Europe. As to America, it is possible that it was in touch with our old continents either by Behring Strait or by Atlantis which disappeared in a great catastrophe. At any rate when Mexico was conquered by Cortes it was the centre of a great commercial activity. According to Cortes the market at Tlateluco could hold 60,000 persons, and that of Mexico city 200,000.[1]

But alongside invasions we must place merchants and seek to understand the reasons which made a clan or a tribe make to another tempting offers. As far as the clan is concerned, commerce is in a manner the monopoly of the community. There is nothing individual about it. In Australia to-day, a young man trained expressly for the task is authorized to trade in the name of all with a representative similarly chosen of a neighbouring clan. He is in a measure invested with a public office. He is a negotiator who has received full powers from his principals. Now suppose a clan has made a successful raid. It has too many possessions, beasts, garments, prisoners. It wants to get rid of some of them. An exchange would be profitable. Here is the determining motive. Commerce thus appears to us in the beginning intimately related to theft. It is not merely the savages of Oceania who, seeing before them objects which tempt them, try to get them by force or by guile, like the native whom Wallis tells of who seized the braided hat of a British officer and threw himself and it into the sea so that it could not be taken from him. It is not only the natives of Polynesia who snatch iron from the hands of sailors and barrel hoops. In the beginning even the most commercially minded peoples betray traces of raid and rape. The Phœnicians like the Greeks, made their debut as pirates, and it is not without significance that Hermes among the Greeks and Mercury among the Romans were at once the gods of merchants and of thieves.

Later, when the peoples become more civilized and have

[1] Letourneau, p. 203.

L

many possessions that are superfluous, either fruits of the earth or manufactured articles, they have fresh inducement to trade. They think of exports and from that moment there is on sea and on land a coming and going not unlike that which takes place in the veins and arteries of the human body.

Such were the causes which produced trade, and made it regular. What now were its methods ? The oldest method without any doubt is by barter and barter by depositing the goods at a fixed place is the primitive form. Herodotus has described this system, at once naive and complicated, which is the result of profound mistrust and yet gives evidence of very great confidence. He tells it as the Carthaginians reported it : " There is, they said, a place in Libya beyond the Pillars of Heracles, where are people with whom they trade. They discharge their cargo, arrange it on the beach, re-embark, and light a smoky fire. The natives, when they see the smoke, come down to the beach and deposit gold as payment for the goods, and then retire. The Carthaginians return, examine the gold and, if they think it equivalent in value to the goods, they take it up and depart. If they think that there is not enough, they return to their ship and wait. The natives return and add more gold until the foreign merchants are content. Never is there sharp practice either on one side or the other. The one side will not touch the gold until it equals their goods in value ; the others do not touch the goods until the gold has been accepted and removed." [1] For many a day it was the fashion to call Herodotus a lying Greek. But the evidence is too strong for his story to be disbelieved. In the seventeenth century a traveller, Claude Jannequin (1648), mentioned the method as still in force in the same district, and since then it has been found in operation in Ceylon among the Veddas, although they, to obtain still greater security, work at night, and indicate their views by signs. Similar practices have been found among the Eskimos, the natives of Borneo, the Chinese, the American Indians who use it to exchange deer skins for salted meat, the Abyssinians who used it in the sixth century of our era, and the Chilian Indians where the method had been further

[1] Herod., iv, 16.

refined. When the traders arrived at a village they advised the chief, who informed his subjects by sound of trumpet. The natives appeared, made their choice of the goods offered, and then withdrew to their huts. When the merchants were ready to go, those who had taken goods brought what they proposed to give in exchange.[1]

Such dumb barter where buyers and sellers struck a bargain without speaking, and without seeing each other, led rapidly to more direct methods. By a natural process, argument was added. Barter was the occasion for prolonged discussion, and even to-day one can find discussion raging in the villages, when the village girl who wants to buy a dress will have twenty bits of material displayed, will ask a reduction, will go away, come back again, and finally, after two hours' argument, make her purchase. We might cite, too, those epic duels in the fairs between the horse dealer and the peasant over a horse which, according to the former is magnificent, stout, strong, inured to toil, and a lamb to manage and, according to the latter is a poor wreck of a brute with neither strength nor health. The famous dialogue of Rabelais between Panurge and the sheep-seller is a brilliant satire on these interminable arguments where as many untruths as words are exchanged.

Certain practices, like that which consists of striking one hand into the other and spitting on the ground, concluded the bargain, and appear to go back to remote antiquity. The Eskimo who buys a knife licks it twice, no doubt in token of ownership. Among certain Ethiopian tribes the ox which is bought and the pearls which are given in payment are spat upon. Besides there comes into existence a mysterious language expressed by touch or the movement of the fingers, a language which permits business to be done at night without a word being spoken. Sometimes even in broad daylight the bargainers cover their hands with a handkerchief, and keep their faces impenetrably impassive in order to disappoint the curiosity of a neighbour, and hide from him the price accepted.

Little by little commercial relations were established between the different peoples. Boats sailed from maritime countries, especially from those whose territory was small

[1] Letourneau.

and unproductive, as was the case both with Tyre and
Athens. Caravans crossed the seas of sands organized
under a leader, and including armed guards, interpreters,
scribes, and priests, the chief, like the master of a ship, being
able to trace his route by the sky. Then without prejudice
to these long expeditions there were created centres of
exchange, markets. At first these were on the frontier
between two peoples in a place that was considered neutral
and sacred. Sometimes it was beneath the walls of a temple,
and even when war was raging enemies could meet here.
No quarrelling was permitted. A safe conduct was given to
all who went or came. There was a regular police system,
and any attempts at theft or violence were severely punished.
Such is the appearance of the market among all the half-
civilized peoples. By its establishment internal trade
developed. When there were several villages or something
resembling a town in a country, the inhabitants of surrounding
districts who wanted to sell or buy met at one place which
gradually became a centre of business. People came there
by necessity or for amusement. Races, languages, ideas
were mingled here just as much as the products of the town
and the products of the country.

At that point, necessity, the mother of inventions,
produces fresh ones, the weights, the measures, and the
science of numbers. The measures are taken from the
human body, man, as it were, projecting himself on the
goods to be measured. The thumb, the foot, the elbow-
length, the pace, the fathom, the ell indicate approximate
lengths. They are not exact, precise. The same can be
said of the measures applied to the soil which were indispensable to the farmer,—the perch which is six feet long
like the goad one applied to the oxen, the acre which
represents the extent that an ox can plough in a day, the mile,
determined by the length that a good runner could cover
without resting.

By processes not dissimilar the science of numbers was
born. Some tribes among the modern primitives know only
1, 2, 3. But afterwards they doubled, trebled, and arrived
at the dozen and that is why no doubt the figure 36 is still
popular. In societies which were already settled, a duodecimal
system was created which seems to be of astronomical

origin. The division of the year into twelve months and of
the hour into sixty minutes (5+12); the sale of certain
classes of goods by the dozen and the gross (12+12) are
evidence of its existence. But the majority of peoples
counted easily up to 5 by using the fingers of one hand.
By using two hands they arrived at the decimal system.[1]
This is not merely conjecture. In South America certain tribes
say " a hand " instead of five ; " two hands " instead of
six ; " two hands and a foot " instead of fifteen ; " two
hands and two feet " instead of twenty. This system of
counting by twenties has been in use among many peoples,
particularly the Aztecs and the ancient Gauls, and it is
from the latter that the French expression " four-twenties "
for eighty ; " six-twenties " for one hundred and twenty,
and " fifteen-twenties " for three hundred are derived.
Other nations to the fingers added the ankle, the knee, the
hip, the wrist, the neck, the chest. For more complicated
figures recourse was had to flags and feathers which marked
dozens or hundreds as was the case in Mexico or to little
pebbles,—compare the derivation of the word *calculate*—,
or to seeds or to shells strung on a rope, a method similar
to that whereby to-day we initiate the very young into the
mysteries of arithmetic.

For measures of volume various types of vessels gave
sufficient approximations. As to weights the choice of a
basic weight was difficult. Weight was first estimated by
the eye and the hand. Then a bar of metal, a ring, a nut,
sometimes a grain of corn, barley or rice, became familiar
units. The word *grain* still remains in our languages to
denote a very small weight. But greater exactitude was
necessary. The need of an instrument was felt which would
record the exact weight. The scale was invented fairly early.
It was known to the Greeks of Homeric times, but the
Mexicans had not yet discovered it when the European
invasion took place.

Money was the next development from weights and
measures. The moment barter became common, when it
was not merely a question of buyer and seller, but of a great
number of persons who were conducting trade in the most
varied classes of goods, a common measure of value had to

---

[1] Deniker, p. 264. Espinas, *Origines de la technologie*, p. 58.

be found. One or several standards which were easily divisible and more or less approved by the frequenters of the markets became necessary. Otherwise difficulties without number resulted. As long as barter in kind existed it was necessary to harmonize supplies and demands which did not coincide.[1] What one man wanted was not what the other wanted, and often a third had to be called in to serve as intermediary. The first money which came into circulation was objects which one was sure of being able to exchange, which represented a known value which was easy to reckon, which could be easily transported, and which were plentiful enough to supply trading needs, and yet rare enough never to lose their value by becoming too common. At the beginning there were no objects which could be universally exchanged. Certain moneys were assigned to certain classes of goods. Thus in the Solomon Islands cowrie shells are the only currency in which one can purchase a wife, secure allies, or pay compensation for a death.[2] The trade is regulated. A lance is exchanged for a bracelet, a pig for a knife, etc. So there is no need to be astonished when we find a great variety of currency among primitive men.

We shall mention here only the principal ones. We may distinguish between objects of luxury and objects of utility. The former which meet the general desire of man, and especially of woman, for adornment, are at first the shells gathered on the sea shore, the cowries which rank as money among the Papus of South America as well as in Oceania and Africa. The quantity of shells which have been found in the tombs of our ancestors lead one to believe that they have been sought for and valued from the earliest times. To-day, sometimes small, sometimes big, and threaded on to cords they have a very variable value. When they have been worked and cut, as is done by the Kanakas of New Caledonia, they are very valuable indeed.

Then come pearls, precious stones, and the glass beads made in their image. Over 400 sorts of the latter have been counted. Add to that, feathers supplied by the parroquets and birds of paradise, dyed mats manufactured for the purpose, cotton which can be cut into small pieces and which is very attractive when dyed a brilliant scarlet,

[1] Letourneau, p. 817.   [2] Lévy-Brühl.

cloth of camel hair or goat hair, furs, jewels of all kinds which are often amulets, a class to which the Egyptian scarabs belong. Then there is a transition to objects of utility, bundles of flax for weaving and, according to the district, coveted foods or spices—in Mexico, coca seeds and bars of bronze ; in the Far East tea in bricks ; in Abyssinia black pepper, and in the centre of Africa salt which is so greatly appreciated that war will be made to obtain it, and which is replaced, if it cannot be got, by plant ash. There were also living moneys—sheep, pigs, and especially cows. The Latin word *pecunia* which means money, has the same root as the word *pecus*, which means cattle. And among cattle slaves were often reckoned. In quite modern times an elephant tusk was worth so many slaves. The word *capital* or *cheptel* which means the possession of so many head of cattle, also indicated the possession of so many head of human cattle. Among the objects of utility which men wanted were weapons and tools. We know that they were much in demand among our remote ancestors and their descendants have not much changed in this respect. Daggers, axes, iron lances, iron spades, iron wire, brass wire, nails, performed the function of money among the backward peoples. Metal, which is more solid and more easily handled than the wares in use before its discovery, became predominant before it became common and kept its predominance. Sticks of copper, ingots of bronze, bars of iron and gold dust everywhere triumphed in the market.[1] In an island off New Guinea a small boy of about 12 years of age has been offered for a bit of iron and more than one black man or woman has been bought for a small quantity of silver.

In the distant ages when history begins to touch prehistory, the metals cut or weighed were long in use in China, in Egypt, in Chaldæa. Gradually gold and silver ousted the others from use, or reduced them as was the case with copper, bronze and iron to a very inferior position. Then a further step forward was taken. The necessity of weighing the bars of silver and ingots of gold or gold dust, appeared too laborious. The idea was conceived of stamping on these pieces of metal a certificate of genuineness which would inspire

[1] Letourneau, p. 34.

confidence and prove that this or that piece had this or that weight or value. This rendered the scales unnecessary for money ; men began, as the phrase is, to strike or coin it. In China, for instance, the copper money was early marked with symbols which rendered other proof of its value unnecessary. In Lydia, where Pactolus flowed, where Crœsus, richest monarch of his time, was ruler, the money was stamped with the fox, the symbol of Bassareus, a local god, and possibly an ancient totem. That happened about the middle of the sixth century before our era. The acceptance of such money with its official stamp implied an act of faith in the authority, city or ruler, which had stamped it. And in certain cases the tacit promise thus given by the authority was sufficient to give value to objects which had not that intrinsic value. In times of crisis, in sieges, in Carthage and in China, leather coins marked with the state arms were put in circulation, and this miracle has been reproduced many a time since. Paper money, the banknote, seems to have existed in China at a remote date. The bill of exchange was in use at Nineveh and Babylon, and money, in virtue of its status as universal merchandise, became itself an object of trade and speculation. The bankers whose trade it was to sell money and credit appear with history. In many countries the temples enriched by the offerings of the faithful possessed considerable treasures, and the priests assumed the rôle of bankers. This was so in Babylon, at Delphi and in Jerusalem. The Temple in the last named city became a money-changer's bureau and the traders whom Jesus drove from the sacred precinct were bankers who had set up their establishments within its walls.

With money appeared the practice of lending at interest. In primitive societies lending exists, but it is amicable and free between neighbour and neighbour ; it is a mark of solidarity between members of the same clan, between the inhabitants of the same village. No doubt a service rendered was often recognized by a present. A share of the fruit gathered was willingly given to one who had loaned a basket or a ladder to enable cherries, plums, or apples to be gathered.[1] Gradually, however, the present became habitual, regular,

[1] Tarde, ii, p. 358.

and then obligatory. It was agreed, if a ewe, a cow, a
female slave was loaned, that when they were returned
any young to which they might have given birth would be
sent back with them. The Greek word which means the
interest on a sum loaned is *tokos*. It also means birth or
living product, and so is applied to the sum which reproduces
itself or, as the popular saying is, has children. Whenever
interest appeared it tended to become very high. In China
it was 36 per cent ; among the Kabyle 30 per cent to 50 per
cent, in India 15 per cent to 60 per cent ; among the
Greeks and Romans 30 per cent to 40 per cent were quite
average rates. Among the Hebrews, as among most of the
primitive peoples, no tenderness, no scruple was ever displayed
towards the stranger. It is true that in Egypt the debt was
considered as cancelled when the interest payments reached
double the capital, and that among the Hebrews the creditor
was warned not to deprive the debtor of his cloak. None
the less, the levying of interest almost everywhere was
complicated by the extraordinary rights recognized to the
creditor, rights which concerned not merely the goods but
the person of the debtor. The luckless man who could
not pay his debt could be sold, reduced to slavery and cut
in pieces. The pound of flesh which Shylock claimed to take
from the body of Antonio is not simply a poetic invention ;
primitive legislations allowed this bloody manner of payment,
and it is not so long ago that in France imprisonment for
debt gave the creditor rights on the body of his debtor.

I have carried the story down into history to let it appear
how in different countries and at different times commercial
customs have been established, customs whose origin lies
very far back in time and whose sequence, so far as we can
establish it, indicates not indeed a continuous evolution,
but a broad picture of civilization to which numberless peoples
have supplied this or that detail. Humanity's evolution
consists of partial and local evolutions, the tendency of which
is to link up and to complete one another.

I should finish the chapter on commerce here did I not
think it worth while to sum up the good effects and bad
that it had on civilization. It was the inspiration to travel,
to the development of navigation. It wove between the

nations " ties of gold and silk ". It contributed powerfully to the mingling and fusion of races, customs, and ideas. It carried throughout the world the various local discoveries. It awoke the desire of imitation. In all these respects it has been an instrument of progress. Born of theft originally, but later the result of industry and agriculture which supplied goods for exchange, it reacted on these to their great advantage by opening to them outlets for expansion. It thus raised the general level of existence, taught man to exploit the resources of the earth, and generally improved conditions of life. I have already told how under its influence arithmetic progressed because it was needed for reckoning. As much might be said of its influence on writing which was necessary for contracts. The alphabet which conquered Europe and more than half of the civilized world, was perfected and spread by the commercial peoples, the Phœnicians and the Greeks.

While one cannot deny the benefits which commerce has brought to man, one cannot say that all its results were beneficial. It inspired the destruction of certain species of animals whose skins fetched high prices. It has wasted much innocent and useful life which was the adornment and wealth of the earth. It has been the cause of countless atrocities to provide slaves for lands whose inhabitants had decided to live on the work of others. It gave free rein to greed of gain, to the desire for wealth irrespective of the means of getting it, and so to fraud, to the adulteration and falsification of goods, to usury. Thereby it contributed to the degradation of character. It developed a mercantile mentality which was harsh and base. Within every society where it predominated, it favoured the oppression of the poor by the rich. It has been the great instrument to preserve inequality. Outside the frontiers it urged to violence, to the abuse of force and cunning. Unable to forget the raids and piracies from which it originated it has always been eager for lucrative conquests. Commerce on the grand scale with its implacable competition and the strategic manœuvres by which it is carried on, is, says Théodule Ribot, one of the forms of war. Merchants are often a bellicose class, as they were in Mexico and Carthage. Often they have been the precursors of armies in the countries to which they came as seemingly harmless guests. Commerce has been the cause of terrible wars. It is stained with much blood. Those who seek to pass a verdict on it must balance this profit and loss account but it is not my task to establish which is the greater. It is enough to have shown how it began.

BIBLIOGRAPHY

DENIKER, Work already cited.
ESPINAS (A.), *Origines de la technologie.*
HERODOTUS, lib. iv, c. 116.
LETOURNEAU, *L'évolution du commerce.*
LÉVY-BRÜHL, *La mentalité primitive.*
RIBOT (Théodule), *Essai sur l'imagination créatrice.*
The travels of Cook and Wallis.

CHAPTER X

The Origin of the Arts

IN primitive societies the work is not only manual: it is intellectual as well. The invention of the tools and methods which allowed man to make a weapon, a vessel, a hut, demanded, and proves the existence of, great mental activity. Toil itself is equally not merely utilitarian; it may be inspired by motives which are connected with the desire to satisfy a physical need, but which sometimes rise above that. This is true of a whole series of works which have an artistic character, that is to say, they are capable of giving that particular kind of pleasure which is attached to a feeling for the beautiful.

What is the origin of those arts which appeal to our intellects and to our senses, some like drawing, engraving, sculpture, painting, and dancing appealing to the eye, some like music and poetry appealing to the ear, and others like drama appealing to all the senses at once? Their origin seems to me to be very complex, and the error of those who have sought to discover it appears to consist in the fact that they have over-simplified it and have so perceived only a portion of the truth.

It is certain that all the arts respond to a sentiment that is inborn in man, to that which urges him to adorn himself, and makes him wish to appear beautiful; and, when I say man, I mean woman to be included. This sentiment is shared also by many animals. It is revealed especially in the mating season. Then the peacock displays his gorgeous tail, the nightingale sings its sweetest song, the dunghill cock dances before the hen which he wishes to attract, the tabby cat makes itself sleek and assumes wanton attitudes.

All that appertains to adornment, to that coquetry which Renan declared was the most charming of the fine arts, was encouraged by the legitimate desire of man and woman to appear desirable to one another. Painting and tattooing of the body, variety of costumes, collars, bracelets, and jewels of all kinds, perfumes owe to it their birth. Nor is that all. The mysteries of reproduction gave birth to certain cults, to certain hieratic representations of the organs of pleasure. They are found in the shape of statues or amulettes.

Building on these undeniable facts the philosopher physician of Vienna, Freud, has claimed that the development of all the arts can be explained by the expansion of sexual desire. Such at least is the thesis maintained by his disciples going in the manner of disciples beyond what the master taught. The thesis is defensible for certain forms of art. Among the dances there are some which represent the provocation, the resistance, the ruses, the retreats in what can be called the duel which, for greater or less time, is fought between lovers before they come together. One can also maintain that much poetry and song has been inspired by love. One can even admit in the manner of an old English print which I have seen, and which was boldly called " The origin of painting," that painting arose because the hand of a woman in love was inspired to trace on the wall the portrait of her beloved. But one cannot help smiling at this idyllic conception, and observing that love seems to have been a secondary motive in the oldest poetry, that in it it plays a very subdued part, and that the triumphant victory which it has had especially in Austria and France in the novel and the drama, is a very late event betraying the fact that the civilization in which this occurs is very advanced in every sense of the word. It is quite clear that a mass of artistic productions, war-songs, religious painting, and dancing, cannot be brought under this narrow formula in which some have tried to confine their origin.

If we enlarge the formula, however, in placing joy in life at the origin of art, in extending the taste for adornment to the things which surround man, and are used by him, we can explain why he loved to sing and dance, to decorate his pottery with geometric lines, and then with brilliant colours and even going the length of covering with pictures the entrances to the caverns in which he lived. But that would not explain why, in the grottoes, the bas-reliefs, the clay statues and the most brilliant paintings are relegated to the darkest depths often to places which are practically inaccessible and resemble sanctuaries. Here is a mysterious fact which does not fit our second formula. Without rejecting it we must for certain forms of art seek a different reason for their existence.

It has been said, especially by Karl Bücher in his book *Rythmus und Arbeit*, that art is the flower of labour, and that in two different ways. In the first place it arises from individual work. The worker, especially in those distant times when he was a jack of all trades, took trouble to make, and took pride in making, something fine. He thus marked his work with a personal trademark and thereby he gave it an artistic character. More, when he succeeded, he happened to vent his feelings of delight by a more or less rudimentary song, which was, as Ruskin says, an expression of the pleasure he found in his work.

But co-operative work especially became a rhythmic toil from which different forms of art were derived. Rhythm which is a succession of regular movements performed in time, can be considered a universal law of, nature. Day and night, cold and heat, the ebb and flow of the sea, succeed one another with a persistence that no longer impresses us because we have grown so accustomed to it. Rhythm is also a law of human nature. The air in our lungs, the blood in our arteries, and our veins have their periodic unceasing ebb and flow. When we walk our arms without any conscious effort on our part follow the motions of our legs. Symmetry is taught us by our bodies where the two eyes, the two arms, the two legs can pass for a form of rhythm, and in the plastic arts the repetition of the same lines, of the same motifs, is a special case of it. Symmetry is rhythm in space and rhythm is symmetry in time.

Now rhythm which is more visible because it is movement, is essential to labour, says Bücher, even to individual labour. The smith who beats the iron on the anvil, the housewife who beats the linen in the wash-house, make their blows fall at regular intervals. Even more rhythmical is co-operative work. Threshers, rowers, and the like must co-ordinate their actions and then rhythm is no longer merely the regularizing of labour ; it makes it easier, lightens it, enlivens it, makes it more disciplined, more productive, and renders semi-automatic activities which without its aid would be jerky, intermittent, and capricious. It creates a sense of rivalry, and yet a sense of solidarity among the workers ; it encourages and fortifies the weaker by compelling them to keep up with the stronger and so prevents them dropping out. Watch the masons perched on the steps of a ladder throwing the bricks from hand to hand ; there is no distraction, no pause. Each must catch and pass on what is caught ; they form a human group which has become an ordered whole, organized and harmonious, as it were a living mechanism which acts with the sureness of perfection.

The rhythm in labour is accompanied often with inarticulate cries, exclamations, and gasps, which coincide with the moment of supreme effort. Thus the woodman or the baker punctuates his toil with significant " Ha's ". Then when several individuals are engaged on the same task the ejaculations become a sort of song and fall into natural cadence. Who has not heard the boatmen hauling a shallop, or workmen driving in a stake with strokes of the mallet ? To begin with, these are songs without words, then words perch like birds on the melody which is cut into lengths separated by a pause and frequently interrupted by a refrain. They express the joyous or sad thoughts of the workers. A little later, musical instruments will aid the voices and thus music and poetry seem to have been born of toil.

Referring the present to the past, Bücher gives numberless proofs in support of his thesis. He shows that among the negroes, the Malays, and the Arabs, it is the practice when loading or unloading a boat, when leading camels or horses to the watering place to add music and song in solo or chorus to the task. He reminds us of the Greek bas-relief which represents four women baking bread to the sound of the flute. He does not forget to mention that in every country there exist songs peculiar to one trade or another ; spinners, weavers, ropemakers, camelmen, boatmen all have their songs, and he cites that of the washerwomen which Zola gives in *L'Assommoir* :

> Pan ! Pan ! Margot au lavoir
> Pan ! Pan ! à coups de battoir
> Pan ! Pan ! va laver son cœur
> Pan ! Pan ! tout noir de douleur.

He declares that among the modern primitives every task which is at all complicated is made easier by the tom-tom, the drum, the tarbouk, or the clapping of hands.

It would be easy to add in support of this thesis fresh arguments,—the songs which according to Rousseau in the *Nouvelle Héloise* accompanied the stripping of hemp in the Vaud : the songs which according to Mistral in the *Mireille* are sung at the gathering of the mulberry leaves or those which in Provence to-day are sung by the young girls as they gather orange blossom or those which are heard in the evenings in the villages when the nuts are cracked or the sonorous refrain which in Auvergne is called *la Grande*, and which the ploughman roars out in the fields, or the songs of Béranger and of Pierre Dupont whose refrain is taken up in chorus in the Paris studios and to which the strokes of the sculptor's hammer keep time.

Bücher says further that among our ancestors as among the uncivilized peoples of to-day, song, dance, and labour were intimately connected, that at their feasts they performed what were regular pantomimes in which the daily tasks were represented—sowing, harvest, the building of a boat or a hut and, especially, the pursuit of an animal whose flight, resistance, agony, and death was represented by one of the participants. He might have added that certain popular or childish catches are relics of days when daily tasks were acted. I remember having seen in 1925 at Venice on the Côte d'Azur the dances of the workers' guilds, in which female weavers, spinners, basketmakers, and gardeners reproduced in singing the attitudes and motions which were conventional in their professions. Most French people have heard bands of boys and girls singing—

> Savez-vous planter les choux
> À la mode, à la mode,
> Savez-vous planter les choux
> À la mode de chez nous ?

They are, says the song, planted with the hands, then with the feet, with the knees, with the nose, and the little band, as the droll lines succeed each other, perform all the movements which they indicate and act the various tasks which they prescribe.

M

Bücher, therefore, concludes that the first verses were made in imitation of the rise and fall of tools. In the combination of short and long syllables which form a verse in Greek and Latin, in rhyme which serves as metronome in French poetry, in Italian, and in the poetry of many other peoples, one can recognize the rhythm of feet trampling the linen or the grapes or of the hammer striking the anvil or the flail falling on the ears of corn. Thus in the early days of humanity, in public festivals and rejoicings, which served to break the monotony of ordinary life, song which expressed the feelings of a crowd or an individual became lyric poetry; the story which related episodes of war or hunting became epic poetry; the pantomime which gave a lively imitation of what we may call a slice of life was the embryo of drama.

Bücher's theory has real value. Strongly criticized in Germany by Meyer and in France by Olivier Leroy, it should be modified, but it ought not to be simply dismissed. Artist and artisan are the same thing in primitive societies and even as late as our own Middle Ages. Even to-day the worker who makes his own weapons, tools, furniture, or clothing makes them his boast. It is his pleasure to care for them, to make them beautiful. He has the joy, like the artist or the poet, of being really a creator, and that is the explanation of that puzzle which when first encountered, baffled the scientists that, among men of the quaternary period and especially among those of the Magdalenian epoch, there were sculptures which betrayed at once a sharp sense of reality and a refined taste. The artist had put part of his soul into the rock on which he painted.

After having made utensils which answered to a need, man then tried to add something of beauty to them. At first his pottery was very rough, then he decorated it, rendered it more delicate and more elegant, and following the rule that one invention leads to another, the art of pottery in which he handled clay and learned how to make it assume various shapes, led to modelling and sculpture. Thus, too, tattooing and the dyeing of cloths led to painting, as painting itself led to writing.

That recognized, we can modify Bücher's theory. The festivals on which he relies cannot be considered labour any more than dancing can be.   The pictures which represent animals and men have little to do with rhythm.   The picking of leaves or spinning, tasks at which the worker often sang, have nothing rhythmic about them.   The war songs which roused men's courage as did the violins which Condé had played at the assault on Lerida cannot be connected with labour, and, when a task is done to music, it is the music which gives the time to the task, and not *vice versa*.

FIG. 12.—Colossal statues on Easter Island.

To religion occasionally had been attributed the honour of having produced the arts.   Certainly magic which, in the beginnings, is mixed up with religion, seems to have inspired the paintings of the prehistoric caverns, which are, as it were, an anticipation of the capture of the game.   Magic also produced a mass of incantations, intended to ward off plague, or ensure victory, a good harvest, or successful hunting.   Everywhere the religious ceremonies, the songs by which they were accompanied, the ritual dances such as those depicted in the Altamira grotto or those which David danced before the ark, the statues rough enough, it is true, which represent divinities, the amulets which hung at men's necks, have an æsthetic as well as a religious character. It has also been noted that temples are among the most magnificent monuments that man has erected, that the sacrifices which took place there, were really sacred dramas, that dramatic poetry in Greece as in France and many other countries developed from the religious rites and festivals.

These facts must be admitted. But while recognizing that religion, whose importance in early days was enormous, was very favourable to the growth of certain forms of art, we cannot claim for it the honour of having given birth to war or love poetry, nor to what we may call professional

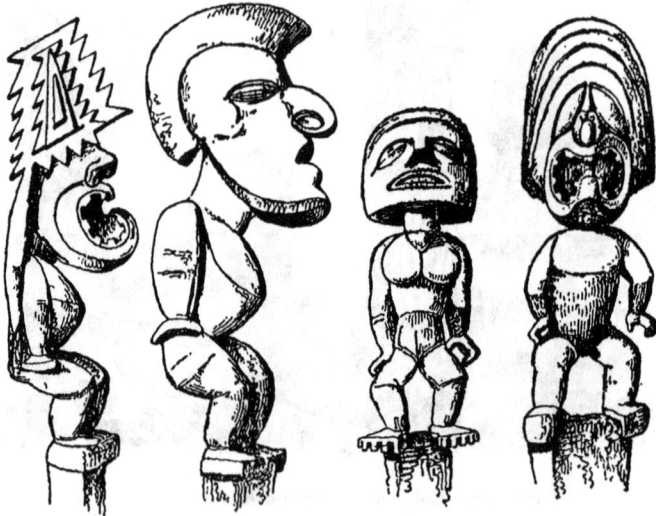

Fig. 18.—Fetishes of Hawaii (*Voyage Pittoresque*).

poetry, that is, poetry connected with a trade. Apart from religious art there has been secular art, laïc and disinterested. It is, for instance, quite impossible to find any magical meaning in a rock sculpture which represents a mother holding her child by the hand.

It has also been said that art depends on the method of production, or to enlarge this formula which comes from historical materialism, from the kind of life led by the people.[1] It is certain, for instance, that the nomads never practised architecture, but excelled in metalwork, leatherwork, and

[1] This thesis is strongly championed by Ernest Gross.

carpet-making. It is equally certain that the fisher peoples more than any other were the makers of barcarolles and poems telling tales of travel. But while that shows that there is a connection between the economic life of a people and the forms which art takes among them, it gives us no clue to the origin of the fine arts which in the last resort it is necessary to relate to a powerful instinct in man, to a desire which is unconscious which leads him to reproduce life in all its forms. Labour and rhythm are elements in it. Religion uses it for its own ends. The kind of occupation of a people determines its expression, but it is at the very deeps of human nature itself that we must search for the creative force which produces art.

That said, we must now determine the beginning of the various arts from the direct and indirect documents which we possess. The plastic arts—in the caves, on the rocks, in the tombs—have left precious remains whose number is constantly increasing. So far it is among the men of the Magdalenian epoch that they seem for the first time to have, in our regions at least, reached a higher level. Man seems first to have ornamented the objects which he used for the same reason and in the same way as he adorned his body with painting and tattooing. The ornamentation was in the beginning very simple. Lines of dots, parallel grooves, zigzags, stripes, and lozenges constituted a geometric design which was for an individual an owner's mark, but which also gave him a feeling of pleasure and appeared to him to make the article beautiful. From this first stage, man passed gradually to drawing figures. What first inspired him to reproduce the figures that he saw around him? Perhaps he got the idea from seeing his shadow cast by the sun on the ground, or seeing his face reflected in clear water. Perhaps a freak of nature suddenly confronted him with a shape which he thought he could recognize. Anyone who has visited the caves, has found himself surrounded by elephants, hippopotami, and seals, which were only stalactites and stalagmites. The eyes of man found in what surrounded him strange resemblances. How many mountains have a shape which recalls that of a lion's head, a policeman's helmet, or the profile of Napoleon! To the fact that it has a vague resemblance to the human figure, the root of the mandragora owes its reputation for marvellous properties which popular superstition attributes to it. Many sculptors of prehistoric times used roughnesses and flatnesses of the rock which suggested animal forms, which the artist took pains to perfect.

Drawing with charcoal, chalk, and ochre was no doubt the first way in which man endeavoured to express his vision of the world around him. But it is possible that modelling from which developed sculpture was practised equally early. On horn, bone, soft stone, and then on ivory and on the horns of stag and reindeer, man adorned his weapons,—and also those mysterious articles which we call *bâtons de commandement*, without daring to be dogmatic on their real use—with pictures in relief of animals, worked for the most part with the saw. But he did not confine himself to these tiny sculptures to which we can compare the tiny figures of bears and mammoths found in Moravia and elsewhere. In the caves appear bas-reliefs which represent in little big animals and hunting scenes, while in full relief we find statues of men and women, clay bisons which were only sketches and are small in size, and were then executed in natural size.

On the other hand, drawing gave birth to engraving, which is seen on the rocks in the open air, on the walls of the caves, and, as in America, on shells, or, elsewhere, on bone. The first of these have practically all disappeared as a result of the elements, although here and there it is still possible to recognize on a rock a herd of horses or the outline of a lioness. The second still remain but are covered over with drawing upon drawing, probably because the surface which presented itself as suitable to the early artists was so small, or because they disliked their first attempts and persistently emended them, or because a layer of paint which later scaled off showed up the contours of the last work and concealed all the earlier ones.

Lines begin to be used to indicate shadow or the hairs on the skins of animals. Then engraving is combined with painting. On the walls of the inner galleries of the caves are visible prints of hands of which the fingers are mutilated or bent back. Sometimes the hands were dipped in red liquid and then pressed on the rocks ; sometimes they were simply sketched round with red or black on the smooth surface of the rock, such hands as one finds imprinted on the Australian rocks and which perhaps were believed to ward off the evil eye. Tubes of ochre have been found in the caves and the painter's brushes and the smooth slabs of stone that served as palettes. Even when painting in which at first only one colour was used, became many coloured, the colours do not vary much. There is little more than red and yellow, which mixed with black give brown. But is it quite possible that other colours were used, but having been of vegetable origin the sun or the damp destroyed them. Red is the dominant colour. The colour of blood, it was the emblem of life and perhaps of survival.

The objects represented are for the most part animals, those which the artists were most accustomed to see, reindeer, horses singly or in herds, mammoths, bears, boars, marmots, ibex, antelopes, chamois, bisons, aurochs, and less frequently carnivora such as wolves, lions, hyenas, rhinoceri. As living and as recognizable are the pictures of fish, trout, pike, and eels. Were some of these animals venerated totems ? It is possible. Some (the male following the female) seem to have been designed with a view to increasing reproduction. But for the majority it seems likely that the motive for painting them on the walls was to snare, paralyse, and render them more easily slaughtered, especially as often the animal is depicted wounded in the middle of traps, snares, and nets, into which before the hunt began he, by courteous magical formulæ and promises of good treatment, was invited to fall and allow himself to be taken.

Vegetables are rarely depicted in the caves and equally rarely, at least among the Magdalenian paintings, do we find figures of men and women. Was this because man did not yet know how to draw them ? It would be surprising if he did not, when he could depict so faithfully both the shape and the motions of animals. But plants had very little interest for tribes which were essentially carnivorous hunters, and as to the infrequency of drawings of the human figure, we may suppose that, as to draw a living thing was practically to secure a lien on it in the flesh it was forbidden among certain tribes to depict men and women. The Koran much later affords us an instance of this religious ban, of this *tabu*, as the Polynesians would call it. In Persia, Chardin saw a carpet on which a female figure was depicted, but it had been deprived of an eye so that it was not an absolute reproduction of the actual human being.

Among other groups earlier in date to the Magdalenians, for example, among the Aurignacians, statues of men and women were common, but they seem to have been intentionally deformed. The women are Venuses *à la* Hottentot,[1] whose breasts, haunches, and rump, although among negroes these are actually of great size, seem to be intentionally exaggerated so much so indeed that we may consider the statues as emblems of fecundity. In Spain at Cogul and many other places, paintings of groups are to be seen which are said to represent ritual dances and in which scenes of war, troops of men and women attacking beasts and placing a yoke upon them, allow one to suspect a magical motive.

This manner of applying art to utilitarian ends is doubtless not foreign to the general evolution which quaternary art which was at first innocent of such motives, seems to have followed. Influenced by many circumstances and in particular by the religious ideas of the times what began by a scrupulous imitation of reality gradually departed therefrom. There was at first intentional deformation. The engraver found himself torn between what he saw and what he had seen. Memory conflicted with impression. In drawing the profile of an animal he gave it two ears as if he was looking at it in full face, forgetting that in a profile drawing one ear would hide the other. He represented the arrow heads which struck the bison or the horse when actually they would have been buried out of sight in the animal's flesh. He even went so far as to represent, as if its body had been transparent, the internal organs of a trout or an elephant. This is the explanation why, in the Egyptian paintings, so many heads are seen in profile although the body is depicted as facing one ; perspective which diminishes the stature of persons in proportion as they are further away, was unknown to the primitives.

To the deformation of what was seen, a deformation which arose from carelessness, was soon added another

---

[1] E.g. the Venus of Brassempouy, the statues of Vistonice, etc.

type of deformation which was intentional. It arises from what is called *stylization*, that is to say, the actual is simplified, abridged, transformed, and represented in a schematic and conventional way. That we may observe in passing is the ordinary development of art down to our own day. It begins by the imitation of nature; it gradually departs from it; it copies and makes unnatural its own works; it falls then into symbolism, into conventions, it ends by losing sight altogether of the life which it thought to express. Then a vigorous return to realism or to naturalism brings it back again to its eternally changing model; it bathes in the Fountain of Youth and begins once again the same evolution.

This is what happened among the primitives just as it happens among their descendants. Stylization is sometimes the result of lack of endeavour. The artist confines himself to reproducing approximately an earlier work; he reduces it to certain essential characteristics. We see a type of horse's head degenerate into a trident; the fish gradually changes into a simple ellipse with a dot replacing the eye. Art returns to its beginning to a geometric decoration in which the original model is quite unrecognizable. But it is this development, let us not forget, that will lead to writing; the letters of the alphabet are only amputated, mutilated, and distorted pictures.

But at the back of these deformations there was also mystical ideas. As in Egypt, in Assyria, and in Greece, gods were represented with the head of a jackal and goddesses with the head of a lioness, winged bulls had human faces and centaurs, satyrs, and chimæras were depicted by the artist, so among primitive paintings we find symbolic pieces whose meaning it is very difficult to discover. In many examples of American or European pottery we can see a taste for the grotesque and the monstrous, a desire to provoke amusement or terror. We have vessels with the head or body of animals in the form of polyps or dragons, clay pipes in the shape of a tapir and the like. With this tendency we may connect the paintings which represent men wearing masks or disguised as chamois and dancers having a horse's tail or a stag's antlers.

If we turn now to architecture, we find that it also is

not solely practical and utilitarian, devoted solely to the building of houses and the fortifying of villages. It is also, and especially, funerary and religious. It was in memory of the dead that the dolmens were built in which a covered corridor leads to a sepulchral chamber and similarly with these mounds or tumuli where heaps of stones or pyramids sheltered the bones of the dead, these subterranean cities which are the vast cemeteries of Egypt or these pits with several storeys which were caves for the dead in Peru. In many places, for reasons which we do not yet understand, stand menhirs, elevated stones sometimes single, sometimes placed in a circle and painted with red circles with a black spot in the centre, sometimes in a shape like that of a tortoise, or set up in rows as at Carnac. They remain enigmas. We know only that they were sacred monuments which preceded the temples and the palaces. At Saint Sernin in the Aveyron a menhir which was perhaps an idol roughly represents a woman. We may connect it, perhaps, with the colossal rock statues of Easter Island.

But temples and palaces, whenever the larger human groups were organized into societies, copied in stone the buildings which had earlier been erected in wood, as one can see in Yucatan, and made them of enormous size. There the art of the painter, the sculptor, the goldsmith, the potter, displayed all their resources, all their magnificence. For gods and chiefs nothing was too beautiful or too costly, and as a crowd of slaves was employed to adorn these dwelling-places of the great ones of earth and heaven, the peoples admired themselves in their works which bore witness to their sojourn upon earth.

The other arts, music, dancing, poetry, were connected above all with the festivals which were occasioned by a victory, a successful hunting or fishing expedition, or among the agricultural peoples by the various tasks of the year, ploughing, sowing, harvest. Later still among nations which had acquired some astronomical knowledge they were occasioned by the phenomena of the sun's annual course.

In poet fashion Lucretius [1] has described the first pleasures of the human groups : " Often, therefore, stretched in groups on the soft grass hard by a stream of water under

---

[1] *De rerum natura*, v, 1392–1405 (Rouse's translation).

the branches of a tall tree, they made merry at cheap cost, above all when the weather smiled and the season of the year painted the green herbage with flowers. Then was the time for jest, for gossip, for pleasant peals of laughter. For then the rustic muse was in its prime : then they would wreathe head and shoulders with woven garlands of flowers prompted by joyous playfulness and they would march out moving their limbs out of time [1] and beating mother earth stiffly with stiff foot." No accounts of these rustic gatherings have come down to us but the narratives of travellers allow us to make the picture precise and complete. According to Letourneau they included what is really an opera ballet, in which song, musical instruments, dancing, and pantomimes unite to express the collective joy of the people. The whole is a very complex work of art which sometimes degenerates into wild orgy—witness the bacchic orgies among the Greeks or the corroboris of Australia—and the elements of which tend to become dissociated in virtue of the law of the division of labour which obtains here as elsewhere.

In these exuberances of the crowd the individual was not stifled. Skill in music, for instance, placed a man above his fellows, a skill that to-day is very unevenly distributed and, if we cast a glance at contemporary primitives, we shall see the Bushman deriving real pleasure from his solitary playing on the *gora* when he listens, having stopped up one ear, to a melodious but scarcely perceptible sound which he produces " by breathing on a stem of a feather fixed between a vibrating string and a handle fitted to a calabash ".[2] The player of the lyre, the drum, the tarbouk, the reed flute, produced melodies to which the listeners kept time by clapping their hands or striking cymbals.[3] Similarly in singing, the

---

[1] Here the poet probably went wrong. Time among the primitives is beaten and kept with rigorous exactness.

[2] Lalo, p. 308.

[3] It is well known what quantities of musical instruments have been recovered from the tombs—conches and trumpets of hoarse note, wooden rattles or metal ones reminding one of children's rattles, or the bells of the jester, flutes made of human or animal bones, whistles in baked clay, castanets and the like with their dry sound, drums and tambourines made of the skin of an ass or a doe, clashing cymbals. If one adds to these stringed instruments of wood or tortoiseshell, one has here an orchestra the volume of whose sound was no doubt increased by the shouting and clapping of the audience. The tune was thus gradually doubled, as it were, by more or less uncouth song.

individual won fame by his solo while the crowd sang the refrain in chorus, and in the dance and the pantomime an individual participant by superior agility, by skill in improvising words or gestures or by his powers of imitation, revealed individual gifts and ideas amid the evolutions of his companions.[1]

If we try to class the different sources of inspiration from which came those artistic and poetic manifestations in which the group and the individual shared in equally, we meet first religion. Prayers were in rhythm and were sung. Before the fetishes the sacred dances were performed. Magical incantations promised rain or victory over animals or other men. Then comes war; rousing songs, pantomimes of fighting with brandishing of arms, death cries, and dances round captives and trophies. Then comes labour. The departure to the hunt was acted, or the building of a canoe, or a hut, or the gestures of a man sowing, or ploughing, or at his trade, and thus, apart from the festivals in which the whole clan was interested, there arose certain individuals or certain groups who, to lighten their daily toil, invented songs which brought music into the family workshop. Finally, as sexual attraction never loses its hold over men, love produced the dances and songs in which it was expressed.

Now in these festivals of which the furious celebrations of modern savages can give us some idea, three elements were united which later separated. There was first the exaltation of the self, an eruption of burning feeling which expressed itself in words unlike ordinary words and from it came lyric poetry. Then the narrative of some heroic episode recited amid wild enthusiasm, became epic poetry. Finally, the imitation of life in its sad or its joyous aspects, the frequent sacrifice of prisoners solemnly put to death, or drunkenness which produces jest and also madness gave impetus to drama.

Such—completed and confirmed by what travellers have told us of the uncivilized peoples of to-day—is the picture which the first artistic efforts of our ancestors present to us. These efforts, according to the peoples who made them,

[1] The part played by woman who, to amuse her children, becomes a maker both of dolls and songs ought not to be forgotten.

were more or less happy, but wherever they were made, they bore witness to a mentality which raised man from above the animals from whom in his beginnings it was impossible to distinguish him. They opened to him a world of dream and beauty in which he was far away from the daily realities of life in this world. They placed him on the road which led to culture and civilization.

BIBLIOGRAPHY

BÉGOUEN (Comte), *Les modelages en argile de la caverne de Montespan ; La magie dans aux temps prehistoriques.*

BREUIL (Abbé), *L'évolution de l'art quaternaire*, Paris, 1909 ; *L'art à ses débuts.*

BUCHER, *Rythmus und Arbeit.*

BURKITT, *Prehistory* (Cambridge, 1925).

CAPITAN. A number of studies of which he himself has drawn up a list (Paris, 1924).

GROSS (Ernest), *Les débuts de l'art.*

HADDON, *Evolutions in Art illustrated by the Life-histories of Designs* (1895).

LALO (Ch.), *L'art et la vie sociale* (Paris, 1926).

LEROY (Olivier), *Essai d'introduction critique à l'étude de l'économie primitive* (Paris, 1925).

LETOURNEAU, *Evolution de l'éducation.*

LUBBOCK, *Prehistoric Man.*

LUCRETIUS, *De rerum natura*, lib. v.

LUQUET, *L'art et la religion des hommes fossiles.*

MORGAN (J. de), *Les premières civilizations* (Paris, 1909).

REINACH (Salomon), " L'art et la magie " (in *Mythes et Religions*).

CHAPTER XI

The Origin of Science

KNOWLEDGE which is a condition of the power to act had very modest beginnings. The body of knowledge was formed only very slowly; just as vegetable mould is formed by innumerable generations of fallen leaves, so the fertile ground on which the sciences were finally to bloom took centuries to form. The very little knowledge that was amassed appears to us to remain for ages buried under conjecture and error and fantastic notions which seem like the visions that haunt a sick bed. The scientific spirit which consists in considering as true only what can be demonstrated, a spirit which is not very prevalent even to-day, was conspicuously lacking in primitive man.

But we must not accuse him of being irrational. In presence of a phenomenon which made an impression upon him, he tried to explain it to himself. He sought to reach back from the event to the determining cause. He had the essential instinct of the seeker, and he would willingly have agreed with the poet who said: "Happy are they who know the why of things."

He had the faculty of observation; he had acute senses which enabled him to make sufficiently exact affirmations, but he was the dupe of appearances. He took them easily for realities. Thus when he saw the stars moving, he believed that the earth stood still in the centre of the universe. He said, just as we say to-day, that the sun rises, that the sun sets, without suspecting that he himself was turning round the king of the heavens. Equally he regarded man as another centre around which nature gravitated, and as a being to which could be related all that existed around it. Starting from that point primitive man possessed a logic which he applied imperturbably. He unhesitatingly made deductions from a conception which was not foolish, but simply was childish, and which was imposed on his intelligence by superficial consideration of his surroundings.

Think of primitive man confronting the myriad marvels

which for him were incomprehensible—tempest, flood, the germination of plants, the reproduction of animals, the volcanoes, the earthquakes, the eclipses. How with his limited experience could he explain these ? He humanized, personalized the causes which he did not understand. He conceived them in his own image. He saw in them a will at work, benevolent or malevolent, but always more powerful than his own. He attributed to invisible and superhuman forces all that was unusual and disturbing.

Thus all his knowledge was a medley of precise observation and mystical belief, of practical wisdom and frail imagination. Science and faith are at the beginning inextricably mingled.

Who were these terrible beings who lay in wait for and dominated wretched humanity ? First of all, there were the dead who wandered underground, who were prone to ascend from the tomb and to scour hill and valley by night, to scare the hapless traveller lost in the darkness, to torment in their beds those of whose conduct they had had cause to complain while they lived under the sunlight. It was from a desire to imprison them in their tombs that man placed heavy stones on the graves or tied the dead body with ropes. It was in order to prevent them having desire to return to the earth that he killed and buried with them their wives, their horses, their slaves, and all the articles which could be of use to them in their underground life, that care was taken to provide food and drink so that they might take a liking to their new abode.

There were also other spirits at once superior and akin to man. There were the great chiefs whom the lightning, the hurricane, and the rain obeyed. It was necessary to court and conciliate by prayers, by offerings, by sacrifices, these gods or demons who could at will be either benevolent or malevolent. At need they had to be constrained by magical incantation to meet the wishes of their humble worshippers, or, at least, to abandon their evil designs. If the moon were eclipsed, it was because she was devoured by a monster whom one had to frighten by shooting arrows at him or by raising a terrific din.[1]

[1] From the account of the travels on the banks of the Niger in 1830-2 of the brothers Lander, I extract the following (*Le Niger*, p. 434). In the middle

Between the mysterious powers who acted incessantly on human destiny and men who could never escape their all-powerful influence there arose a class of intermediaries. These are the priests and the magicians. The former, possessors of knowledge which they could transmit only orally, and which was accessible only to the initiated, interpreters of dreams sent from on high, of omens which unveiled the future, of oracles given out by women whose nervous sensibility and predisposition to mysticism rendered liable to religious exaltation—sibyls, mænads, pythonesses—, quickly secured an almost unbounded domination over the credulous and docile masses. The temples which were also observatories, libraries, clinics, museums, and treasure-houses, became among the primitive communities buildings more revered than the palaces of even the most powerful chiefs. In every country performers of sacrifice who took upon themselves to purify the people and render the divinities propitious to it, surrounded with solemn rites all the important acts of human life, regulated initiation, marriage, burial, and created prescriptions and interdictions which became the bases of public morals, law, and hygiene.

of the night, the narrative says, the travellers were aroused by the news that the sun was dragging the moon across the sky : there was an eclipse of the moon. " The natives thronged into our courtyard, some fully convinced that the end of the world was at hand, others that this phenomenon at least portended the coming of a great calamity. The local scientists increased the general terror by their explanations. They declared that the moon, tired of the path which she traversed across the sky, which was difficult, steep, and bristling with obstacles, had seized a favourable moment and this very night had left the old ways to trespass on the path of the sun. The sun, much annoyed at this intrusion, had attacked the imprudent queen of the night, had shrouded her in darkness, and was eating up her rays so as to force her to return to her old path. Consequently the thing to do was to terrify the sun and compel him to allow the moon to cross the heavens in the old peaceful way.

" The natives formed a great circle, three deep, whirled round with the speed of a top, crying, shouting, groaning with all the might of their African lungs. They flung themselves about as if possessed, twisted their bodies and their limbs in every sort of way, leaped up, struck the ground with their feet, and stretched up their arms to heaven. Outside the circle boys and girls, striking empty calabashes one against the other, ran about madly and howled bitterly. Bands of men wore themselves out of breath by blowing huge trumpets or bull horns which emitted raucous and discordant noises. Others induced old cracked drums to produce horrible groans, while iron triangles and chains, clashed against one another, gave forth notes more sinister than any others in this diabolic welter of sound. A European who did not know Africa and found himself suddenly in the midst of these people, might well have deemed himself in the power of a legion of demons celebrating by an orgy the arrival of a damned soul, so terrible was the appearance of this fear-maddened crowd, so infernal was the din it made."

N

Thus we can understand how they obtained a privileged position and enjoyed powers and honours which assured them the most important place in society. They succeeded in getting into their hands both spiritual and temporal power.

The magicians competed with the priests in the working of miracles, the sorceresses were the rivals of the priestesses; sometimes the two rôles were confused. As a rule, however, the magician was regarded with fear rather than respect. Men knew that he possessed secrets which could cure or cause illness, strike an enemy at a distance, stop the flow of blood from a wound, render a man invulnerable and light in the heart an inextinguishable flame of love. But men knew also that the magician abused his powers and many a time he was pursued and executed for having caused a plague or destroyed some great personage. As societies became more policed, the sorcerer and the sorceress did not disappear, but they sank more and more into the despised classes among the servants of evil powers and the smugglers of the supernatural.

What, however, was the contribution of priests and magicians to the sum of human knowledge? There is no doubt that the sorcerers and the miracle workers were often clever curers of disease, fervent adepts of occultism, forerunners of the scientists who study hypnosis and suggestion, able by methods kept carefully secret to emerge triumphant from the ordeal of fire or boiling water, an ordeal later on to be forced on Savonarola by the people of Florence. Certainly they made more than one discovery about the hidden potentialities of human nature.

More obvious and greater are the services for which we owe gratitude to the priest. For a long time the temple is the home of science. Just as in mediaeval times the word *clerk* meant scholar, so in the beginning the priests is he who transmits to future generations the discoveries of the past. It is curious to note that the first automatic machines, gates opening of themselves by the aid of cords and pulleys, and by the aid of compressed air, had their origin in ceremonies of worship. Nor must we forget above all that writing developed within the security of the sanctuary.

At the same time, while we pay a tribute of gratitude to

the members of the priestly class we cannot but regret that, thanks to the secrecy which they used and abused in these distant days, they kept to a small minority what might have been the possession of the whole community, and also that, by using methods which were completely theological, they believed that they could make permanent what they believed to be truth, that they said " I know " when they should have said " I think ", and that they proceeded to make bold and unprovable affirmations on subjects like the origin of the world and many another, which were beyond their scope, that thus and by the tyranny of ritual, they often paralysed human inventiveness, that they cursed the tree of knowledge and forbade man to touch it. They were the conservers of the ancestral tradition, but often were also the obstacles to necessary innovation.

More, they are responsible in measure for more than one divagation of human thought. They encouraged the sophism *Post hoc, ergo propter hoc.* Two results followed, the one giving birth to the other. They are in great part responsible for the practice of seeking guidance for action in the entrails of victims and in the appetite of the sacred fowls, or by observing the direction taken by smoke or the steam from boiling water, for ordeals of which the mediaeval judgments of God are survivals, which made a man prove his innocence by walking through a furnace without being burned. Many popular superstitions regarding the virtues of amulets and magical formulæ go back to the days of the priests who, instead of fighting them, actually, and into our own time, favoured and helped to spread them. That is why the human spirit in its onward march has incessantly to free itself from the bandages in which a clerical class has sought to stifle it. It has been well said by Salomon Reinach, " Human history is the progress of laïcisation."

Having said all this on the mystical nature which newborn science reveals itself as in general possessing, let us examine briefly the different branches of knowledge. What escape most easily from the mystical influence are technical ideas which the progress of the arts and crafts steadily multiply. No doubt a magical motive is not absent from the sculptures and paintings on prehistoric rocks. No doubt there did exist a sort of agricultural magic which ruled over the domestication of plants and animals, which prescribed certain religious rites for the fertilization of the fields, which, for example, ordained that the seeds should be brooded over by women who increased the fertility of the soil by lying upon it. No doubt, too, the blending of metals or the solemn marriage of a people to the sea implied a belief in the intervention of unknown forces which were believed by man to be animated with benevolent or malevolent feeling towards him. The gods or goddesses which the guilds took as patrons, the ritual which accompanied sowing and harvest and which lasted into our own times, the blessing of the herds before they left for the hill-pastures, of the hounds before the chase, amply prove the hold which religion acquired and kept on the most diverse activities and on those who took part in them.

Nevertheless, there came into existence independently in each one of the occupations of man a series of practical rules of empirical knowledge which increased from year to year, and was transmitted from one generation to another. " Inherited " is the correct word, for these were secrets which were handed by father to son, mysterious procedures which were carefully concealed from the profane and revealed only to the initiate. Even in recent times workers have been known to conceal their methods, and modern works which protect themselves carefully from the glances of the curious are not entirely unknown. As an instance in early days of communication between men practising the same trade, and analogies between their works we may cite the Limeuil excavations, where MM. Capitan and Peyrony discovered and studied the workshop of sculptors whose technique is so precise that it is possible to talk of a school of art.

Otherwise as one might guess, it is not theory which at that remote date interests and makes progress. Science for science's sake, disinterested science, becomes possible only when the toil of the manual worker creates leisure for the toil of the intellectual worker. It is in the applied sciences whose utility was immediate and obvious that we find a steady increase of ideas amassed by experience. But here, too, we see the mixed character mentioned above, the perpetual confusion of exact data and weird imaginings.

If we begin by the less complex sciences which must have

been the first to be studied, we see that of numbers, so necessary to commerce, developing rapidly enough, yet we find grafted on to it all sorts of beliefs. Uneven numbers are pleasing to the gods; hence the quantities of triads and trinities—the three Graces, the three Fates, the three judges in Hades, the three divine persons in Egypt, in India, in Christianity, the three theological virtues. The number seven has equally many properties and is no less in favour—the seven against Thebes, the seven-branched candlestick, the city on seven hills, the seven sacraments, the seven deadly sins, the seven gifts of the Holy Spirit, the seven sorrows of the Virgin, the seven days of creation, the seven lean kine and the seven fat kine, the seven ages of man. The number one thousand was also the source of many terrors and many hopes. An entire philosophy, transcendant and symbolic, had for basis the combination of numbers which was quite sufficient to explain the universe. Geometry which was indispensable in Egypt for the delimination of the fields after the Nile floods and necessary elsewhere for like purposes, seems to have existed among peoples that had as yet no culture.

Astronomy which was necessary for travellers on the sea and in the desert seems very early to have aroused and held the attention of men. Without the aid of instruments, the conception of the lunar year was reached, and then that of the solar year which competed with the earlier. The towers consecrated to Baal had seven storeys which bore the names of the five planets which were known and of the sun and moon whose names fell to the two highest storeys which shone with silver and gold. In America, as in the Old World, the peoples learned how to make calendars which measured time with sufficient accuracy and we cannot fail to admire the effort of thought and observation which such calculation implied.

But with the study of celestial phenomena the mystical element was again bound up. It was claimed that the future could be read in the movements of stars and planets. It was believed that the destiny of the babe depended on the position occupied by the planets at the moment of its birth. Astronomy had astrology for companion. The horoscope varies according to the day on which one is born.

The day of the sun holds promise of happiness and good fortune. In Germany *Sontags Kind* means a child born under a lucky star. The moon is the inspirer of dreams; it produces lunatics. Mars naturally is connected with war; Mercury with commerce and diseases; Jupiter with good fortune, wealth, and power; Venus with love and Saturn with knowledge, and it seems that in mediaeval times there was a special perfume for each day in the week.

Physics and chemistry afford us a similar picture. The illusory theories that surround the four elements, earth, fire, air, and water, are well-known. If the blending of metals produces definite results it is none the less true that alchemy was intimately allied to chemistry and turned men's mind to investigations in which, hoping to discover how to turn lead into gold, the seekers discovered by chance substances and combinations and even principles which had a wonderful future.

Medical science, whose need is always urgently felt, could not fail to find eager students. Scholars have been astonished to find on fossil men proofs that primitive men knew how to set a dislocated or broken limb and even to perform the delicate operation of trepanning. Surgery attained a certain competence. The amputation of the fingers, ovariotomy, the cæsarian operation were performed by the primitive doctors. As to medicine, properly so-called, which is an art rather than a science, and which has to act on organs which it knows only imperfectly, the most singular remedies were in use. The physician used simples and experimented in vegetable cures; he even used some that appeared to him panaceas, like the sage which was believed to be able to combat death itself. It is possible that thermal streams were used at an early date, streams which inspired equally fear, astonishment, and worship.

But in this domain, more perhaps than in others, imagination ran riot. From the beliefs which still survive and from the practices of savages one may conclude that our forefathers believed that from drugs in which were nail-parings, the blood of the owl and the bat, or fat from the body of a man who had been hanged, produced astounding results. Meteoritic stones aided women in childbirth. Talismans, plaques of metal on which were engraven magical figures and signs rendered a man invulnerable or cured wounds more efficiently than any balsam. Herbs gathered at midnight by the light of the moon on a certain day of the month would miraculously stay the course of a fever. Formulæ of bizarre words, the sense of which was unknown to those who pronounced them, would stop the flow of blood from an artery. Amulets protected men against accident, the evil eye or the weavers of spells who were responsible for deadly and mysterious disease. The medicine man, the healers and charlatans who sold charms shared with the priest a power which they owed as much to sorcery as to knowledge of really curative methods such as bleeding or the clyster.

Natural history and geography were also made wider by fantastic speculation. By the side of precise orientations, by the cardinal points and the stakes of wood which marked definitely the national boundary, by the side of information often very exact on the habits of one game-animal or another, appears a profound ignorance of countries not very far away and tales of fabulous animals, many-headed hydras, winged dragons, sirens, phœnices arising from their ashes after having been burned on the pyre. The tales of travellers were filled with improbable episodes, a circumstance which gave rise to the proverb : *A beau mentir qui vient de loin.* What Homer tells of the Cyclops, the Laestrygons, or the sorceress Circe does honour to the imagination of the poet, but it helped very little to instruct men regarding the position and customs of distant lands.[1] The boldest seamen like the Phœnicians kept their route secret, and legend asserts that one of the Phœnician ships was deliberately sunk lest a Greek ship which was tracking it, should learn the way to the lands whence came amber and tin.

As to the ethical and political sciences which even now so little deserve the name of sciences, they existed only in an embryonic state in the maxims and precepts in which were condensed the practices and experiences of previous generations. Naturally the priest was their mouthpiece and theology stifled and took the place of what one day was to become philosophy. The prescriptions of custom were extremely rigid, even when they did not appear as did the

[1] Deniker, p. 267.

Ten Commandments amid the crash of thunder and the quiver of lightning, and the superstitious suppositions on the origin of the world, on a gradually organized chaos and on a creation of something out of nothing, on the existence of rival principles, good and evil, light and darkness, contending for the domination of the world, resolved themselves into sacred dogmas often contradictory, but proclaimed untouchable truth by the peoples which adopted them.

In a word the scraps of knowledge existing without any connection between them and mixed with grave error, scarcely begin to be organized in pre-history. Yet the mind of man was singularly active and the day when the invention of writing allowed him to render safer the communication of the first essentials of civilization, to fear no longer or, at least, fear less, the loss of knowledge acquired, these scraps formed already a respectable mass which henceforward went on rapidly increasing. Written documents, the explorations of traders and seamen, even the wars and invasions which brought races into hostile contact, and often ended by the fusion of conquerors and conquered, were so many elements which conspired to help on the growth of knowledge and aided humanity to see itself and its surroundings clearly. We ought to greet with respect this dawn, a pale dawn indeed, of the intellectual light.

BIBLIOGRAPHY

DENIKER, Works already cited.

GRAND-CARTERET, *L'histoire, la vie, les mœurs et la curiosité* (vol. i).

LANOYEL (F. de), *Le Niger et les explorations dans l'Afrique Centrale* (1858).

LÉVY-BRÜHL, Works already cited.

REINACH (Salomon), Works already cited.

CHAPTER XII

THE FIRST HUMAN SOCIETIES

WHAT were the conditions under which the first men lived ? We can only guess at them. Excavation tells us nothing about them and the study of savage peoples brings us little more light, for all those whom we are able to observe live in organized societies. Was there, as Karl Bücher supposed, a period when men searched individually for food, or were the first men, like horses, reindeer, and monkeys, banded in herds, seeking together the food they needed, as Oliver Leroy, that keen critic of Bücher, believes ? The documents which we have at our disposal are not sufficient to enable us to reach a definite conclusion. It is possible that the course of events on islands differed from that on the mainland ; but it is, and perhaps always will be, impossible to have accurate knowledge of the beginnings of human civilization.

Nevertheless it is advisable for the study of man's primitive economic life to lay down principles which may serve us as guides. In the beginning man appears to us very much as he is to-day, as an individual, that is to say, a being distinct from and separated from others, forming a self-contained whole, living a distinct life, and as a social being, that is to say, living by preference and by necessity in a society.

On the one hand, he seeks his own personal interest. He seeks to conserve and develop his personality. On the other hand he is drawn towards his like by a mysterious and powerful sense of kinship, by an obscure force which is a law of life and which draws together beings of kindred nature. As individual he is egoist ; he relates everything to himself and makes war for existence against his like who become his rivals and his enemies. As social being, he combines to preserve existence with them and they then become his allies and his friends.

All his actions spring from this double conception. It

makes him to other men now a wolf, now a brother. It is the motive of quarrel and war and also of solidarity and co-operation. It creates individual property and, side by side therewith, collective property, as well as family property which is an intermediate form.

It is easy to imagine how man, having everywhere the same tendencies, seeking to realize for himself or for a group of which he is a member this desire for existence and well-being, which is the motive force of all living creatures, must everywhere end by organizing identical societies. But to do so is to be grossly misled. The civilizations which man has created are infinitely diverse. Why ? Because the human races while they are composed of individuals capable of rational process, are very unequally endowed both physically and intellectually, above all because the environment in which they live is infinitely diverse : aridity and humidity, warmth and light, the violence and direction of the winds, electrical radiation, latitude and altitude, fauna and flora, plain and hill, nearness and remoteness from the sea, relative isolation or easy means of communication with other lands— here are elements which constantly vary, which act both on the body and on the mind, which determine this or that form of existence. No doubt man in his turn acts and reacts on his environment and tends to mould it in this or that direction ; but his receptivity, his power of adaptation, drive him to a compromise between what he desires and what is permitted by the conditions under which he lives.

The result is that elaborate monographs on all the different civilizations would be necessary to reveal all the laws of human evolution, that we must beware of hasty generalizations, that it is, for instance, very rash to ascribe to primitive mentality general characteristics which can be present in one sort of climate but not in another. Thus one hears constantly the statement that primitive man was lazy. That can be maintained when one is dealing with fortunate islands like Tahiti, where life is easy and there is no necessity to work. But elsewhere, where primitive man had to do everything for himself, where, with clumsy tools, he had to fell and cut up a tree, where he had to spend days in scraping the skin of an animal and months in building a canoe or polishing a stone axe, he had to submit to slow and painful toil which was no game, but served precise and practical ends. Similarly when he invented and perfected his set of rudimentary, but already complicated, tools, he gave evidence of possessing a foresight which has too often been denied him.

There is, therefore, no reason for astonishment if, when we try to discover the customs either of our ancestors or of prehistoric survivals, we meet a host of exceptions and contradictions. While we need not despair of their ultimate explanation we must state them, yet without forgetting that there are certain common characteristics which we can perceive in the societies scattered over the world, and that there does exist a certain number of ascertained facts on which we can build the knowledge of the future.

Whether there were at first amorphous groupings with a certain promiscuity from which the family slowly emerged, or whether the family trinity—father, mother, and children—was the original cell, which by increasing and comprising several generations became a clan of people having the same origin and was the first human society, it is impossible to say in the actual state of our knowledge, and it is not of much importance for the purpose of this book. What we have to discover is the relations of the persons who composed the family group or clan, relations which varied greatly according to time and place and which we must deduce from a study of the societies first constituted.

We may ask, first of all, in what countries the first civilizations arose. Their rising depends primarily on geographical conditions. The temperate zones seem to have been their cradle and in these zones we must include countries where altitude or the influence of the sea tempers tropical heat. It is possible that a continent now disappeared, Atlantis, existed in former times where to-day the waves of the Atlantic roll, and that at its disappearance it left in the east and the west peoples and inventions which survived it in Europe and America. To-day more than half of the human race is grouped between the 20th and the 40th degrees of north latitude, and the reason why there is not a similar state of things in the southern hemisphere is because there the ocean takes up the bulk of the space.[1]

[1] v. the works of Febvre and Haddon.

The environment is less favourable in the zones near the tropics which contain deserts marked by oases, green islands in seas of sand. But it becomes actually hostile in the equatorial region where man is oppressed by the constant extreme heat as well as by the exuberant vegetation of virgin forests and the enormity of giant rivers, or in the arctic and antarctic zones where land and sea are covered with ice and the only vegetation is lichen, the food of the reindeer, moss and dwarfed trees. We cannot place reliance on such vague and easy generalization. We must examine the conditions of life and labour that existed for both sexes in the different societies existing in primitive times.

Attempts have been made to classify these societies by species and several types have been distinguished. But it is not correct to consider these as regularly succeeding one another. If man sometimes does pass from one to another, equally often the types have developed side by side without it being possible for us to say this is the earlier, this the later. Nor is it correct to regard them as clearly separated. If this type or that is marked by certain characteristics which are peculiar to it, it is the rule rather than the exception that related types are inextricably mingled. But we can differentiate them according to the principal occupation of the individuals composing them, or, since it is a history of labour that we are writing, according to the kind of toil which by preference or by necessity they undergo in order to live. Hunter peoples, fishers and sailors, shepherds, farmers, all these having industries created by their special needs, have been the originators of customs which are characteristic of the various groups and differentiate them the one from the other. We shall examine these different civilizations and try to show what was in each the organization of the family, of production, and of property. But first of all we shall note what they have in common.

What is common to all of them, what appears to have existed everywhere, is the clan and totemism. The clan is composed of individuals who recognize a common ancestor. It is an extension of the family. Let us suppose that it includes not only the first pair and their children but also their married children and their grandchildren, that it includes two or three generations allied by blood relationship, and, more, having adopted members who may be clients seeking protection or slaves, who were originally prisoners of war. Then it becomes the clan, a group whose members are homogeneous, united and enjoy rights equally to the extent that not only is it prohibited for a member to kill or injure another member, but an injury done to one member must be avenged by all. The clan thus unites under the same name which is taken from an animal, a plant, or something regarded as living, like rain, lightning, or a river, human beings having, or considering themselves as having, a common ancestor who is thought to be the object or the animal from which the name of the clan is taken. The American Indians call that object *totem*. The Iroquois relate how the tortoise, the emblem and protector of their group, was transformed into a man. The totem was sacred, was *tabu*. If it was an animal, that animal could not be killed and eaten save on certain solemn occasions, when a sort of communion ceremony was held in which the clan fed on its flesh and acquired its qualities.

There is evidence enough to presume that totemism has been universal, for it has been found in America, in Australia, in ancient Egypt, among the Eskimos, and traces have been found of it among the Greeks, the Romans, the Celts, and the Germans. The clan, composed of related groups, appears to have had the same universality. The clan had neighbours which could have birth similar to its own or which were branches detached from the one parent stem. If a common danger threatened them, if a military leader was able to weld them together, the clans thus federated became a tribe in which the clans were swallowed up. The clans could be masculine or feminine, that is to say, affiliation and inheritance could be established through the mother or the father. Uterine affiliation seems to be the more ancient, although one cannot say so definitely. But it seems natural that the female was in the beginning the pivot of the family. Maternity was easier to determine than paternity. The husband recognized and accepted the child and the strange custom of the *couvade* which, as it exists among the Basques, condemns the male to remain in bed and receive attention and congratulation when the female gives birth to a child, or the *amphidromia* of the Greeks, in which the father ran round the hearth holding the new-born babe, are possibly not only rites intended to ward off evil spirits, but modes of paternal acceptance, ceremonies of recognition, reminiscences of ancient times when it was possible for Telemachus to reply, when asked who was his father, " *Men say* that I am the son of Odysseus."

In such a case the maternal uncle had sometimes more rights over the children than the father, and the nephew, the son of the brother or the sister of the wife, was often preferred to what we should call the direct heir. The son-in-law also had advantages at the expense of the son. In ancient Greece, Agamemnon and Menelaus wedded daughters of kings to whose thrones they succeeded, and the kings of Rome were succeeded not by their sons but by their sons-in-law.

This system in which woman occupied the predominant place in the clan and in the family had been called *matriarchal*. But the word is ambiguous. It does not mean that woman exercised what we may call political power ; she does not appear actually ruling, as the Amazons of legend did, or as taking in deliberations a place equal to that of the men as she does among the Iroquois.[1]

In the feminine clan was it monogamy or polygamy that ruled ? Monogamy appears to have been the rule. A man had to be wealthy before he could afford several wives and many children. Now in the beginning equality was the rule in the clan ; there were no great differences of wealth. Marriage, if we may judge from the studies made in Australia and elsewhere, was hedged about with precise and complicated regulations. While the clan was isolated, cousins and sometimes brother and sister necessarily married. What is called *endogamy* (marriage within the clan) must have existed in the beginning and was completed by the rape of foreign women considered as spoils of war. This is the opinion of Frazer, who found the system existing among the Arunta, one of the most backward of the Australian tribes. Its existence has also been noted in Egypt and Peru. But whenever many distinct clans came into existence, custom introduced *exogamy*, that is, the males of one clan sought their wives in another clan carefully indicated to them.

[1] Cf. too, the customs of the Yassai of Azerbaijan.

No doubt it is a projection into the past of modern ideas to ascribe the rule of exogamy as inspired by the desire to avoid incest and degeneration. Such moral and hygienic considerations are essentially modern. For lack of a better explanation, one may adopt that of Durckheim who considers that the interdiction against shedding the blood of a member of the clan was extended to include the shedding of blood involved in marriage with a virgin.

When we try to get a precise idea of the status of the male in the feminine clans, we find that at his marriage he passed into the service of his parents-in-law, that he laboured for them, lived in their house, or at least went there to visit his wife who remained in the maternal home. He was to a certain extent in economic dependence upon them. Consequently there is no need to wonder that he sought to substitute within the clan paternal affiliation and authority for the system whose main characteristics I have outlined.

The clan exercised over its members an authority practically without limit. Their lives were regulated in their smallest details and restricted by customs which had to be obeyed. But the eternal conflict between the general and the individual interest none the less existed and that struggle of the individual against the collectivity which surrounds, maintains, and confines his life in a frame of iron, that struggle which arises from the dual nature of man, brings changes : it is the cause of slow but radical social transformations.

Where the masculine clan gained the victory over the feminine, a victory which was not universal, it was won by the effort of the male desiring to possess his own in his own home and taking there first of all his children and then his wife. Certain changes in the mode of production, in the nature of the work that devolved upon the sexes, favoured, as we shall see, this development. Woman then became subject to man. In many countries man had the privilege of roasting and eating the prey, while woman had to be content with cooked vegetables and fruits which sometimes she prepared apart. In Australia, when the clan moved, it was woman who bore the stakes and skins, the materials of the next home, and who carried, besides the little children, the bag in which was stowed the poor utensils of the household, while man walked unburdened by anything save his weapons. But it was also his duty to explore the route, to try the ford which made the river passable, to beat the thickets and be ever ready to attack or defend. When the goal of the journey was reached it was woman who set up the portable home.

In short the patriarchal system gave complete authority to the father who was king of the house and absolute mastery of his wife and his children. Inheritance was in the male line and the woman, often purchased, became the property of the husband. Thus possessed, and even inherited if she became a widow by the son or brother of the deceased, she fell to a subordinate position.

Between these two extremes, *patriarchate* and *matriarchate*, the organization of the primitive family swings. That said regarding an evolution which appears to have been general, we shall pass on to show how civilization and mentality have taken a different development according as the peoples varied in type.

Let us begin with the *hunter peoples*. These most probably had a mode of life most akin to that of the first men, a wandering life in search of food. To-day they are represented only by the Pygmies and the Bushmen in Africa and by the Ainus in the Kurile Islands in Asia. The pygmies are still nomads.[1] They are woolly-haired, short-thighed, broad-buttocked, with a height of 4 ft. 9 in.—a smallness of stature ascribed by an English observer to the fact that they lived shaded from the sun in the depths of the tropical forest and that they pass long hours standing motionless in pursuit of game. They never remain longer than fifteen days in the tiny villages where the women build huts with branches which they drive into the ground and cover with thick leaves. They live practically entirely on the game which they kill. They cannot, however, be regarded as a pure type of hunter people for they eat fruit and roots also, and buy salt and tobacco from their neighbours. Monogamy is the rule among them and the restricted family—father, mother, children—is the basis of their rudimentary organization.

If we go back now from these, the last of the hunter

[1] *V.* Lowie.

O

peoples, to their predecessors in history and prehistory, we see the latter wandering across the grassy steppes and sandy deserts. In pursuit of the game which flies from them, they must perpetually be moving onward whenever they have killed out all the game around their encampments. They remain nomads by necessity. They are the peoples of the tent. They scarcely halt in their wanderings. They are birds of passage. They are attracted by fruitful and sun-bathed lands. They are invaders or the cause of invasions. It was the Asiatic hordes, Huns and Mongols, who, driving other nomads before them, precipitated the catastrophe in which the Roman Empire went down before the barbarians. If they have contact with settled peoples it is usually a hostile contact. If they have need of food or anything else, a raid will equip them. Robbers and pillagers, they reap their harvests with the lance and the sword.

After their domestication of the horse and the camel they lose a little their character of brigands and become leaders of caravans. They even become clever traders who can make their toiling neighbours work to their profit. But the old hostility which set the nomad at once against other nomads and against settled peoples still lives on. In our day it is seen in the war of insults which is waged in Algeria between the nomads of the Sahara and the peasants of the Tell. The latter cry: " O filthy Arabs, drinkers of curdled milk, you are always on the move like locusts. Your trade is the brigand's; you eat only dates; if we shut our markets to you, you would die of starvation. We rule you by the belly." To which the men of the desert answer: " O you naked beggars, always seeking wool and camel's hair and dates, what a life is your life! You dwell ever in the same place in the midst of excrement and eaten up by lice. Yours is the slave's trade. Endlessly you toil. In winter you till, in summer you reap." [1]

This hostility, however, does not prevent the two groups having a certain solidarity of interest. But it must be recognized that their adventurous lives give the nomads a special mentality. They desire space, liberty, the unknown. In our own day the Beduin have retained this character of daring and independence. One of their poets has written

[1] Daumas, p. 278.

this panegyric of the chase in which there rings the echo of a passion inherited from a distant past. " The chase frees the mind from the cares that burden it. It adds to the quickness of the intelligence. It brings joy, scatters sorrow and makes the doctor superfluous for it keeps the body perpetually well. It makes good horsemen for it teaches a man to leap swiftly into the saddle, to dismount in a twinkling, to ride at a gallop across precipice and rock, over crags and bushes. Who devotes himself to the chase gains every day in courage. He learns to mock at accident." [1]

Never attached to the soil the hunter peoples know no other property than their tents, their weapons, their horses or their camels, and that part of the spoil which was allotted them after the chase. The prey is his who killed it, and if several were in at a death there were precise rules which assigned to each his portion according to the place where his arrow or his javelin had struck. In the daily life there was always this spirit of equality which, however, did not prevent their yielding implicit obedience towards a chief chosen to conduct an expedition. But on ordinary occasions all took part in deliberation and decision. The folk of old owned no other authority save that of age and experience. Among them there was neither poor nor rich. The tribe would have been ashamed to have in its ranks beggars and paupers. All were hospitable : the guest, perhaps because he seemed a nomad like themselves, is a messenger from heaven. Woe to him who receives him ill. The host will ruin himself to entertain the guest properly before he will hand over to another the sacred duty with the admission that he cannot fulfil it. There is no other industry but the working of skins and metals except the sewing which the women do at odd moments. Pelts, weapons, a few household utensils, a few jewels for the women who are beasts of pleasure when they are not beasts of burden, that is all which is necessary to these wanderers who do not believe in heavy baggage.

Next to the hunter peoples we place the people who are *fishers* and *sailors*, especially since the chase and fishing are closely connected. These peoples settle on the coasts

---

[1] Ibid., p. 105.

of the sea, the great lakes, the rivers. They are tied to the
zone of water which they exploit. They have fixed abodes
on land ; they return regularly to their port of departure.
Thus Eskimos, Lapps, Fuegans, and the natives on the
shore of Tanganyika cannot be considered nomads. The
type has been noted in ancient Crete and among modern
savages on the Pacific coasts from Alaska to the south of
California, in the north-west of Siberia and in Kamchatka.

The products of the sea or the lake provide them with
food in plenty and so they form dense enough centres of
population in which a new type of civilization appears.
The division of labour among the sexes is precise. Among
the Eskimos and the Greenlanders the male hunts the seal,
the moose, and the whale ; he makes tools, houses, boats ;
he prepares the skins of the bigger animals and in the long
nights of winter plays the part of painter and sculptor. The
female cultivates the plants, fishes for small fish, cooks,
looks after the children, and everything appertaining to
the toilet, guides the great family barge which is like a
floating house, works at the skins of small animals like the
muskrat and of sea birds. The clans who possess totems,
are for the most part, masculine. Man enjoys a marked
superiority.

Among several of these peoples production outstripped
consumption ; the surplus became the object of barter. Hence
arose, as always happens where trade exists, inequality of
wealth. The organization of the family soon felt the effect
of it. Marriage became based on purchase. Sometimes
the price asked was so high that several purchasers combined
to pay the sum asked by the parents and so a single woman
had several husbands.[1] But as a rule it was the opposite
which happened : a rich man bought two or three wives.
For the most part they were harshly treated. The property
of the husband, they were really slaves and they had to
gain by toil the money they had cost.

In the less severe climates the coast peoples soon became
sailors, especially if they inhabited an archipelago or a
much indented coast. These, like the hunters, had desire

---

[1] Polyandry is found in Dahomey but only in the case of princesses of its
royal house (Paul Marty, " Etudes sur l'Islam au Dahomey," *Revue du
Monde musulman*, 1926).

for adventure and contempt of danger. Boldly they advanced over the salty desert. Their chiefs solemnly wedded the sea by throwing a ring into it. Again, like the hunters, they had small respect for the property of others. They began, like the Greeks and Phœnicians, by being pirates.[1] They raided the boats they met on their journeys and the countries at which they disembarked. But they were also invaders who drove the earlier inhabitants from a corner of land or occupied parts till then uninhabited ; they settled in trading stations and colonies along the coasts. Yet they remained bound to the land whence they had come ; they spread its customs and its products. Now in the mother city it often happened that a more or less refined civilization had developed. The sea is the great highway along which this was carried into the world. This was the part played in history by the Mediterranean.

As a result of the long absences imposed on sailors, woman among these peoples is more respected, and plays a greater part. Consequently she has a higher place in society.[2] Also, a further consequence of these expeditions into far-off lands, to which can be exported and from which can be imported various types of goods, the mother-land often became the centre of a prosperous industry and commerce.

The *shepherd peoples* to whom we come next are partially nomadic. They drive their herds before them to wherever they see pastures and even when they partially settle down, they live in the plains in winter and in the highlands in summer. This double life exists even to-day. In Provence, in Languedoc and in Spain when the hot weather begins, shepherds and flocks go off to the high land where the grass which has remained under snow for a longer time, resists more effectively the scorching of the sun. Even yet it is possible to find in the Alps of the Valais, for instance, villages which are divided into two parts each on a different level. The lower part is inhabited in winter, the higher is inhabited in summer, when the cattle go to the mountain pastures and is abandoned again in the autumn.

---

[1] *V*. Thucydides.
[2] The Cretan civilization affords an example of this.

The life of the shepherds is less precarious than that of the hunters since they have at their doorstep, as it were, beasts which they can milk or kill at need. But they also have to defend themselves against robbers, against wild beasts, against cold and diseases which ravage the cattle and against drought which ruins the pastures.

In the beginning the tasks of men and women were different. As was natural the care of the smaller cattle and the poultry fell to the women. The men had charge of the cows and the bulls, and employed the whip, the stick, and the dog. In certain African countries, in Uganda for instance, only man as a rule milks the cows and almost everywhere to him is reserved the right of driving goats and sheep to pasture.[1] He it is, too, who lives in the hills in a hut or a tent, while the woman remains in the valley, weaving cloth from sheep wool the shearing of which is a man's task.

The preponderant part played by the man in a shepherd civilization had as consequence the patriarchal organization of the family. The man either " lifted " his wife, and this rape remained a symbolic ceremonial among many peoples, or he bought her. Among the Kalmucks[2] the price was high enough ; a woman cost fifteen horses, fifteen cows, three camels, twenty sheep, so that to have daughters of marriageable age was a sure means of increasing one's flocks and herds. But once become the property of her husband, the woman was frequently despised and ill-treated ; sometimes her brothers were obliged to interfere on her behalf as in the classic tale of Bluebeard. In the event of adultery she was punished by death. She could be repudiated if she was barren, and then the husband was repaid her price, as if he had made a bad bargain. As to the man, he could, if he were rich, have several wives, of whom one was his favourite and the mistress of the others. The children like the mother were servants of the father.

In this society appears the collective holding of the soil which the tribe uses during its seasonal migrations and on which it declares it has an exclusive right and, as the same causes continue to have the same effects throughout the centuries, it is still quite common in the highlands to find

[1] The young girls of Sinai in the Bible are an exception.
[2] Gross, p. 105.

a mountain pasture possessed and used by the entire population of a village. But side by side with this collective property exists private property in cattle and sometimes slaves, houses, and articles of personal use. This right of individual property is pushed so far among some peoples that among some of the American Indian tribes father, mother, and children possess individually a cat, a hen, a chicken, a dog, or a cow. Thus, even thus early, there is no question of equality in a shepherd community. There are poor and rich, according to the number and value of beasts possessed, or according to the number of slaves owned.

The clan exists among the shepherds but the restricted family appears to be more important. There is no stable political organization. If the shepherds sometimes unite under one chief to fight a foreign foe, the union is purely temporary, and ordinarily authority is shared by the heads of families.

In another sphere of ideas, the life of the shepherds is to a certain extent a life of contemplation. The shepherd who watches his flocks at night to protect them from wild beasts and robbers, has to pass long hours in idleness, in watching the herds of the planets and the stars cross the sky. Like the sailors he follows the march of the constellations. He becomes the observer and the worshipper of these mysterious stars which move on above his head. It is no chance that the shepherds of Chaldæa were the first to think of an astral religion and to construct that lunar calendar which was in force for long in Greece as in Assyria, and of which our week and the twenty-eight days of February are the stubborn remains.

It remains to speak of the *farmer peoples*. In what land did they originate ? Perhaps on some sun-bathed plateau, then in valleys where well watered, alluvial land lent itself to cultivation. China, India, and less remote from us, Mesopotamia and Egypt, have been the destined lands where agriculture could develop.

But among the farmer peoples two types must be distinguished which sometimes correspond to two successive phases of evolution, but which at any rate constitute two different civilizations. There is cultivation by the hoe in which man does not use cattle, and there is cultivation by the plough in which man is aided by animals who provide tractor power and manure.[1]

The first type, which the Europeans found among the American Indians, still exists in China, where human excrement replaces animal dung, in India, in Oceania, in Africa, and among the Eskimos and Fuegans, and it still exists among ourselves, even alongside a more advanced and more complicated type, among peasants who cultivate unaided a tiny piece of soil. These farmers who used only the human arm and the most simple tools were sometimes semi-nomadic. When the earth which they tilled and reaped of its harvest, appeared exhausted, they went on to seek virgin soil. This is seen in several parts of Africa, among the Fangs, for instance, but it is exceptional. For the most part, the peoples who sought their chief nurture from the soil settled down by their fields and by the trees which they cultivated and whose fruits they gathered.

With these begins a more stable and more regular civilization. Houses appear instead of tents and huts, and fortified villages, almost towns and also a new social organization. Land no longer remains undivided among the members of the clan or tribe which retains only, to use a juridical expression, the *eminent domain*, and which also maintains as communal property prairie or forest. It is family property that obtains generally, but reformed by allotments or periodical divisions in which newcomers and those who by some accident are without land can have their claims met and receive their share. In more than one country it is the village community thus regulated which is substituted for the clan community; in India, for instance, ancient Egypt, Russia, etc.

One cannot therefore say with Rousseau: " The man who first enclosed a plot of ground and was ready to say ' That is mine ' and then found folk simple enough to believe him, was the true founder of a civil society." Everything points to the fact that collective property in land preceded individual ownership and the civil society which regulated such ownership is earlier than either. Nor is it true to say with Proudhon, " Property is theft." The appropriation of articles for personal use—weapons, tools, clothing, furniture,

---

[1] The third type, agriculture by machinery, is still in its early stages.

houses—is as old as man himself, and should not be considered illegitimate and, as to land, if all collective or individual appropriation is regarded as expropriation of all other human beings, it must be recognized that the people, the tribe, and the family anticipated the individual in seizing it and dividing it out.

How did individual ownership of land come to exist beside communal ownership ? Simply enough. The man who, beyond the land already cultivated and divided, won from the forest or the heath another piece of land was authorized to retain it as his own possession, to exploit it for his own profit and this reclaimer of land was possibly a more active and more skilful worker than his neighbours or a braver chief whose exploits had won him more slaves. Hence arose private estates which went on increasing in number.

One must not conclude that the farmer peoples were invariably pacific. They were easily attracted to new lands where life would be easier ; they had, above all, to defend themselves against the shepherd or hunter peoples who regarded as a promised land a region where the earth yielded food for the nation every year. According to the Bible, Abel, the farmer, is killed by Cain, the raiser of cattle, and the fertile land where grew the legendary grapes of Canaan was attacked and occupied by the Hebrews who had been desert nomads for forty years. In such an instance the conquerors are usurpers who take the place of the conquered peoples, and settle in the latter's country. If they cannot seize the land, the nomads must be content with plundering it at the expense of the settled peoples.

In a society which is firmly settled on the land, but is forced to exploit it by the aid of human power alone, the family acquires a peculiar character. Woman, the mother of agriculture, which is derived from the process of gathering food, has sometimes a very high status. She is equal and sometimes superior to the father. The feminine clans with inheritance in the uterine line are very numerous at this stage of civilization. Women can own land ; the mother has authority over her children ; sometimes over her husband. There are even tribes among whom a man who has violated the laws of marriage is punished by the women.

Only gradually did man emancipate himself in these groups and become predominant. The process began at the top.[1] I mean to say, it happened thus. A man who had inherited from his mother considerable possessions, instead of buying his wife by a more or less prolonged service with his future parents-in-law,[2] paid for her so many bushels of grain, and then, instead of going to live in the house where his wife was born, instead of seeing his children grow up in the clan of their mother, he proceeded to live and have them live with him in his own house, and so gradually drew them and his wife into his own clan. To put it differently, by a slow transition the masculine clan gradually won predominance. Society is advancing towards the partiarchal state in which woman is subordinate,. but in which, at first, as she works in the fields and brings with her possibilities of inheritance, she has the right to a certain consideration which is not refused her.

Technical progress accelerates the change in the domestic hierarchy. For cultivation that progress consists in the introduction of the plough, oxen and manure. The same causes which led in the shepherd civilization to the triumph of the patriarchal system favour its triumph here. In primitive Mexico as in ancient China, among the Greeks and the Romans, the Celts and the Germans, everywhere the clan, the *genos*, the *gens*, is organized under paternal authority, with inheritance in the masculine line and rights of primogeniture.

The father is the absolute master of his wife and of his children ; he can repudiate the one, sell or put to death the others. He keeps for himself besides work in the fields, the chase, fishing, war, public life, in short, the occupations which are held to be the most noble. He is the unchallenged chief, not merely of his family, but of the domestic cult which assures the family's continuance. He alone has political rights which he exercises along with other heads of families. He leaves to his wife the task of grinding the corn and making bread, a toilsome occupation which she will transfer where she is able to slaves. He abandons in her favour that part of the cooking which he long kept to himself and the

---

[1] Gross, p. 177, et seq.
[2] Cf. the Bible story of Jacob.

weaving of material which was originally a man's work.
To him also is reserved the grafting of trees, the felling of
trunks, and the guidance of chariots. The woman, as it
were, second master of the house, takes charge of the garden,
the kitchen, and the poultry, has the care of the children,
control of the servants, sees to the maintenance of clothing,
the making of butter, cheese, and preserved fruits, and
plays the part of assistant at the time of haymaking, harvest,
vintage, and the like. The two sexes have thus two distinct
spheres of activity, and as duties pass by inheritance from
father to son, and from mother to daughter, the result is
the development of different aptitudes in the man and the
woman. In general, then, one is led to believe that the
customs of to-day, or at least those of yesterday, are not very
remote from those obtaining then—the woman, minister of
the interior, presiding over the food, arranging, preparing,
cleaning, and mending all that is needed in the domestic
life, and the man concerning himself with things that are
exterior, in particular taking charge of industrial and
agricultural production and keeping in his own hands
commerce and political power.

But it is to little purpose that the woman has kept at
home an authority which is the reflection of that possessed
by her husband; she has diminished in status and even
the Roman matron, respected as a member of the governing
oligarchy, is reduced to lower rank and confined to the home.
" She spins wool and keeps the house," was the saying in
ancient Rome. The duty of woman, it was said in old
Japan, is to obey and be silent.

Under this system the central power is in the hands of the
heads of the great families. The assembly of the elders with
a king whom it elects, whom it seeks to keep subordinate
to itself and whom it sometimes succeeds in dispensing with,
directs the affairs of the community. The ownership of the
land apart from conquered territory which belongs to the
city, is practically entirely family ownership to the extent
that it cannot be alienated. It remains undivided,
administered by the father and after him by the eldest
son. It is a sort of deposit of which the family enjoys the
interest. The pride and ambition of the big landowner
is to make his domestic economy self-sufficient, to produce

on his own fields with the aid of his cattle, his children, his grandchildren, clients and slaves, all that his family needs, grain, fruit, and flesh to nourish it, wool, flax, hemp to make its garments, wood to heat the house, and to serve as material for furniture, presses, and casks.

In such a society, ancestor worship is the rule, but it is accompanied by worship of the forces of nature with which the farmer has incessantly to struggle or co-operate.

This organization, which is a profound modification of the primitive equalitarian clan system, is in turn dissolved in several different ways. First of all, the fact that property in land becomes the basis of society produces an unexpected result. The territorial division is gradually substituted for the clan. Instead of community of blood it is now the community of residence, and of interests that bind men. Thus were formed in ancient Egypt the districts called *nomes*, thus were created the *demes* of Attica, thus in Incan Peru the simultaneous existence of both systems can be observed. The clan shorn of its power, fallen from its high estate, gradually sinks till it is nothing more than a pious brotherhood revering the same ancestors. Then as can be seen in ancient Egypt, a military leader, a king, put at the head of a confederation of clans, absorbs the powers possessed before his advent by the other chiefs. His *totem* becomes the most important. The hawk which is his emblem, conquers the elephant, the ibis, and the crocodile. It is absolute semi-divine monarchy which arises with privileged positions within it for priests and soldiers. With certain differences locally, that is what happened in Assyria, in India, in China, in Mexico, and in Peru, where the process is combined with the maintenance and organization of a vast communist system.

But the dissolution of the clans did not always result in the founding of great empires. In other lands, especially in mountainous countries divided by nature into sections which only with difficulty communicated with one another, there arose as many cities, as many sovereign states, as there were sections. The word *polis* in Greece signifies both city and state. Henceforward the City has an interest and a religion superior to that of the clans and families. Urban economy which raises to pre-eminence commerce and industry is substituted for the self-sufficient economy of the great landed proprietor. Within the city walls are united inhabitants very different in origin and position. Besides the family chiefs with their lands and slaves are men who have no means of existence, except their arms and their brains. Proprietors and proletarians exist side by side.

The latter are the younger sons who by virtue of the right of primogeniture find themselves lacking possessions, home or cult, when they seek to free themselves from the perpetual dependence which is their lot ; the strangers, the banished, the illegitimate whom the city does not recognize as its children ; the artisans and merchants who oppose to landed property their personal property and their individualist activity. These disinherited and these creators of new wealth unite against a system under which they are nothing. In Attica, and soon all over Greece, there is a fierce struggle between the Eupatrides, the well-born, the aristocrats, and the pioneers of democracy who sometimes give themselves a popular leader to break the resistance of their enemies. In Rome there is the centuries-long conflict between patricians and plebeians led to the assault by their tribunes until the day when here, too, there is founded a great empire whose sovereign will be as absolute as a Pharaoh of Egypt or a king of Assyria, who like them will live as a military and religious chief and will die a god.

But that takes us very far from the primitive societies, although in Europe in the regression caused by the barbarian invasion we shall see the proprietor-nobles reappear priding themselves on being kings on their domain and producing on it all that is necessary, and later still the queen-cities, the urban republics of Italy and Flanders, although everywhere among the backward peoples the clan system has survived till our own day. It is time to stay our steps. But I have said enough to indicate the strict relation that exists between the kind of life and labour enjoyed by a people and the social institutions it creates. Certainly there are anomalies to explain, details which here and there do not harmonize. But although there was a number of little states jealously preserving their original shape, all the societies on our planet approach more or less to the types briefly described in these pages, and in bringing our rapid survey to a close it is permissible to formulate a few generalizations which can be applied to all the various types of human civilization.

If we seek to discover whence arose the social inequality which early reveals itself among our ancestors, the essential cause of it is clearly the indestructible inequality which exists among human beings in strength, beauty, intelligence, virtue ; inequality of fact and difference of aptitude which produced unequal situations and different functions, but which do not prevent the individuals being equal in law as members of the same species having the same needs, the same tendencies, the same desire to live and be happy. There is here a double conception which is not yet everywhere understood and admitted, since the diehard still seems to be ignorant of the fact that those better endowed by chance or by birth have not merely no more rights than others, but actually have more duties towards those who surround them.

Besides this essential cause and arising from it, there are others. We have seen that the organization of property, the development of industry and of commerce placed in the hands of certain individuals wealth and power which were the means of domination over others ; they favoured the growth of distinct classes which ended by placing in opposition the possessors of land and the possessors of goods and then raised against both those who had no land nor any capital save that which was in their arms and their brains.

More, and here is a second cause of inequality, the division of labour which arose spontaneously whenever several workers were engaged on the same task, or whenever several tasks fell to a group of workers, acted vigorously to the same end. The moment that a task is done in common, there exists discipline, authority, subordination, and mutual dependence, and different rôles are assigned to different workers whose labour is now divided, and becomes relatively detailed. From the moment, too, that the workers are numerous enough in a society to be able to cease to be jacks of all trades, there arises a specialization which increases as the society becomes greater and more complicated. As a result there is a primary separation between *masculine* and *feminine* labour. We have explained this, and there is no need to return to it. Then comes a second separation between

muscular work and *brain* work.   Everywhere certain forms
of activity demanding keen intellectual ability and less
strength and manual dexterity, become professions and
even create special castes.   Thus doctors, priests, sorcerers,
and anti-sorcerers, clever observers of nature or bolder
exploiters of the credulity of their neighbours, early acquire
a very important place in society.   Equally there arise from
the ordinary mass men better endowed than others with
regard to this art or that, painters, sculptors, musicians,
singers, dancers.   They enjoy a certain consideration, but
without ever winning the respect won by the so-called see-ers
into the future and miracle workers, who claim to be the
necessary intermediaries and interpreters between men and
the gods.

Below these are the manual trades whose workers become
united and join together in colleges, guilds, and professional
fraternities.   Most important are those who make a serious
apprenticeship a condition of joining the craft, because their
craft involves complicated work ;   these are the blacksmiths,
the potters, the goldsmiths, etc.   Employing different tools
and producing work which is different, these manual workers
have also different social status and those who handle the
most precious material are also those who rise highest in the
social scale.   The inequality which results is increased by
the circumstance that the specialist who devotes himself
to a task which is always the same, ends by acquiring a great
technical skill, produces more work in less time and work
which is of higher quality and more value.   Thus the division
of labour has for result the creation of classes which are
distinguished by their occupations, their tastes, and their
incomes.

There remains a third cause of inequality—violence and
especially that collective violence which is war.   It creates
a caste of warriors who are ranked sometimes above, sometimes a little below, the priests.   The caste is seen in India,
Egypt, etc.   War also creates a class of pariahs, for the use
of force ends in the appropriation of the goods and persons
of the vanquished.

Primitive men were in general very exclusive.   To the
members of a clan, the stranger unless he presented himself
in the rôle of the passing guest, was as a rule the enemy.
The Hellenes considered as barbarians all the peoples who

were not of their race : the Hebrews and after them the Christians, considered as outcasts all who were not of their religion. The communally organized clans when they wanted to get rid of inconvenient or dangerous neighbours, either slew them or adopted them to replace the warriors who had fallen in battle. Usually the right of the stronger was implacably exercised against them. If they were not massacred at once, if they were not kept to be eaten or to be ceremonially sacrificed, they were reduced to the position of beasts of burden ; they became living tools, slaves.

As has been justly remarked [1] slavery implies a certain degree of civilization ; it implies that men have reached the conception and the means of making profit out of the slave. But the slave was made to work ; on his shoulders was thrown the bulk of the burden which weighed on men and even more of the burden which weighed on women.

The possession of man by man once established developed. Sometimes slavery was increased by a more or less individual act, an act of brigandage, a raid, or a piratical descent in which men, but especially women and children, were made captive. Sometimes the act was one of people against people by a war which in case of victory had two different but analogous results. Either entire populations were enslaved on the spot, remaining in their own land, but compelled to toil for their new masters—this was the slavery of which the God Terminus half buried in the soil, half above it, can serve as emblem, for the slaves were bound to and, as it were incorporated in, the domain which they cultivated or to the trade of which they worked to the profit of others, were half-free, half-subject to fixed service owed to their masters—or the inhabitants of the conquered land were led away, dispersed, and sold ; they lost at once home and liberty. This is slavery, properly so-called. Nothing was more usual after the capture of a town. Andromache, after the burning of Troy, became the slave of the son of Achilles, and endured the fate which Hector had predicted. " Then in Argos thou wilt spin the web for another ; thy heart full of bitterness thou wilt draw water from the well ; a hard necessity will weigh on thee, and the passer-by seeing thy tears will cry ' Behold the wife of Hector who excelled all the Trojans in battle '."

[1] Letourneau, *L'évolution de l'esclavage.*

Slavery thus brought about by war which is its main source, was also otherwise nourished. First the slaves multiplied by the birth of children born in slavery by what we may call the annual increase of the human cattle, and then by the sale of free-born children and adults. In the case of children the father was sometimes too poor to keep them, and exposed and abandoned them, as was frequently the case with female children among the Arabs before Mahomet. Certain merchants, the precursors of the negro slave dealers, conducted a trade in children. In the classical comedies, the recognized denouement is at a given point in the action where the hero or the heroine is recognized by name by the parents to whom he or she has been sold. As to the grown man, he could become a slave if he could not pay a merciless creditor, if he had committed some serious crime or married a female slave, or if, to free himself from hunger, he gave himself to a master to be sure of having food every day.

One must not forget that slavery was the cornerstone of all ancient societies, and that the boldest thinkers never dreamed that it could be done away with, so difficult is it for man to conceive a social state other than the one he knows.

Shall we try now to sum up how labour was organized in these societies, if indeed we can apply the term to what was still in many places an undefined thing? We can say that free labour and slave labour existed side by side just as there existed individual labour and collective labour. Individual labour which is the rule in agriculture on a small scale and in small industries, which is usual among artisans and artists, united in guilds and fraternities, which is less frequent among hunters and fishers, is generally free. Collective labour is still done in part at least by free-born persons at the time of sowing, haymaking, harvest, and vintage, but when it is a case of irrigating land, or fortifying a village or a town, or erecting a menhir or a pyramid, of making a road, or building a temple or a palace, or exploiting a mine, discipline is necessary and a hierarchy of those who command and those who obey, and which is more, as a general rule this sort of work is left to slaves who work under the lash and the rod.

Thus from its origins labour has had very different aspects, and its diversity goes on increasing.

P

Fig. 14.—Engraving made for a dinner to Gabriel de Mortillet in 1907.

BIBLIOGRAPHY

BUCHER (Karl), *Etudes d'histoire et d'économie politique.*
CONTENAU, FOUGERE, P., GROUSSET, JOUGUET, and LESQUIER, *Les premières civilizations.*
DAVY and MORET, *Des clans aux empires.*
DURCKHEIM, *Année sociologique.*
FEBVRE, Work already cited.
FUSTEL DE COULANGE, *La cité antique.*
GROSS (E.), *Die Formen der Familie und die Frauen der Wissenschaft.*
HADDON, *Man past and present.*
LEROY (Olivier), Work already cited.
LOWIE, *On the Trail of the Pigmies.*
TARDE (G.), *Psychologie économique.*

CONCLUSION

AT the moment when human societies enter into history, we see them composed of strongly differentiated social classes. History is the story of the political and economic conflict and collaboration between the classes, but we only catch a glimpse of its beginnings. All the rest lies beyond the limits set to this book.

The most advanced peoples in China, in Assyria, in Egypt, invented something new which had the most tremendous consequences, the art of transferring human thought to stone, brick, parchment, wood, wax, or that substance at once so fragile and so lasting, papyrus. Many other nations made essays in the same direction, but none of these had any future. In Mexico, as among the Scandinavians and perhaps among the menhir-builders,[1] graven signs have been found of which we do not always recognize the meaning, and the most part of which will remain for ever dead letters. But in China, in the Middle East, and in Egypt, the essays developed into systems the success of which has lasted till our day. We cannot go into detail on these essays here. It must suffice to indicate the progress made by the human mind in this invention of writing.

In the beginning the most rudimentary means were adopted to preserve the memory of things that had happened. Menhir building is probably one of them, but to cause human thought to be transferred in space required something very different. First of all sticks notched in a certain fashion, or strings of shells of different sorts, served as means of communication over a long distance. In ancient Peru messages were transmitted by means of bunches of cords whose knots, colour, and arrangement had specific meaning to the initiated.

Then came designs and pictures representing people and things, from which developed means of expressing a series

---

[1] M. and Mme. Saint-Just Péquart in collaboration with M. le Rouzic, *Corpus de signes gravés des monuments monolithiques du morbihan.*

of facts and ideas, the attitude and the relative positions of the figures permitting the recipient to understand the message of the sender. A famous petition [1] addressed in 1849 by the Chippewa Indians to the Congress of the United States in this dumb but not very precise language, permits one to estimate the advantages and inconveniences of the method. A further step forward was taken when for the pictures of the sun, the man, the house, figures at first completely drawn, was substituted a conventional abbreviation. From hieroglyphs which, as the name indicates, were sacred

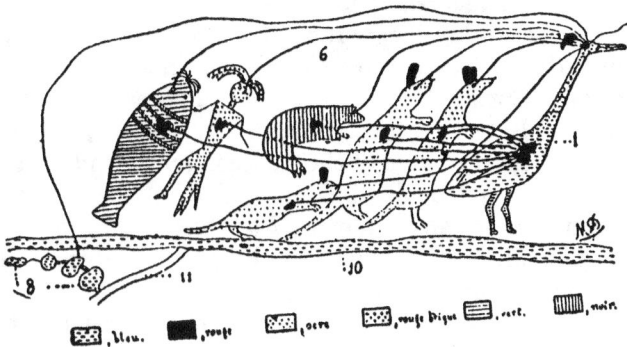

FIG. 15.—The different clans to the number of seven are represented by their totems. Two series of lines the one going from the eye of the totems, the other from their necks and ending at the eye and the heart of the totem of the chief clan which is in front, indicate that all the petitioners hold the same views and have the same sentiments. As to the object of the petition a line beginning at the eye of the principle petitioner indicates that it concerns the possession of little lakes (marked in blue), which lie beside a large river and near a road which is marked in white (*after Schoolcraft*).

letters whose key was held only by initiates, man passed to a writing more popular and more within the reach of the ordinary individual.

But the most essential step forward was taken when the sign lost its original sense and became a representation of the sound which expressed the thing or the person. From that day writing from being ideographic became phonetic. Instead of appealing simply to the eye it appealed at the same time to the ear.

[1] *V*. Beuchat or Deniker.

Then finally, the trading peoples needing a writing that could be rapidly set down and at the same time was capable of being understood for use in contracts and accounts, there was invented the alphabet which carried far and wide by the Phœnicians and the Greeks, conquered all Europe and the greater part of our planet. All other alphabets except the Arab, the Chinese, and the Japanese, have yielded to the one in use among ourselves.

On the day when a people learns how to preserve in written documents the memory of what it had accomplished, it passes out of pre-history. Again I may remind the reader that the date of this transition varies for the various nations of which none to-day is ignorant of the art of writing. I do not think that I exaggerate when I say that this invention was as important for humanity as that of speech, but for this book it sounds the curfew. I end here the short account which I have tried to give of the first conquests and creations which man secured by his labour, and which constitute his chief claim to glory and renown. I am well aware that there are many details to be added to the picture which I have tried to draw, but the historian, and above all the pre-historian, must never cherish the illusion that he can construct something complete and definite, something that is for eternity. He ought to consider himself fortunate if he can reach a level from which his successors will be able to pass higher and come nearer to truth.

INDEX

A

Fig. 16. Mousterian scraper.

Fig. 17.   Pecten, after C. Fremont, *Les Outils Prehistoriques* (Paris, 1901).

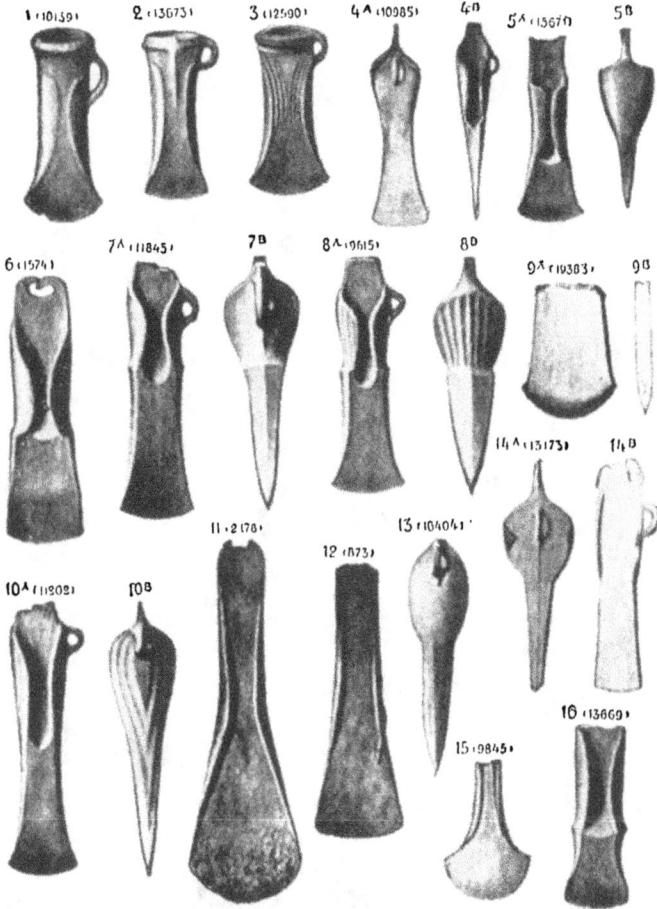

Fig. 18. Lacustran remains from the Lausanne museum. Varieties of
axes of the bronze period.

Fig. 19. The *escargotière* of Mechta-el-Arbi. The great 25 metre trench (Archæological Society of Constantine, 1925).

Fig. 20. Method of making fire by sawing (Malabar Coast).

Fig. 21. Method of making fire by boring (Rawack), after C. Frémont,
Origine et Évolution des Outils (Paris, 1913).

Fig. 22. Two skins used as bellows in Africa, after Frémont, *Origine et Évolution de la Soufflerie* (Paris, 1917).

Fig. 23. Papuans tilling with pointed sticks (photo. by Haddon).

Fig. 24. Dolmen of Aubergenville reconstructed in the moat of the Château of Saint-Germain.

THE HISTORY OF CIVILIZATION

Titles in the series

For Product Safety Concerns and Information please contact our EU
representative GPSR@taylorandfrancis.com
Taylor & Francis Verlag GmbH, Kaufingerstraße 24, 80331 München, Germany

* 9 7 8 0 4 1 5 8 6 9 6 8 3 *